Crises in Campus Management

edited by
George J. Mauer

The Praeger Special Studies program—utilizing the most modern and efficient book production techniques and a selective worldwide distribution network—makes available to the academic, government, and business communities significant, timely research in U.S. and international economic, social, and political development.

Crises in Campus Management

Case Studies in the Administration of Colleges and Universities

Praeger Publishers   New York   Washington   London

PRAEGER SPECIAL STUDIES IN U.S. ECONOMIC, SOCIAL, AND POLITICAL ISSUES

Library of Congress Cataloging in Publication Data
Main entry under title:

Crises in campus management.

    (Praeger special studies in U.S. economic, social, and
political issues)
    Bibliography: p.
    Includes index.
    CONTENTS: Introduction: Mauer, G. J. Higher education
administration. —Universities in transition: Hanson, H. P.
From the expanding university to the steady state university
Case, C. W. Trials and tribulations of university reorganization.
Barbe, R. H. The metropolitan state university. Goodall, L. E.
Inter-campus relations in multi-campus universities. [etc.]
    1. Universities and colleges—United States—Administration—
Addresses, essays, lectures. I. Mauer, George J.
LB2341.C85   378.73   75-23981
ISBN 0-275-55710-3

PRAEGER PUBLISHERS
111 Fourth Avenue, New York, N.Y. 10003, U.S.A.

Published in the United States of America in 1976
by Praeger Publishers, Inc.

© 1976 by George J. Mauer

Printed in the United States of America

Those familiar with the literature of higher education administration are well aware of the paucity of published accounts on the
experiences of those who manage the college and university. They
also know the reasons for this void: few academic administrators
have either the time or the desire to articulate the troublesome nature
of their work, and few others care to rationalize their professional
behavior. As a result, the preponderance of recorded information in
this field, whether researched from without or analyzed from within
the academic arena, tends to be theoretical or descriptive in nature
if not purely statistical. Thus the real world of ongoing collegiate
management remains something of a mystery to external observers,
and oftentimes a source of frustration to internal participants. This
incongruity among individuals in institutions dedicated to the pursuit
of truth has led Nevitt Sanford, for one, to observe in The American
College: "Our greatest lack, in this social sphere, is of knowledge
of the inner workings of colleges considered as large organizations."
Although many attempts have been made to bridge or to fill that
gap, most often by way of presidential memoirs, it is clear that the
quality and quantity of those efforts to date have been insufficient.
Academic insight into the respective disciplines is far superior to the
level of awareness of the administrative context in which it flourishes.
Such a condition is not conducive to esprit de corps in academe, nor
is it a tribute to the conduct of higher learning. So it was toward the
resolution of this dilemma that this collection of case studies was
conceived. On the one hand it is believed that it can contribute to a
broadening of the base of scholastic work in higher education administration; on the other hand it is hoped that it will add depth to the
perspective of those engaged in advanced inquiry. The extent to which
these optimistic notions may be realized will be to the credit of the
collaborators in this effort. All academic administrators, past or
present, they offer the reader a unique set of studies: each of their
case studies is grounded in actual experience; the context is a specific
problem area common to most other academic institutions; and the
treatment of the subject will be found to transcend all levels of the
college or university organizational hierarchy.
Those unaware of the literary production in this field will not
know that the application of the case study method to learning experience in higher education administration is a phenomenon of very
recent origin. Despite the utilization of this technique or tool of

analysis in the academic training of business executives, lawyers, and government bureaucrats dating back many decades, it was not until 1955 that Ronald Bauer's <u>Cases in College Administration</u> paved the way for the broader application of the method in the preparation and upgrading of campus managers. Although that work was predicated upon a unidimensional view of multiple events, namely those of the author alone, the book nevertheless served to point up the usefulness of casework in promoting the cause of more effective academic administration.

The utility of the case study method is most evident in the development of management skills, and especially in simulated decision making situations. Moreover, it permits reasoning by analogy, affords an awareness of self and of the interrelationships between theory and practice, and allows the serious learner an opportunity to sense some of the trauma brought about by human confrontations. Herein those prospects are multiplied by the diversity of experience of the authors, and potentially by the imagination of the analyst. That no other book can attest to such a framework may be prima facie evidence of the uniqueness of this venture, but more importantly it is an uncomplimentary reminder of a peculiarity of the profession.

We are hopeful that affected academicians and practitioners will find the contents to be instructive and useful. Surely the governance of our colleges and universities would be improved if all concerned would be attentive to management problems and related studies. But apathy takes its toll in all professions, with the likely result that the principal beneficiaries of this work will be the aspiring academic administrator, both abroad and among the 2,400 senior institutions of higher learning and the 1,200 junior and community colleges across the United States. To suggest that each of the tens of thousands of administrators therein would necessarily profit from this book is to presume more than we know about our colleagues. However, it is equally valid to submit that none are above lifelong learning, nor inclined to wantonly disregard substantive commentaries that bear upon their livelihood.

To set the stage for the consideration of these case studies in higher education administration, an introduction follows to reflect upon the contemporary state of collegiate affairs, to cite the conditions and circumstances of the current academic implosion, and to detail the methodology employed in the selection of the authors of the subsequent studies. Thereafter the book is organized into five parts, each concerned with a different theme significant to postsecondary education management, and each composed of four case studies with prefatory comments and follow-up inquiries. The cases, with few exceptions, were prepared especially for this book. Moreover, they are reasonably brief and to the point, suitable for classwork as well as institutes and seminars, and factual despite the need of some writers to allude to the fictitious to protect the innocent. The conclusion summarizes the implications of the cases and commentaries. Finally, for the benefit of interested persons, a selected bibliography of some length is appended.

In retrospect, it is fair to surmise that a half-century ago Thorstein Veblen would have characterized this work as essentially a collection of analyses on the mundane tasks of captains of erudition. Unlike his assessment of the role of academic leaders prior to World War I, as expressed so caustically in The Higher Learning in America, this book submits that the tasks of educational administrators today are not anathema nor irrelevant to collegiate affairs. To the contrary, this collective effort is predicated on the proposition that colleges and universities the world over are among the most important of human institutions, and their efficacy is greatly dependent upon sophisticated management.

I would like to thank Eugene Lee and the Institute of Governmental Studies under whose sponsorship this collection of case studies and commentaries was planned and assembled during the writer's year of postdoctorate work at the University of California, Berkeley. In addition, I am indebted to Lyman Glenny and James Stone of the College of Education at Berkeley for inspirational thoughts gathered during my visitations to their program in higher education administration. However, they may be pleased to learn that I remain solely responsible for my following assessments and deductions.

CONTENTS

1

HIGHER EDUCATION ADMINISTRATION: AN OVERVIEW AND ANALYTICAL APPROACH

George J. Mauer

Higher education in the United States has entered a new era. Gone for now are the luxuries of the 1960s and early 1970s, which included a deluge of students on campus accompanied by peak appropriations, expanded curricula and a concomitant number of faculty, and greatly increased physical improvements supported by record expenditures. While previously, for leaders of the colleges and universities, the principal task of management was a rational allocation of resources toward meeting the needs of growing academic communities, that preoccupation is no longer primary.

Owing to the end of the post-World War II "baby boom" and the subsequent decline in the rate of propagation, coupled with the onset of national economic austerity, the age of prosperity on campus has been replaced by an era of retrenchment. For the immediate and foreseeable future, the consequences and ramifications are increasingly evident: while some institutions of higher learning have been forced to close for lack of sufficient students, others now struggle for survival with a static or dwindling enrollment; new academic programs are no longer sacrosanct, nor are suggestions to enlarge the curriculum; and faculty positions, heretofore plentiful, are being frozen or consciously reduced.

Of course the common denominator of these reversals is the dollar, or, more properly stated, insufficient income to meet the rising tide of costs. Thus for the contemporary administrator a relatively new set of problems is begging for solutions. Although available resources still must be allocated, which activities and programs should be given higher priority? Shall academic offerings be stabilized or reduced, and which among them might be eliminated or subjected to major surgery? Where are the excesses on campus—

in the number of faculty, in physical facilities, or perhaps in the intercollegiate athletic program? How long might this difficult period
continue? And which disciplines are more likely to be affected, both
in terms of the anticipated needs of students and those of society?

These and other equally hard questions cannot be left unanswered
nor the answers unheeded, and the onus for positive action is clearly
on the managers of the academic enterprise. Not unlike their contemporaries in business and industry, the leaders of our institutions
of higher learning are beset today with a bewildering array of organizational aspirations together with apparent contradictions: new ends
and static means, quests for quality in the face of mass production,
provision of equal opportunity in situations of limited capability, and
the desire for modernization despite unrelenting inflation.

In practical terms, these challenges must be met with reasoned
policy, shrewd financial planning, and sophisticated administration.
Of necessity the progressive enterprise cannot afford less than a
contemplative reevaluation of its objectives, the courage to pursue
the findings of such an appraisal, and a commitment to continually
adjust to ever-changing realities. To do otherwise is to become
obsolete and to beckon obscurity.

For higher education, the birthplace of change and not infrequently a forerunner of its implementation, the responsibility for
rational reaction is particularly great. And some institutions already
have begun to set the tone for others to consider. In recognition of
the fact that prior approaches and future requirements tend to be
incompatible, many colleges and universities have adopted significant
measures both to remedy inadequacies and face up to the trends of
the times. As will soon become apparent, these innovations have not
evolved by mere chance or by intellectual gaming. Rather, they have
arisen as a result of considerable soul-searching and undoubtedly
much heartache, for seldom is change unanimously desired or
unanimously endorsed.

Illustrative of actions, rather than rhetoric, recently undertaken
by concerned leaders on a variety of campuses are a bevy of reforms
that affect the very philosophy if not the function and form of our institutions of higher learning. Whether attributable to native uprisings
or the need to attract more future alumni, the more important changes
are occurring in the educational process. Teachers are officially
being reminded of their primary professional obligation, that of
assisting students in their intellectual growth, both inside and outside
the classroom. As a result, curricula content and methods of effective
communication have come under closer scrutiny, leading more often
than not to revisions and modifications to better meet the objective of
meaningful learning experiences. Old notes and stale lectures are
giving way to joint professor-student preparations and dynamic

discourse. Waning too is the proliferation of dubious programs for academic degrees, the traditional time frame for earning credits and credentials, and the strictly campus-oriented opportunities for the pursuit of truth. Although the weaning of the learner may soon see its day, it appears that we have not as yet reversed the influence of the "progressives" in offering algebra in the third grade and spelling in our graduate schools!

To the consternation of some, the redefinition of objectives and approaches also has led to reorganization to facilitate new purposes and procedures. Heretofore independent disciplines are being consolidated under more broadly based interdisciplinary departments, some divisions are in process of being altered while others have been abolished, and even entire colleges are now extinct or undergoing the need to justify their existence. And publicly disposed agencies, in the form of the various centers, bureaus, and institutes, are being reconsidered while many members of their staff are relocated. Economy and efficiency undoubtedly underlie these and similar efforts, and may be due cause for such measures on those grounds alone. However, if reorganization in academe does not ultimately further the cause of teaching effectiveness and student learning, it may well be indicative of myopic management.

A number of new developments peripheral to the purely academic are similarly well underway. Of special interest to faculties, the sanctimonious state of tenure is increasingly being scrutinized almost everywhere; and if no longer being conferred at all, it is surely being proffered with greater care and less frequency. Sabbatical leaves too are on the wane, as is the routine of automatic salary increases. On the campuses of multiversities, some teachers are feeling the pain of encouraged relocation, while on unicampus colleges the pressure is building in favor of consortia with others to staff both general and specialized degree programs. Some institutions, acting out their total desperation, have resorted to the rationing of stationery, paper clips, and rubber bands. These conditions, coupled with the likes of lowering the mandatory retirement age and actual decreases in the effective value of insurance programs, have prompted greater interest among many faculty, staff, and students in collective bargaining and representation on institutional boards of control.

Of course administrators in higher education are far from oblivious to these developments, and indeed they too suffer or enjoy the resultant trials and tribulations. To manage a static or receding enterprise replete with contracting budgets and both internal and external woes is, after all, not conducive to attaining senior citizenship and it severely tests the skill and patience of the most competent of administrators. Therefore it comes as no surprise that considerable turnover affects their ranks, and this may serve to explain why more surviving incumbents are spending as much time on campus these days as off. And as candidates for such auspicious employment are finding, the politics of selection is giving way to professional measurements of capabilities, for more than ever there is a heightened awareness that management and leadership talents hold greater utility than does patronage and prior acquiescence.

To be sure, there is not an institution of higher learning in the nation that singularly can lay claim to all of the change in academe described above. Indeed only a handful of our colleges and universities can opt for a majority of the changes. Moreover, it should be emphasized that not all would necessarily profit by even the better of such trends, and only a very careful examination of the unique circumstances of a given campus could determine their applicability. But this is not to suggest that complacency should supersede introspection, or that rhetoric should be permitted to rationalize deficiencies. These dispositions are characteristic of those academic communities which elect to linger in the limbo of yesteryear and thereby to guarantee their continuing anonymity. To the contrary, what is needed today, at least as much as ever before, is a frank appraisal of the status and direction of the college or university, and a determined effort to make it a truly meaningful educational environment. Surely some campuses have realized that ambition. Others have serious-minded people at work on it. But for the balance these words are not comforting, for therein the search for significance all too often leaves their administrators and educators as nervous as clams at low tide.

NATURE AND FUNCTION OF HIGHER EDUCATION ADMINISTRATION

To the casual observer the college or university is perhaps better known for its more obvious characteristics: students and professors, buildings and grounds, intercollegiate and extracurricular activities. To friends of the institution, it is also a center of learning, a setting for the intellectual development of man, and a corporate body of scholars dedicated to the pursuit of truth and its dissemination for the benefit of society. To the unfriendly, it is a haven for radicals, a source of perpetual aggravation, and a place where eggheads apparently have found something more intriguing than sex!

Be that as it may, among the less visible on campus is the myriad of personnel who hold positions of administrative leadership in our institutions of higher education. Charged with the overall management of collegiate affairs on and off the campus, they are basically concerned with responsibilities supportive of the academic objectives in teaching, research, and public service. On the typical campus, these officers include the president or chancellor and his immediate assistants; vice presidents or provosts for academic affairs, administration, finance, or development; deans of the respective colleges and professional schools; divisional or department heads of each of the disciplines; and directors of the complementary agencies ranging from admissions and library services to bureaus and institutes. These officers are among many others who fulfill the policy objectives of the academic institution.

Policy in academe emanates from a wide variety of sources or power centers, both formally and informally as well as individually and collectively. Of course ultimate decision making rests in a board of control, be it designated the regents or trustees. This body, in turn, is normally beholding to a legislature or corporation, replete with the political influence that relationship implies. In either a public or private institution, the frequently presumed independence of the governing board is occasionally restricted by others in external officialdom; such impositions are often cited with regard to gubernatorial or entrepreneurial interests, programs of the federal government, policies of affiliated regional associations, and the whims of selected philanthropic organizations and individuals.

Also, the policy choices of institutions of higher education are affected by individuals and groups more directly concerned about their welfare. In addition to all administrators, these include members of the faculty and especially their senate, the alumni and their association, local community leaders, and the various student leaders and their organizations. These groups, though most often less persuasive than external groups, are seldom ignored by those who make the final decisions in academe. Problematic though this be for the rational resolution of choices, the matrix of institutional policy makers is inherently sound as it properly depicts the very real interdependency of diverse interests in higher education. The attentive administrator will keep all in proper perspective and appropriate bounds, for otherwise, undemocratic decisions will lead to academic dysfunctions.

Whatever the policy determinants, the administrator is obliged to carry them out. This does not preclude the likelihood of administrative influence at the inception, development, or execution of policy. For as the student of administrative behavior is well aware, the impact of policy can be mellowed or exaggerated by those who implement it. Thus policy and administration become, in fact, an inseparable process, and one in which the actors and the interplay will vary with the nature and circumstance of the problem under consideration.

Policy administration, however important it be, is but one of the multiple functions of the executive, whether in education, government, or business. Leadership in the direction of desired goals also

is fundamental, for without it any organization will soon become pur-
poseless and stagnant. It clearly requires a capacity to synthesize
from among alternative courses of action, to vigorously prevail upon
higher authority to accept the outcome, and then to effectively communicate that decision to those who will assist in its fulfillment. Concomitant with this task, particularly among administrators in higher
education, is the need to facilitate, encourage, and support all methods and programs that advance teaching and learning, as well as
research and service, in and beyond their academic institution.

Procedurally, these objectives are accomplished by serious and
persistent attention to ever-changing individual and societal needs.
Such admonitions in turn will call for frequent adjustments in organiz-
ing and staffing personnel, coordinating and directing their efforts,
budgeting and reporting new planning, and gaining feedback on the
effect of each successive step toward meeting the expressed goals of
students and faculty. Ultimately this should mean that policy is effectively translated into more relevant curricula, improved teaching and
learning, and better use of all facilities and equipment. But all too
often these aspirations are thwarted by shortsightedness, inappropriate
organization and methods, poor systems of communication, divisive-
ness within the ranks, and sometimes events and personalities outside
academe.

Perhaps overriding the technical aspects of collegiate management, not all academic communities are privileged in having at the
helm the unique combination of abilities that characterize the more
successful administrators. As put pointedly in the preface of Raymond
Gibson's The Challenge of Leadership in Higher Education: "The
college administrator must be, first of all, an educated man with a
fundamental understanding of the broad divisions of knowledge; and
secondly, a man who has certain technical skills which are indispens-
able if one is to avoid anarchy in the management of facilities, buildings and budgets, and great social skills necessary for providing
leadership among intellectuals on the one hand and ordinary citizens
on the other." To these qualities one might add integrity, impartiality,
and the courage to use good judgment.

Qualifications such as these are not common. They necessitate
a general education beyond the formal and a breadth of insight unattain-
able within the scope of any singular discipline. In sum, they demand
a comprehensive view not only of the history and development of
higher education, but of the contributions of the arts and sciences, the
theory and practice of administration, and perhaps more fundamentally
the nature and evolution of man and society. Suffice it to say that in
this age of specialization few are so prepared, leaving most with an
operational framework which is not wholly conducive to a higher level
of achievement.

To those who may quarrel with this assertion, they should be reminded that training in the profession of higher education administration is relatively new. As a result, most who presently serve in positions of authority in academe, and especially those at lower levels, are products of the traditional disciplines, albeit subsequently modified by increasingly responsible work in collegiate management. That institutions generally have survived and prospered under such leadership is a credit to the resourcefulness of the incumbents. That some colleges and universities have foundered, however, is indicative of a problem still largely unmet.

As John Perkins admonished in an article in the Harvard Educational Review some eighteen years ago: "It is high time that administration in higher education was recognized for what it is—a vitally necessary function, one of the most difficult of all areas of administrative activity, and an undertaking to be consciously prepared for." Yet to this day there are relatively few advanced programs in the field, though more admittedly for those at the top than those below in the hierarchy, and the piecemeal approach of internships, workshops, and conferences for the training and upgrading of executives in academe are useful but nevertheless insufficient means toward meeting a critical need.

Meanwhile, experience or in-service work remains the major vehicle in preparing most higher education administrators for their complex duties. To the extent that this method has satisfied the graduates of the university of hard knocks, one should not complain. But to the extent that it may come at the expense of less than effective service, not to mention concrete examples of mismanagement and corruption, some should continue to be concerned. Besides, successful administrators tend to promote greater achievement throughout their institution, whereas the unsuccessful most often produce only anxiety. But perhaps this is an exaggeration, for one really doesn't know the meaning of anxiety until he is caught in a topless sports car entirely surrounded by tall and vicious dogs! On second thought, some administrators have come to learn that feeling, particularly when they have found themselves far out of step with the board of control or with faculty and students.

A PREVIEW OF THE CASE STUDY APPROACH

The foregoing overview of higher education and its administration was not intended to exhaust or to pinpoint all of the difficulties that confront the contemporary academic community. Rather, these observations were designed to dramatize a time frame and related issues, both of which are preconditions for a fuller awareness of the setting in which the college and university administrator must now function. Thus the rationale was to offer a perspective on institutional problems and governance in the 1970s in order that even the unacquainted reader might gain further insight into the troublesome roles of those who manage the tenuous state of campus affairs.

Now we can proceed to consider how that might be better understood. To assume the existence of one best way to accomplish an objective is to advocate the cause of scientific management. Although this school of thought has much support and a measure of validity in investigating some kinds of human activity, it has limited utility in analysis of the administrative arts. Likewise business and public administration offer useful perspectives on the management of the college and university, but care must be taken not to exaggerate the transferability of their principles and practices.

In the traditional social sciences, where liberal education generally takes precedence over the more marketable preparatory work of other divisions of the arts and sciences, caution also must be exercised in recognizing the limitations of each discipline and the approach thereto. For example, the historian will properly advise that there is much value in reflecting on the what, when, and where of prior events. But as relevant as this view is, it alone is inadequate in contemplating matters of present and future consequence. Similarly, the organizationist tends to stress how goals are attained, the politicist wants to know who attains them, and the behavioralist asks "why." Again each of these orientations holds merit, but must be considered narrow if conceptualized without benefit of complementary studies. Such studies would include, though not exclusively, the findings of psychologists and sociologists with regard to individual motivations and group activities within organizational life, and the manner in which each affect and are affected by bureaucratic structures.

For these reasons the methodological approach to the study of higher education administration would better be eclectic. That is, rather than to laud the present training of most in the profession, it is suggested that only a multidisciplinary orientation can begin to offer the insights necessary for a comprehensive view of the world of collegiate management. Should existing programs in the field encompass such breadth and depth of inquiry, future administrators will be more likely to cope effectively with the problems and needs of modern higher education. Parenthetically, if the case studies to follow are not read, analyzed, evaluated, and explored in that light, this fault should not be attributed to the respective authors.

To further explain the methodology that underlies this effort, a few additional thoughts are in order. As Clark Kerr observed in 1963 in the foreword to <u>The Uses of the University</u>: "The University has been a remarkably unstudied institution until very recently." It might have been added that administration, at least in terms of its practical application, remains among the university's lesser examined phenomena. Descriptive commentaries on the subject are plentiful, as are statistical summaries, but analytical work on higher education administration unfortunately is minimal. And it is in direct response to that condition, and toward filling that vacuum, that this collaborative study was undertaken.

With some notable exceptions, it is not often that an opportunity is afforded higher education administrators, at varying levels, to make a meaningful contribution to the advancement of their profession beyond their campuses and states. Aside from formal and sometimes informal conferences with colleagues, an occasional book or article, and public addresses, administrators have little real opportunity to communicate with peers and learners—at "gut" level—regarding the accomplishments and failures of their stewardship. This is because such revelations are among the remaining taboos of academe, necessitating their pronouncement in terms of generalities and thereby leaving the reader or listener only a modicum of insight into the cause-and-effect relationships of the subjects they treat.

Given this sad state of the art, coupled with an awareness that many in the profession would wish to improve upon it, the editor elected to use this channel of communication to bridge the gap between those who have something substantive to offer and those who would give serious thought to it. Subsequently, a prescribed number of higher education administrators, as well as a particular kind of official, were sought out and invited to contribute a study on a phase of their professional experience which would add scope and depth to the general perception of such roles in collegiate management. The result is at hand.

Thus the rationale of this effort becomes evident. Our libraries are lacking in pragmatic accounts of the many and varied administrative problems that characterize and beset the campuses across the country, and relatively little is known about the periodic and recurring events that place extraordinary demands upon the higher education official and test both his skill and patience. As a result, there is a wealth of insight that evolves from these challenges to academic decision makers, nearly all of which is destined for unrecorded history. Rather than lose the instructional value of such lessons, this collaborative effort was undertaken.

Consultation with well-informed and concerned colleagues led to the conclusion that the case study method would best serve the purpose of this work. That is, by soliciting problem-oriented administrative cases, especially prepared by those personally affected, it would be feasible to communicate a meaningful appreciation of managerial

difficulties in academe and simultaneously to foster a keener awareness of the positive and negative approaches thereto. Hopefully they
also will serve in helping to minimize the alternative recourse of
many to the often painful process of trial and error.

Surely not all or necessarily the most important of administrative
activities are claimed by this approach. But more vital is the frame
of reference it seeks to impart. If the casework effectively furthers
that end, it will be a contribution to the art of management in college
and university affairs. However, such an assessment is properly left
to the critics, for the writers are convinced only that this technique
of disseminating knowledge is relatively unique in the literature of
higher education administration.

CLASSIFICATION OF COLLABORATORS

Because it is highly presumptuous of any individual to purport
to render an authoritative account on all facets of higher education
administration, it was obvious from the outset that only a collective
effort could possibly meet the objectives of this endeavor. Moreover,
it was equally clear that careful attention had to be given to the selection of potential contributors, particularly with regard to their positions and the kind, size, and location of their academic institutions.
In the interest of balance, and in recognition of limitations, special
guidelines were drawn and systematically pursued.

Four-year institutions of higher learning became the focus of
our interest, notwithstanding our awareness of the natural application
that administration holds for the ever-increasing number of community
and junior colleges. The national boundaries fixed our geographical
limits. Thereafter the task of determining a representative group of
analysts was tedious, despite the recourse to computer sampling. To
establish our affinity for equal opportunity, a concerted effort was
made to select cooperatives on the basis of their region of the country,
the kind of academic institution represented, its size, and the position
of the contributing official within it. The resultant collection of essays
are authored by a reasonable facsimile of our model. Over one-third
of the states are represented. Private and denominational schools
are numbered with those that are state-controlled in approximate
proportion to their relative strength nationwide. The colleges and
universities range in enrollment from a few hundred to over twenty
thousand. And most importantly, the administrators are representative of the principals normally found on campus, and fortunately they
possess diverse academic backgrounds and professional experience
in higher education.

As a group the authors are, with few exceptions, members of central administration. The presidents or chancellors, and to a lesser extent the vice presidents or provosts, may be said to hold a comparable perspective vis-a-vis the management of the academic enterprise. That view is universitywide or collegewide, and is affected by both internal and external affairs. That their orientation nevertheless will differ is attributable not only to the human condition, but also to the kind, size, and location of their institution, not to mention the nature of the problems peculiar thereto.

Subordinate to top management on campus is a host of supporting personnel worthy of note. As mentioned previously, these include the heads of a number of agencies essential to the orderly functioning of academe. Among them are the directors of admissions, personnel, accounting, libraries, etc., whose task it is to render supportive services to the academic community in compliance with the directives of higher authority. Surely these persons cannot be overlooked in an overview of higher education administration, for clearly they too are engaged in the making and execution of institutional policy. However, there are realistic limits in the conduct of research and analysis, and for the purpose of this work it was concluded that the higher officials would prove to be more appropriate communicators.

The deans in American colleges and universities are yet another breed. Although some serve in generalist capacities, and thereby may be considered a part of central administration, most are physically and psychologically a part of the collegiate university, that is, at the helm of and dedicated to one of the many academic or professional schools. Their resulting role is one of quasi-central and quasi-collegiate administrative responsibility, depending upon their position and predilections. Moreover, their attachment to the charge of education tends to be stronger than that of higher administrators, for few become divorced from their prior disciplinary interests. Thus any classification of deans, administratively speaking, is tenuous at best, although at least within the college they represent, their perspective is as broad as its purview.

Similar to the status of most deans, that of chairpersons of collegiate departments is not theoretically or effectively a part of central administration. Thus unlike comparable European institutions, wherein the locus of authority is vested in the college and generally is devoid of administrators superimposed thereon, the American system of higher educational organization causes the academic function to be subservient to the administrative. Of course, there are exceptions to this distinction, notably in some of our major universities. Therein one can find examples of policy decisions by deans and chairpersons, as well as by directors of bureaus and institutes, which are made and administered without review by higher authority. So in a fashion it can be argued that we have some semblance of the collegiate university, but at least in theory we cannot ignore the prerogative of higher administrators to override the wishes of subordinates should a confrontation arise.

Because the department head is clearly an integral part of collegiate management, whether of the foreign or domestic style, it must be noted that a concerted effort was made to enlist a representative number of them in our case studies. However, owing to inadequate and insufficient replies, the reader will observe that only a few have been accommodated. Of some importance are the reasons which apparently underlie the reluctance of department heads to offer a rendition on their experience. Although some surely cannot speak for all, it is worthwhile to summarize the explanations of those who elected to decline an invitation to participate in this effort. Essentially they advised that in addition to other restraints on their time they chose to refrain from making such a contribution because they sincerely questioned the significance of their position in higher education administration; they did not really believe themselves to be administrators as opposed to their being academicians; and they doubted very much if many of their colleagues viewed their plight to the contrary.

If these assertions are valid, they constitute a serious indictment of one of the basic assumptions regarding the development and execution of policy in higher education, namely the functional existence of a level of management purported to be essential to the rational administration of institutional objectives. And this consideration resurrects some questions long avoided by the profession and especially among those who espouse organizational orthodoxy. With all due respect to the position, who fills it and who made that determination? What credentials supported the appointment and what objective evidence exists to validate its appropriateness? How many chairpersons are enthusiastic about the role and how many can attest to substantive contributions growing out of their tenure?

To the extent that these persons are effective administrators, rather than academic housekeepers, there is no cause for alarm. To the degree that the secretary or a departmental business manager might function as well, there is room for innovative thought. For if the basis of selection is reward for extraordinary service in teaching or research, that judgment is both misguided and irrational. Extrication from the classroom or library under such circumstances is not likely to improve the chairperson's net effect in meeting the needs of students or the institution. Also, if the choice is predicated upon senior status, the whim of a superior, a compromise among colleagues, or the desire to promote up and out, the price in terms of leadership for the department and for the college and university is likely to be great.

It is not the purpose here to resolve this potential dilemma. Perhaps this is not a problem at all. However, it is an area of inquiry that should command far greater attention than has been given it to date. After all, administration is more than routine activity. Indeed it is partly that, but it is much more an obligation to creatively plan, organize, staff, direct, coordinate, budget, and review, and thereby to contribute to the goals of the organization be it an academic department or a larger entity. If a lesser effort is exerted by an administrator at any level, the time for reevaluation of the position and its incumbent is long overdue.

UTILITY OF CASE STUDIES

Attentive students of business and public administration have long been aware of the value of case studies in the training of individuals for positions of authority in private and public organizations. Postgraduate executives also have learned the merit of this educational approach toward upgrading their perceptiveness and skills. Although it is equally applicable for higher education administrators, whether for novices or veterans, the use of this method in preparing the former and expanding the horizons of the latter is far less prevalent.

Whether utilized in the classroom, in special conferences or workshops, or in independent reading, case studies entail a wide variety of instructive analyses which can contribute much insight and understanding to one's perception of higher education administration. Being both timely and timeless, the problematic aspect of these cases, and more importantly the favorable or fatal responses thereto, can prove useful for the edification of peers, as a reference for those who aspire to similar service, and otherwise as a source of information for those generally interested in the concerns and reactions of the administrative mind.

Lest these conclusions appear to be overdrawn, perhaps the words of a few administrators invited but unable to contribute to this work will attest to the merit of this approach. The dean of a northern college noted: "I fully realize the importance of the case study method in analyzing managerial problems." Added an eastern college vice president: "The book of case studies will be most valuable as a training tool for administrators." And a western college vice president observed: "Surely there can be no argument with the basic premise that real-life case studies can be of great instructional value to others who occupy the no-where land of college administration."

In addition, we feel obliged to acknowledge our appreciation for the words of those who unknowingly have given further impetus to the pursuit of this task. Indicative of the fear that continues to hamper the cause of open inquiry, one president of a northern private university was compelled to write: "It seems to me the better part of judgement that I not commit myself to such a candid public disclosure." And it would appear, on the other hand, that humility has not lost its place in academe, for as the dean of a western public university has admitted: "I remain a neophyte and hopefully a reasonably good student of administration. Like many others I have learned and practice much of the art from the 'saddle,' hence I have no desire to perpetuate such ignorance through a publication. Let the masters be our teachers, and hopefully in your search you will identify more of them than you can accept to assist in the development of a volume from which the rest of us who attempt to function in such capacity can learn."

Suffice it to conclude that all of the authors of this work would quickly disavow the presumptuous title of a master. On the other hand it is readily apparent that none is reticent about being candid. Hopefully their efforts will encourage more humility and less inhibition in the field of higher education administration, private as well as public. If some men and women may also be moved to effectively correct maladies in the administration of higher education, then this work will have been even more worthwhile.

At the midpoint in the decade of the 1970s, it became common knowledge among academicians and collegiate administrators that most institutions of higher learning were experiencing significant change, both in terms of their size and the character of their educational endeavors. The consequences are not unexpected: static or lesser numbers of students require a proportionate faculty and staff, and each in turn means fewer academic programs. The transition from relative affluence and controlled expansion, common to most colleges and universities before the turn of the 1970s, to reasonable austerity and planned contraction thereafter, has prompted a continuing reconsideration of educational goals and economic directions among those institutions concerned about their viability into the 1980s and beyond. Such cautious optimism is well advised, for the direction and degree of the phenomena of change is transitory, and its impact must be constantly reevaluated.

To keynote the problems of change for our colleges and universities, the following four studies address some of the contemporary conditions on the campuses and the reaction of many of their leaders to them. Harold P. Hanson opens this group of studies with a frank appraisal of the new campus realities and some of the resultant challenges today and in the foreseeable future. His exposition sets an important tone, for an understanding of the current and evolving demands upon the academic enterprise permits the making of more rational choices in the allocation of available resources. Along with change there inevitably comes institutional reorganization, either to serve a different clientele, or offer a different product, or enhance efficiency or effectiveness in performance. Similar to other large-scale organizations in society, the college or university must, in timely and appropriate fashion, respond to external trends and internal provocation, one consequence of which is the not altogether painless task of periodically restructuring its agencies and modifying its methods to meet more affirmatively and directly new demands and expectations of the institution. Charles W. Case provides an interesting account of that process and its trials and tribulations in a public institution of higher learning.

For the large educational complex, the question of its function and limitations is incessantly at the forefront of the administrative mind. So it is fitting that Richard H. Barbe and Roy M. Hall offer jointly a pertinent study on the problems encountered at one metropolitan state university which considered the use of its base campus as an operations center for extended educational activities. Leonard E. Goodall anchors this initial group of case studies with an analysis of a wide variety of concerns of importance to administrators and academicians in multiversity settings. His observations on inter-campus relations in multicampus universities reach many fundamental issues that both delight and confound the ablest of collegiate planners and managers.

Collectively, these analyses serve well in communicating a host of problems and resultant challenges that confront academe in the aftermath of changing socioeconomic conditions across America. Analogies on the international scene are no less pertinent. The academic objectives and professional aspirations of institutions and individuals in succeeding generations are, after all, seldom alike, for the development of technology and the norms of subsocieties the world over are by no means static. Nor are the nature and extent of educational and training programs that seek to respond affirmatively to changing needs and expectations. And higher education is not alone in this quest for relevancy in an era of transition, for that must transcend all levels of human development.

2

FROM THE EXPANDING
UNIVERSITY TO THE
STEADY STATE UNIVERSITY
Harold P. Hanson

Basically, there are two cosmological models of the universe that are given credence—the model of the expanding universe and that of the steady state universe. These terms have technical, scientific significance, but even to the lay person they are descriptive and almost self-explanatory. It must be understood, of course, that like the expanding phase, the steady state is not a stagnant condition; rather, it is a state of dynamic equilibrium.

In our microuniverse, the university, we have pragmatic exposure to both of these concepts in action. During the decade of the 1960s, college enrollments in the United States increased from 3.58 million to 7.92 million, a factor greater than two. That was the expanding universe phase—a heady, exhilarating, turbulent time.

In the early 1970s, however, university administrators became aware of the fact that the expansion was coming to an end. It became clear that the exponential growth curve, which everyone had been riding, was necking over into a sigmoidal curve, as all growth curves in nature must. Nationally, a monotonic decline in the absolute number of births had been in effect since 1957, and about six years of plateauing had preceded the 1957 maximum. College administrators, geared and trained for growth, noted with dismay that after 1975 the number of students entering the college-age pool would decline. Shifting priorities and attitudes among the young people of college age were producing precursors of the 1975 maximum as stationary or declining enrollments occurred in many universities. Emptying

---

Harold P. Hanson, Vice President, University of Florida.

elementary and secondary school buildings throughout the nation have
portended a time-displaced analogue for colleges and universities.

No matter how one views the enrollment patterns, it is clear
that the steady state university is in sight. No longer will formula-
generated funds, geared to rising enrollments, be available to develop
new programs, to purchase new equipment, or to hire new faculty
except on a replacement basis. There will be trauma associated with
shifting from the expanding university to the steady state university.
No university can avoid the trauma entirely, but it is an administration's responsibility to minimize the shock as much as possible.

THE UNIVERSITY OF FLORIDA: VITA

The University of Florida is a state-supported land grant school
having roots which go back to 1853. The university offers a broad
spectrum of academic opportunities. In addition to the traditional
arts and sciences programs, it has virtually every major academic
discipline located on its campus including medicine, law, agriculture,
business, engineering, dentistry, pharmacy, education, and journalism. At this writing the university has an enrollment of 25,000 which
is split between 8,000 lower division students, 11,500 upper division
students, and 5,500 graduate and advanced professional students. The
university has a total annual budget of $176 million. It has 2,700
faculty members, of whom half are in the general education budget
and half in medical, agricultural, and related programs. The University of Florida is a selective school that admits freshmen only from
the upper 40 percent of the Florida high school graduating classes;
three-quarters of the freshmen are from the upper 20 percent.

One boundary condition, that has a major impact on the way in
which the University of Florida must meet the challenge of change, is
the fact that it is part of the Florida State University System. The
Florida system consists of nine universities distributed throughout
the state; four of the universities have basically upper division and
beginning graduate programs, while five, including the University of
Florida, run the gamut from lower division to advanced graduate.
The whole system is under the aegis of a board of regents, and a
chancellor provides leadership and direction for the board office.

The University of Florida is the largest and oldest university
in the state, and designates itself as "Florida's first university." As
such it has surging ambitions for national leadership, and its eager
thrusts toward excellence on occasion run contrary to the concepts
and the planning of the administrators of the state system.

The University of Florida has been designated as one of two universities in the state which will emphasize graduate and professional education, but formula funding provides little opportunity for significant upgrading in quality. The struggle which is shaping up nationally between men of goodwill advocating the system approach and men of equal goodwill advocating the autonomous university approach is reflected in the occasional local skirmishes between the University of Florida and the board office. The State University System of Florida is one of the strongest in the nation; it is heartening, though perhaps puzzling, that the faculty of the University of Florida still maintains a spirited aspiration for greatness, and thus far the university has managed to avoid being just another component of the state system. Nevertheless, as a result of being imbedded in the system matrix, the University of Florida has systemwide budgetary constraints which deny to it some measure of the flexibility it needs to meet the exigencies of change.

DIMENSIONS OF THE PROBLEM

The first stage in solving a problem is to recognize the existence of the problem. While much of the rest of the nation has had a clearly established population leveling, particularly in the lower age brackets, Florida is still in an explosive growth phase. When percentage growth and absolute growth are considered together, it is probable that Florida has experienced greater population increase since the mid-1950s than any other state in the nation. About 300,000 people each year now migrate into the state; state officials address themselves to the problem of trying to stem this tide. Florida is the nation's largest housing market, and new housing permits issued in Florida are 25 percent greater than in California, which has three times the population of Florida.

In a climate such as this, it is not immediately obvious to the university faculty that the good days of growth cannot be with us forever. When one examines the circumstances in more detail, however, it becomes clear that the University of Florida's growth period will not be sustained indefinitely.

There are a number of contributory factors involved. First, at this stage, the state's growth is largely due to immigration, and furthermore the age profile of the population influx does not produce a proportional growth in the college student group. Second, more universities (and probably also community colleges) were created in Florida than could be justified economically on the basis of student need. The official projections made in the 1960s regarding the university and community college enrollments for 1980 exceeded reasonable expectations among the college-age pool. Third, there has been a decrease in the percentage of high school students who attend college. In Florida, the number of white male high school graduates who planned to enter college dropped from 62 percent to 54 percent from 1968 to 1971. Since this demographic group constitutes the major portion of the University of Florida's student population, it is clear that this university will be strongly affected. Furthermore, from 1969 to 1972 the overall percentage of Florida's high school graduates entering Florida's public colleges and universities fell steadily from 42.82 percent to 39.02 percent. Thus the leveling-off process is here and in effect.

It was, however, the fall enrollment of 1972 that brought the problem clearly to the attention of administrators and faculty members alike. Instead of the expected regular annual enrollment increase of 1,000 students, the increase was a mere 74. While various voices had been pointing out that continued growth was impossible, it took the nonrealization of the enrollment projection to truly drive home a recognition of reality. Thus when the University of Florida fell a thousand short of meeting its projections, this meant that money and faculty line-items had to be returned to the board office, since state fiscal support is formula generated, and the formula is driven by student enrollment.

Faculty members became aware that what they had considered to be the routine operation of the university was curtailed because the student-generated dollars simply were not there. Further, faculty hearing committees, dealing with denial-of-tenure cases, had recommended that "other" positions be made available to the individuals being denied tenure. They now learned that there simply were no such positions available. Thus an awareness developed which was perhaps not universal but it was wide enough and deep enough to set the stage for faculty response.

The response at the University of Florida took two forms. First, a serious consideration of the problems of the steady state university began. Attitudes, policies, and procedures were changed to adjust to the new realities. Obviously, such quasi-revolutionary changes take time and require faculty support. Consequently this adjustment still continues, and must continue, since it represents the long-term attack on the problem.

Second, for the short term, a major thrust was launched to put off the advent of the steady state. Clearly, the no-growth situation cannot be deferred indefinitely, but it was equally clear that at the University of Florida there was a good chance of phasing into it gracefully through the 1970s. The mitigating factors for the University of Florida were that the state is still growing vigorously and the university had never placed major emphasis on student recruitment. There remained a large reservoir of prospective students who could be attracted to Florida's first university if it were made clear to them not only that there were opportunities at the University of Florida, but also that they were wanted. In the earlier growth phase, the Admissions Office had been so concerned with keeping the quality of students high and the number under control, that they had done little to encourage the obviously qualified student to attend the university. It was hoped that a recruiting effort, which carried with it the caveat of maintaining academic quality, would be successful.

COPING WITH THE STEADY STATE

In the steady state situation, it is clearly the university's obligation and also its opportunity to see that the resources provided by the state are used most effectively. Fundamental to the appropriate and intelligent disposition of resources is the setting of priorities, and basic to the setting of priorities is the gathering of pertinent data. We have then a three-step process: (1) data gathering, (2) setting of priorities, and (3) assigning resources.

The gathering of data involves internal and external sources. The internal source is of course the university itself. To determine where one goes, one must assess where one has been and where one is. This may seem to be the ultimate platitude, but the fact is that universities, where so much research is done, have been notoriously lax over the years in analyzing and finding out about themselves. In most universities, budget and space have been a matter of history, and a cloudy obscure history at that. The decision-makers have rarely asked, "What are we doing now?" let alone "What should we be doing?" It is clear that most universities are recognizing this deficiency; they are learning where they are putting their resources, what happens to their expense dollars, their capital outlay dollars, but there is still much to do.

External sources of data are also a sine qua non for providing critical knowledge for setting priorities. The university is embedded in a milieu that is markedly different from the situation that obtained when universities were being structured and being staffed. This imposes the obligation of ensuring that our university be an integral living part of today's society, not a vestigial relic of a bygone day. We should know what society asks of our graduates in their various professions. We should know how many of these graduates society wants and needs.

To provide these and other types of data, at the University of
Florida, the Office of Academic Affairs, the Registrar's Office, and
the Division of Planning and Analysis embarked on a program of
developing information pertinent to the changing situation. The Division of Planning and Analysis, particularly, embarked on major
studies concerning the students and the state. Vital information is
now available regarding most facets of university existence. While
we still may be surprised by future events, we will better understand
why they happen when they do.

Once we have our data, once we know where we are, what our
assets are, and once we have an idea what demand there is for the
products of our institution, then we are in a position to establish
priorities. At the University of Florida, the decision was made to
accentuate six areas: architecture; the biological sciences; business
administration; the environmental sciences; journalism and communication; and law. This choice is in keeping with the university's mission
as a graduate and professional institution.

When priorities have been established, the task must be faced of
implementing them. Given the priorities, we then consider the
resources which a university possesses. Defining students as a con-
sumer group rather than a resource of a university, the usable
resources are (1) the faculty, (2) operating funds, and (3) space.
These are the resources that must be employed with wisdom and
discretion. Optimum utilization of these resources represents the
true long-term adjustment to steady state conditions.

The faculty represents the most precious asset that a university
has. Phasing into the steady state university will have obvious implications for the faculty. Very hard decisions will have to be made;
consequently the faculty itself must be involved in any policy decisions
which are developed. While there is a strong obligation on the part of
each university to defend and protect individual faculty rights, the
final consideration must be given to the rights of students as consumers
to obtain the best education possible. Classes must be taught by
faculty members who are au courant and vital.

The possibility of a faculty, tenured and titled, growing old
together invokes sentimental images of Mr. Chips, but it is not good
education. Excellence in academics at a university requires a constant throughput of vigorous individuals with bold new ideas. Nationally, in the early 1970s the fraction of tenured faculty in universities
and colleges has climbed from a comfortable one-half to an ominous
two-thirds. About 60 percent of college teachers are now over 40
years old. The corresponding information concerning the University
of Florida is less disturbing because the overall tenure fraction still
is at one-half, although certain academic areas give evidence of being
locked into their present faculty for the next two decades. The median

ages of associate professors and professors have each decreased
during the 1970s. The median age of all tenured faculty is forty-eight,
which means that half of the tenured group is more than two decades
away from retirement.

The approach used at the University of Florida in dealing with
this problem was to familiarize the faculty with the situation, and to
stress the care that would be necessary in initial recruiting and in
granting tenure. A series of studies on the steady state was prepared
and disseminated; every effort is being made to expand the faculty
development program so as to prevent faculty obsolescence; faculty
exchange programs are under consideration; in-service training
programs are being planned and executed; some industrial internships have been instituted to keep faculty knowledgeable in the real-
world application of their disciplines; and tentative efforts to institute
an early retirement program have been launched. It should be noted
that this administration is opposed to any imposition of tenure quotas,
but this carries with it the common obligation of the whole academy
to ensure that tenure be granted only to those for whom a presumption
of continued academic excellence seems strongly justified.

There is a trend observed nationally whereby line-items which
have become vacated by virtue of resignations, nonrenewals, etc.,
revert to a central office of the university. There is a dual purpose
in this. One reason for it is to make certain that there has been
indeed a thorough, conscientious recruiting effort for a qualified
woman or a member of the minority groups; the other reason is that
the line can be reassigned to the area where it is needed and where
the priorities have been established.

This policy was not adopted in toto at the University of Florida
principally because (1) it deemphasizes the central role of departments, and (2) it discourages critical evaluation of individuals being
considered for tenure. Departments must be assured they will not
be penalized for exerting careful selectivity.

A modified approach was used which permits all freed line-items
to remain in the department, but they revert to the level of assistant
professor. The salary savings are taken over by the Office of Academic Affairs to ensure universitywide equity in the assignment of
raises and to allow for administrative input in the application of
university priorities.

Parenthetically, it should also be noted that coping with the
steady state increases the requirement for vigorous and visionary
academic administrators. We have been a longtime advocate of fixed-
term appointments for all academic administrators so as to provide
graceful and timely exits. This has not as yet received general
faculty acceptance.

Operating funds represent the second major resource of a university. While no reallocation of resources is easy in a long-established university, operating funds represent the most flexible asset for reassignment. This resource can be handled mechanically with less personal involvement than is inherent in manipulating the other resources, since with operating funds there is usually less of a continuing commitment in existence. Further, small shifts of funds away from the nonpriority program will usually have undramatic effects, and they often show a gratifying effect on the priority program that receives help. At the University of Florida, the established priority listing has provided an effective framework within which to make the shift of funds.

Space is the third major resource and is probably the most volatile item with which to deal. There is always a great deal of history underlying the present configuration of space. Departments and colleges have been frequently involved in lobbying for their present space, and they may have even obtained the funding, perhaps from the federal government, to erect the various buildings they occupy.

Space is thus an emotional issue. While a faculty member can become depressed and discouraged by not getting sufficient expense and equipment money to run his program, it is on the subject of space that he reacts with passion. Clearly, man has evolved as a territory-defending creature whose territorial instinct is easily inflamed. If an administrator attempts to reassign space, he must be prepared for vigorous if not venomous reaction. On the other hand there is nothing that quite matches the envy and covetousness that arises in the academic animal when he sees space that he needs which he feels is not being used as productively as possible.

To address the problem generally, the Office of Academic Affairs has promulgated the policies given below; this office does not have control of space at the University of Florida, but these policies have played some role in shaping recommendations which have been given due consideration.

1. Space on the campus is not "owned" by any particular academic unit. Its use presents common opportunity to all of the campus community. The only exceptions involve still-current commitments made at the time of funding the original construction.

2. The space generation formula is only a zero-order approximation which relates to the total space on campus. Real need and priorities will provide the higher-order correction.

3. Space may be assigned on a temporary basis to a particular academic unit. This implies that it may be reassigned. There should be a continuing assessment of space needs and potential.

4. No space should lie unused waiting for future use as long as there are current pressing needs that are unsatisfied.

5. Research space should represent the most stable and firm commitment, but an individual who is not using his research area productively must anticipate that it will be assigned to another researcher.

6. A teaching laboratory should not be committed to a department if the utilization of that laboratory is below 30 percent.

7. Offices and research laboratories must not be used for storage. Unless authorized to the contrary, equipment retained in storage and not used for three years should be junked.

8. If usable, suitable space is offered to a have-not group and the space is rejected, the group's space priority will be moved to a lower category.

9. No faculty member shall occupy two offices as long as space is needed by other faculty.

10. Graduate students will not have priority over a regular faculty member in office assignment even if the faculty member is not part of the academic area to which the space has been assigned.

POSTPONING THE STEADY STATE

It has been said that we live in the short run; in the long run we die. Simply because enrollment is apparently due to level off does not necessarily mean, even with formula funding, that there are no short-run solutions. The two main possibilities for increasing the support dollars available to the university are (1) to increase nonformula funds, and (2) increase the enrollment.

First we shall consider the possibility of increasing nonformula funds. There are three avenues within this basis approach: private support, federal funds, and extra-formula state funds. All three avenues are being explored with inconclusive but encouraging results.

In the private sector, the University of Florida has been notably lagging in its efforts. For years, the university leadership felt that it was improper if not unethical to seek private support for a state university. This quaint morality eventually faded, but no concerted major fund drive has been launched as yet, although preparations are underway. At this writing, the fund-raising effort is costing the university substantially more than it is producing, but hopefully this is an initial phase that will be followed by a more productive operation. The first priority for use of private funds if they become available will be to provide student scholarships, support faculty chairs, and augment faculty salaries.

On the other hand, there has long been a canny, aggressive, and successful effort to obtain federal funds. While many schools have been experiencing a decreasing level of federal support, the University of Florida has been successful in raising its federal funding. But the possibility of increasing the flow of federal dollars by any truly substantial amount is not realistic since the University of Florida already receives an amount not much less than what it might possibly get considering the politics of federal fund disbursement and the intrinsic quality of the school. Nevertheless, there is continuing and heightened interest in obtaining federal funds.

The possibility for securing ancillary state funding by extra-formula allocations for university activities is being explored. Currently, the health program and the agriculture program are supported by direct appropriations on a project basis. There is much that the more traditionally academic portions of the university can do in terms of problem solving and project research that could well receive direct allocations from the legislature. A first effort in this direction, to get a quarter of a million dollars for a coastal engineering laboratory, was successful. Subsequent efforts for similar projects have not received board office support. Nevertheless, the university is strongly emphasizing and broadening its role as a service-oriented land grant university that is geared to do programmatic problem-solving research, while in no way slackening the pure research which undergirds its teaching program.

The second possibility for postponing the steady state is by continuing to increase the enrollment. As indicated previously, the university had never made any effort to attract students. With the realization of coming events, the school geared up to recruit vigorously and unabashedly. Large portions of several sessions of the Council of Deans meetings were given over to exhortations for future recruiting efforts, to recriminations about past failures, and to planning strategy.

The registrar and his staff made a serious and effective effort to change the image of their operation. Stung by the charge that they had a "rejection" office rather than an admissions office, the admissions unit developed imaginative and innovative methods of contacting and staying in contact with prospective students. Attitude sessions were conducted by the registrar with the various functionaries under his aegis. Attractive brochures were prepared. Obvious admissions decisions were acted upon with dispatch.

A major defect in the operation of the admission process had been uncovered by an arts and sciences study team. Genuine, but monitored, letters of inquiry were sent by prospective students from Gainesville to the University of Florida Admissions Office, as well as to universities around the nation. It was found that responses were received routinely from the home school long after the natural recruiting rivals of the University of Florida had responded, and at about the same time as responses were received from some of the most distant and unlikely places. This situation has changed.

A further failing lay in the fact that the Registrar's Office ran out of catalogs in the middle of the recruiting season. In previous years this would have been regarded as routine, and indeed prospective students were sent a standard mimeographed card stating that if they still wished to have catalogs after they were printed for the next year, they should write and ask for them. Needless to say, when this situation was uncovered new catalogs were printed for the current year; also interestingly enough a whole new set came out of storage.

A followup procedure was instituted to keep the interest of students who had been informed that they were admissible. A newsletter called Prevues for Future Gators was instituted giving the prospective enrollee information about the university and about things that were happening on campus. The Registrar's Office identified top applicants to the appropriate deans and departmental chairmen so they could follow up on such applicants personally. A black admissions officer was added which rather obviously had something to do with the 30 percent increase in black enrollees.

It seems clear that the concerted effort by the Registrar's Office to make certain that prospective students were genuinely welcomed to the University of Florida was the keystone of the recruitment effort. However, the contribution of the deans of the various colleges should not be overlooked. Various deans embarked on vigorous collegewide recruitment drives. This involved personal letters to prospective students; sending out recruitment teams of students, faculty, and administrators; developing attractive college recruitment literature; and very personal attention to individual prospects and their problems.

The effort was a resounding success. While the other 8 universities in the state system either failed to meet their projections or were just able to, the University of Florida grew by an astonishing 6 percent, or 1,500 students. Perhaps even more remarkable, 85 percent of the growth consisted of new students, in contrast to a five-year average of 22 percent during the years of our strongest growth surge, 1965-69. In previous years the primary driving force behind the enrollment increases was the rapid growth of the available pools of prospective students, not the yield rate from the pools. Studies by the Division of Planning and Analysis indicate that by and large the yield rates had been declining in all areas until the quantum jump in 1973. And this quantum jump was largely the result of a concerted campuswide effort in recruitment.

There were other influences at work as well and it is not clear to what extent they are separable from the recruitment effort. For example, it has been observed nationally that in those states which have a system approach, the older, more established schools have grown or held their own at the expense of the newer institutions. This nationally observed phenomenon probably stems from the perceived value of a degree from a prestigious university and is related to both effective recruiting and changing student attitudes.

Other factors in the growth included the diminution of the adverse national publicity concerning the purported lack of job opportunities for college graduates. Furthermore, a University of Florida decision to permit freshmen to bring cars to the campus, while basically a move away from in loco parentis, was a useful if nonrepeatable component of the recruitment effort.

Perhaps the most gratifying aspect of the recruiting effort is the fact that by every criterion the 1975 crop of students was the best academically that the university has ever had. It is clear that the recruiting was aimed at the highly motivated and highly qualified student.

SUMMARY

Like most state-supported universities whose funds derive from student enrollments, the University of Florida is being forced to face the problem of resource reallocations in a time of no increase in these resources. This poses difficult problems particularly in the area of faculty personnel. A general campus awareness of the problem provides a realistic atmosphere in which, for the most part, solutions can be worked out which are fair to the faculty and which maintain the quality of the school.

Further, it seems that controlled growth is still possible for the University of Florida. The no-growth autumn of 1972 has made the university community aware that the steady state can and will arrive. But, the community also knows that with careful and judicious husbanding of resources at this stage, the shift from the expanding university to the steady state university can be accomplished with a minimum of trauma and disorientation.

3

**TRIALS AND TRIBULATIONS
OF UNIVERSITY REORGANIZATION:
INITIAL STEPS TOWARD
A MATRIX ORGANIZATION**
Charles W. Case

Mountain University was founded in the last decade of the eighteenth century as a private and nondenominational institution. It is located in a small northern state of 450,000 people, whose history has been based on individualism and independence. In 1955 Mountain University became a state university and now receives one-fifth of its financing from the state. Separately, the state also finances four other public colleges and part of an emerging community college.

Mountain University enrolls about 8,000 undergraduate students and around 500 graduate students. Prior to the reorganization process to be recounted herein, the university consisted of the College of Arts and Sciences, the College of Technology, the College of Medicine and the Division of Health Sciences, the College of Education, the College of Agriculture and Home Economics (one of the original land-grant institutions), and the Graduate College. Slightly over one-half of the students in the university were undergraduates in the College of Arts and Sciences. The College of Agriculture and Home Economics also directed the university's Agricultural Extension Service and its Agricultural Experiment Station.

The university's primary commitment has been and is to undergraduate education in the liberal arts and the professions. Many faculty members in the liberal arts have never really accepted the fact that Mountain University is now a public institution. Generally, the four professional schools perceive themselves as state institutions and have committed themselves enthusiastically to service, research,

Charles W. Case, Director of Educational Research, University of Vermont.

and graduate education in addition to their primary commitment to undergraduate education. The Graduate College is responsible for all graduate education in the university.

Like most universities, Mountain University began to feel financial trauma about 1970 due to shrinking federal dollars, decreasing state assistance, and rising costs. It has not, though, experienced a decline in admissions demand.

UNIVERSITY REORGANIZATION
TASK FORCE ESTABLISHED

In 1972 the president and the academic vice president of Mountain University began to analyze the persistent problems they had encountered during the two years that they had been in office. Both men had also served as college deans in the university prior to their current positions—the president as dean of the Medical College and the academic vice president as dean of the College of Arts and Sciences.

Their initial listing of problems included territorial wars among departments, lack of specified missions for colleges, shrinking employment opportunities in engineering, duplication of courses across departments, excessive departmental autonomy, lack of cooperation among colleges, and changes in the agricultural mission. Also some departments seemed to be placed illogically within colleges due to the historical restrictions of a private fund; this had resulted in the basic sciences departments being located in three different colleges.

There was also concern about what balance should exist among the university's three main missions: teaching, research, and service. This issue had become critical due to the rapidly shrinking research monies available to the university. This concern had also caused the university administration to do some preliminary cost analysis of various departments as well as financial projections for the next five years. It was clear that the university could not continue to be all things to all people.

In September 1972, the president commissioned a University Reorganization Task Force to analyze and make recommendations for improving the academic structure so as to more effectively carry out the university's education, research, and service missions. The charge to the task force, which was publicly disseminated, further asked the task force to consult as widely as possible both within and without the university, work as visibly as possible, be receptive to all ideas, and achieve a synthesis of the best thinking relating to both academic approaches and priorities. The task force's recommendations were to be submitted to the president nine weeks later on

December 1, 1972, so that they could be presented to the Board of
Trustees at its December meeting.

The appointed task force consisted of one department chairman
from each of the five colleges, one undergraduate student, an assistant
to the president, and the academic vice president. The representative
from the College of Agriculture and Home Economics was appointed as
the chairman. The members were told to readjust their regular duties
to provide the necessary time for this effort. The committee was
provided a secretary and a budget.

PHASE ONE: THE TASK FORCE PROCESS

The task force spent the first two weeks of its nine-weeks assignment meeting with the president and vice president to further clarify
their perceptions of the problems and to confront them on the short
time period provided for the study—a matter of great concern to many
faculty members on campus. The results of this dialogue were that it
was agreed that a short-term intensive effort would probably yield
recommendations not unlike those that would result from a long-term
effort, that the task force's recommendations would serve as stimuli
for campus discussion prior to final recommendations to be made to
the trustees sometime in the following spring, and that the task force
would not in this first phase focus on horizontal organizational concerns such as the Graduate College or the Division of Continuing Education. The task force then proceeded to expend slightly over 1,000
person-hours to develop its recommendations.

The task force began by examining some of the specific problems
mentioned previously. These were viewed as symptoms of more basic
dysfunctions in organizational structure and processes. Some of the
major dysfunctions identified at this point were overlapping missions
among departments and colleges and lack of cooperative effort. It
was also decided that the current organizational structure reflected a
historical division of knowledge that might not be appropriate to
society's needs of today or tomorrow. Existing decision-making processes in curriculum and budget fostered departmental autonomy which
resulted in a lack of interdependence. The task force spent many
hours clarifying the need for organizational adaptiveness to interdisciplinary education and research, along with the need to preserve
some of the traditional university missions such as the preservation,
transmission, and advancement of disciplines.

Cost effectiveness was a matter of frequent discussion, particularly with regard to the high unit cost of the College of Technology.
Little challenge of a similar nature was raised regarding the sacred

cow of medical education. The duplication of courses and low-enroll-
ment programs were also a matter of concern.

It was felt that the existing organizational rigidity coupled with
an ineffective academic advising system did not encourage students to
take courses outside their own college. There was a strong feeling
that the almost complete relaxation of curriculum requirements
during the late sixties had resulted in even greater departmental
parochialism and narrow educational programs for students.

As the task force began to examine alternative designs for the
removal and addition of colleges and departments, the major concern
focused on the sciences. Two design themes emerged. One set of
designs for collegiate reorganization focused on a sharp distinction
between applied sciences and basic science. These designs usually
tended toward putting all applied sciences (engineering, agriculture,
computer science, business administration) in one College of Applied
Science. All basic sciences (physics, chemistry, biological sciences,
mathematics) would be placed in the College of Arts and Sciences in
these plans. A second plan was to place all sciences, applied and
basic, in one College of Science.

This led to many discussions of the dangers of separating the
sciences from the arts, humanities, and social sciences. C. P. Snow
was often mentioned in this context. The distinction between an
applied and a basic science also became fuzzy when the functions of
education, research, and service were considered for any given
department.

Other alternatives were also briefly considered such as having
only three colleges: the College of Arts and Sciences, the College of
Medicine, and the College of Applied Science, which would include all
existing colleges of applied and professional education except medicine.

At about the four-week mark in the study the campus community
became edgy: What was the task force doing? The rumor mill began.
Paranoia ran rampant: it was said the university would eliminate agriculture or technology or home economics. The task force then began
to meet with faculty, deans, and students to solicit their opinions.
During this time task force members met with eight deans, three
directors, thirty-seven chairpersons, and numerous faculty and students. Generally the suggestions received were of three types: leave
everything as it is, do away with some other department (not one of
the three mentioned above), or eliminate certain duplicative courses.
More of a macroperspective was seldom suggested.

Simultaneously, the task force continued to examine enrollment
trends, the structure of other universities, credit hours generated by
departments, the university's budgets, national employment trends,
and departmental missions.

In its eighth week of operation the task force began writing its recommendations. The report began with a litany of the university's problems discussed above.

The report then stated the guidelines of organizational criteria used by the task force to make its recommendations: (1) Primary academic responsibility for specific disciplines should reside in single administrative units, which must meet the service needs of other programs—a criterion directed toward creating interdependence and avoiding duplication; (2) program size alone does not determine the continuing existence of a program; (3) a major academic unit should consist of departments and programs that participate in the stated mission of that unit; (4) the university should balance its effort between professional studies and liberal arts education with the primary focus on undergraduate education; and (5) cooperation and conjunction should exist between the theoretical and applied areas of disciplines.

The report then outlined the specific problems in each of the existing colleges.

Next a set of general recommendations were made that included the need for curricular breadth, depth, and rigor; recognition of alternative learning and teaching strategies, with less emphasis on FTTE's (full-time teaching equivalents); the need for cross-college curricular decision-making processes; administrative rewarding of interdepartmental cooperation; careful analysis of the potential long-term effects of outside money before its acceptance; help for faculty members in developing new skills and applying their knowledge; and the launching of an intensive study of the possibility of a matrix organization design for the university.

The specific recommendations were preceded with the caveats that they were to stimulate discussion and that the recommended changes must be viewed as evolutionary.

Briefly the specific recommendations focused on dissolving the College of Agriculture and Home Economics and the College of Technology. The word "dissolve" was soon to be an anathema. From this dissolution would emerge the College of Applied Science consisting of the departments in the two former colleges plus business administration and new departments of statistics and computer sciences. The three engineering departments would meld into one department, as would the departments in agriculture except for home economics and forestry. One-half of the program in home economics, those studies dealing with human development, early childhood, and social work, would go to the College of Education, which would be renamed the College of Education and Human Resources. Chemistry and mathematics, formerly in Technology, would go to Arts and Sciences. A new department of biological sciences would be formed in Arts and

Sciences to include botany, zoology, and biochemistry. Other less
major departmental shifts were also recommended.

The recommendations also included the suggestion that a search
committee be formed to secure a new dean for the new college, a
move that was unpopular with the two existing deans in agriculture
and technology.

As will be seen below, the recommendations did clearly stimulate dialogue.

PHASE TWO: THE DIALOGUE

Phase Two of the study began as the trustees, the faculty, and
the public received the report simultaneously. Public reactions were
immediate: "The president was surprised and displeased with some
of the recommendations." "The attempt is to restructure not dissolve."
"I got more than I bargained for." "The trustees felt that agriculture
was being downgraded." "More information is needed." A local editorial stated that the reorganization plan was silly and a clear indication of the antiagricultural and snob attitudes of the academics on
the hill. A U.S. senator admonished: "They can't do away with
agriculture;" and he proceeded to raise the ghost of Justin Morrill!

During the next month over one hundred letters of protest were
received from various agricultural associations in the state. The
reaction on campus was almost completely from agricultural faculty
and students; most other faculty and students did not respond.

In late January 1973 the president suggested a modification of
the task force plan that would have a Division of Applied Sciences
composed of four schools: Agriculture, Natural Resources, Engineering, and Home Economics; the division would be headed up by a
new dean.

Also during January the task force prepared an addendum to
provide further reasons for its recommendations. The addendum
highlighted the enrollment trends and credit hour data over the previous
ten years. It also discussed more fully the self-determined changes
in mission that agricultural departments had made and how such
changes caused them to overlap with other colleges. It also showed
the semantic changes agricultural departments had made in an effort
to drop the term agriculture, including two attempts to change the
college's name. Additional rationale for the other recommendations
was also provided. The addendum ended with, again, a statement of
the need for an intensive study of a matrix organizational design.
Also during January the agricultural deans prepared and disseminated
a counterproposal quite similar to the College of Applied Science plan,

except the expanded college would be the College of Agriculture. This plan did not please the engineering and business administration faculties.

The agricultural committees of the State House of Representatives and the State Senate met with the president and the agricultural dean of the university to let the president know that they did not want any changes in the College of Agriculture. They wanted the dean to continue to report directly to the president, and they wanted a college not a school. The agricultural dean's strategy throughout most of Phase Two was to work through state agriculturalists and faculty, to comment only occasionally to the press, and to avoid direct confrontation with the president.

In February 1973 the president conducted an open meeting. The participants consisted mainly of officers from various agricultural associations and agricultural faculty. The most common appeals and demands were that the university leadership is not agriculturally oriented, agriculture is the backbone of the state's economy, agriculture was being degraded, and agriculture is a way of life. A handful of speakers from the College of Arts and Sciences and the College of Education supported the task force plan.

The trustees met again and expressed more favor with the president's plan, except they wanted business administration added to the School of Engineering. They also suggested that agriculture remain a college.

During this time the state legislature elected three new representatives to the university trustees; the university's downgrading of agriculture became the major issue and three proagriculturists were elected. The governor also publicly supported the College of Agriculture.

In March 1973 it was decided by the president that recommendations would not be taken to the trustees until May or June. Meanwhile the cards and letters continued to come. The mathematics faculty requested its own school. The botany and zoology departments requested to remain separate. Home Economics sought the return of the programs destined for education, except social work. The president met again with the State House and the Senate Agriculture Committees for a rerun of their earlier meeting.

The president and the deans of all the colleges examined the various proposals. They agreed on a revised plan to set up the Division of Applied Sciences along with the College of Agriculture and the Schools of Home Economics, Engineering and Management Science, and Natural Resources.

The task force, which was now meeting very infrequently, suggested to the president that its subsequent study of the Graduate College, Continuing Education, and other horizontal concerns be

postponed until the fall of 1973. The president agreed. This study was
never revived. In April and May the heat of the battle began to subside.
The trustees met again with the president and decided to vote in June.
The president met with the faculty senate and the faculty policy committees to discuss further modifications in the plan and stated that
the revised plan was not a retreat, but an evolution that would require
updating.

The president decided that in June he would request only the
creation of three schools: Natural Resources; Home Economics; and
Engineering, Mathematics, and Business Administration. Also chemistry would go to the College of Arts and Sciences, social work to the
College of Education, and philosophy and religion into two departments. The dean of agriculture would remain so, the chairwoman of
home economics would be director of that area, and the other two
schools would have acting directors. The 1973-74 academic year
would be devoted to further defining the missions of these units. In
August 1973 the trustees approved a name change for education to the
College of Education and Social Services. This college had reacted
during the previous spring and had accomplished its own internal
reorganization to better meet its expanded mission by combining four
programs into one program area and redefining the mission of one
other program area; two programs were left as they were. The final
caveat from some legislators was that they were not pleased with
agriculture losing home economics and forestry, but they would not
retaliate.

SUMMARY

The reorganization process at Mountain University has hopefully
set into motion a heightened awareness of the need for organizational
flexibility with regard to its structure. The process used stimulated
badly needed dialogue and many issues gained added definition. If the
process continues, and there are hopeful indicators that it will, new
transformations in the university's structure and processes will continue to emerge—new patterns of organization that may be more
relevant to today and tomorrow, rather than organizational patterns
based on the needs of yesterday.

The immediate outcomes of this initial effort fell short of the
recommendations provided by the task force. The political dynamics
of the process did result in more minor changes. In essence, the
College of Agriculture lost home economics and forestry, but retained
its college status and dean. These two units gained the autonomy and
a mandate to more specifically define their missions. The new School

of Engineering, Mathematics, and Business Administration is an
amalgamation that offers the possibility of creative programming.

The division of the basic sciences into different college units is
an issue that has not yet been resolved, though chemistry has moved
into the College of Arts and Sciences.

The placement of social work into the renamed College of Education and Social Services, coupled with that college's own internal
reorganization, has already greatly changed its curricular orientation
and its linkages with a variety of social service agencies. This college
also reaffirmed an earlier commitment not to structure itself into
departments, but rather into program areas with specific missions
that are to be reconsidered every three years.

If the reorganization effort remains a process and not an occasional event an evolutionary transformation of the university is
possible.

MATTERS FOR FURTHER CONSIDERATION

Universities, as most are currently structured, clearly represent an intellectual and organizational belief structure that has per-
sisted for many years. As many critics have pointed to the lack of
relevance in universities, few have looked beyond either society's
immediate and future needs or faculty attitudes to examine the rein-
forcing pressures of the universities' organizational structure and
their planning and decision-making processes. We speak of the
rigidity in disciplines and the need for interdisciplinary interaction,
but we do not examine the autonomy that we have vested in departments; nor do we examine our faculty reward systems that reinforce
a discipline bias.

In curricular matters we seldom reexamine our assumptions
about the structure of knowledge; must knowledge forever be classified
in the past? The efforts at planning and evaluation seldom risk fore-
casting future needs; rather most such endeavors focus mainly on
"turf" issues and faculty idiosyncrasies. Seldom do departments ever
define or redefine their departmental mission and how this relates to
the rest of the university. Universities tend to be structured into a
collection of isolated and autonomous tribes.

The task force in this study indicated many times its interest in
the possibility of a matrix organization that would stress the notion
of temporary system structures that bring together interdisciplinary
resources to achieve specific program objectives, and would create
the opportunity for the fluidity of personnel. This possibility needs to
be seriously studied and alternative designs tried. At Mountain

University efforts in this direction have been aided by the process described here. As mentioned before, the College of Education and Social Services has made significant progress in this direction. The College of Medicine has implemented a matrix design that maintains the traditional departments, but they work through interdepartmental program management committees to build and deliver educational programs. The first all-university effort has now begun with the new Living/Learning Center that works with all colleges to provide a number of new and/or interdisciplinary programs of study.

A matrix system or any other structural approach to university transformation necessitates a simultaneous transformation in the processes of planning, evaluation, decision-making, budgeting, and the reward system. Structure and behavior reinforce one another.

4

THE METROPOLITAN STATE
UNIVERSITY: ON BECOMING
AN OPERATIONS CENTER

Richard H. Barbe
Roy M. Hall

GSU is an urban-center university, and as such its problems are almost exactly the same as those facing other institutions and businesses in the city center. Rapid growth and limited land area have caused problems of space, safety, traffic, and the like. As its demands for service have increased, the public has become increasingly unwilling to come to our location for study.

The university has historic relations with the banking, insurance, and commercial sales industries still housed in the city's core. Sixty years ago the state created the university to respond to this need for expertise in the "new science of business." The change from a public business administration college to a multipurpose university has occurred largely since the mid-1960s.

The difficulties associated with a center-city location are not yet reflected in growth figures. Enrollment has increased from 9,000 to 18,000 over the past five years. There is, however, no real competition; the only other local multipurpose university complexes are private and expensive. The university's lower division enrollment has begun to decline; there are three public junior colleges on the periphery of the metropolitan area. While the growth rate is declining, the total is still increasing because of growth at upper, primarily graduate, levels.

The city is youthfully dynamic. So rapid is its growth that while peripheral industrial parks are opening routinely, there is still much new construction in the city's center. The design of what mass

Richard H. Barbe, former Dean, and Roy M. Hall, Dean, Georgia State University.

transportation there is reinforces the vitality of the downtown area—
a convenient, very inexpensive bus system operates spoke-like with
many lines leading directly into the core and almost no lines moving
people circumferentially around the city. Sports, dining, and cultural
activities also help to draw people downtown. Thus far the city has
been able to move both outward at the edges and upward at the center.

NEW DEGREE PROGRAMS

A part of the university's growth was created by the addition of
new degree programs. Professional education and the allied health
professions, particularly, brought large numbers of additional students
into both the baccalaureate and graduate levels.

At the time these programs were added, professionals in the
fields were becoming increasingly concerned for the resolution of the
historic theory-practice distinctions. It was apparent that nurses
couldn't be prepared exclusively in university classrooms nor could
teachers be prepared apart from operating schools. And these schools,
hospitals, and other field agencies had followed population residences
away from the center city. Thus, the best laboratories to support the
new programs were located away from the university, often on the
metropolitan fringe.

Duplicating laboratories so that students can receive on-site
experiences available through other agencies is not economically
feasible. Construction costs in the area are spiralling upwards from
$50 per square foot for high-rise buildings located on land surface
which costs $30 or more per square foot to begin with.

Continuing to accommodate larger numbers of students at one,
inner-city location has aggravated other problems. Parking was the
first, the most obvious, and the most publicized of these. The university's first long-range plan called for parking levels under all new
buildings. The economic unsoundness of this (the bottoms of buildings
must be engineered to support the tops and hence parking under a
building costs more than $30,000 per space) has become apparent.

The construction, by the university, of new parking decks and
the chartering of shuttle buses to move people (for 10¢ a ride) from a
reasonably close stadium parking lot have eased the problem at
present.

Buildings designed to permit the free and quick access of large
numbers of students also permit easy access to people with nonedu-
cational intentions. Security and safety problems increase exponen-
tially as the concentration of students on a central city campus
increases. The cost of theft to the university is a significant budget

item; but the publicity given to attacks on persons poses an even greater problem in that it increases public unwillingness to come to the campus.

In many fields the needs for continuing, in-service, professional training are growing. Teachers, nurses, therapists, and other human welfare workers are all facing growing pressures to continue their educations. And these professionals live, and for the most part work, away from the university's central location.

A teacher's concern for her safety does not lessen her demand on the university to provide additional appropriate experience; it only modifies the geographic basis of the demand—she wants the course to be offered at a location close to where she works or lives.

THE DILEMMA BECOMES CLEAR

The problem, thus, emerged as the dilemma of conflicting alternatives. On the one hand were the forces acting to decentralize some of the university's effort; on the other were the forces and commitments acting to maintain a strong, centrally-located operation. Decentralization was considered to be the only logical alternative; the idea of relocation to a single, more peripheral site was discarded on the basis that the outward movement of the population was occurring about equally in all compass directions. No geographic or political barriers exist which might limit the amount or direction of the city's expansion.

The racial mix of the population is, of course, a factor here as elsewhere. But it is not much of a force influencing the decentralization of university services. Affluent whites and blacks have moved outward in about equal proportions. The residents who remain close-in are increasingly black and poor.

The forces affecting decentralization/centralization, then, were (1) the economic costs of the center-city site, (2) the factors associated with the personal convenience and safety of students, (3) the quality of professional instruction, and (4) some political and legal constraints.

Economic Costs

The university administration has made much of its ability to get a high return on operating funds. The institution maintains, with pride, that it offers almost 40 percent of its student credit-hours

after 4 p.m. The classroom occupancy rate is, roughly, 100 percent
from 9 a.m. through 1 p.m. and from 5 to 7 p.m. on weeknights.
Early mornings and afternoons are light—about 30 percent; late evenings are losing popularity, with occupancy no more than 20 percent of
capacity. Almost no courses are taught on Saturdays.

Class sizes, too, show efficiency. While there is variation
among levels (graduate classes are the smallest) and among schools
(Arts and Sciences has the smallest), the average class size for the
university is about 20. The faculty is teaching-oriented and carries
an average load of slightly more than two such classes per quarter.

Through efficiencies, the cost of providing instruction in the
downtown area is no greater than on small-town, residential campuses.
The faculty's transportation costs are not borne, directly or indirectly,
by the university—salary levels at two other state-assisted universities
are higher. Increased classroom construction costs are, at least
partly, compensated for by relatively high usage rates.

Costs for supporting services are high. The university employs
about twice the security force as that of a larger, nearby, small-town,
state university. Parking decks cost more than parking lots; clerical
and technical services compete for personnel with law and insurance
offices; and maintenance people find it easy to move to construction
employment.

There are no university-related residence halls and there is
little space available on campus for recreation. Food service is provided on a franchise/lease basis by private corporations. Students
go elsewhere in the the city for facilities for both recreation and social
activities.

Convenience and Safety

The size and operating policies of the security force have produced a good record for students' safety. Roving patrols, escort
service, additional fencing, and high-intensity lighting have reduced
parking lot attacks to fewer than one per quarter. Minor incidents
have been reduced by in-person or television monitoring of campus
entrances to screen out unauthorized persons.

But the university's personal safety image is still poor. Publicity
given to attacks in other parts of the downtown area and the expansion,
by rumor, of real but minor incidents into major crises have left
many students, potential students, and husbands or fathers of students
doubtful of the university's ability to keep students safe. Parking on
campus lots and decks has been expanded so that most night students
can park within the university's security system; city buses, for the

most part, don't operate from the area after 7:30 p.m. for lack of
riders—students fear the wait for the bus.

Convenience is also an important factor. The expansion of the
city is multidimensional and the rush-hour traffic flow is also multi-
directional—the five o'clock flow through the city center from northeast to southwest is about as slow as the flow from the center toward
the northeast. A rush-hour trip from the circumference to the campus
is a one-hour drive from almost any direction by almost any alternate
route. Except for people employed by downtown firms, then, after-
work courses are hard to get to. And the newer programs serve
people and agencies that generally are located away from the city core.

Instructional Quality

Professional preparation, at the baccalaureate level, and continuing educational development, at the graduate level, demand appropriate clinical and field experience. The easiest and most effective
way for students to come to understand the relationships between
theory and practice is for the students to move freely from the classroom to the field and back to the classroom during their learning. In
professional fields the interplay of the university with the field is an
imperative in the design of high-quality degrees.

Historically the professional school within this university was
Business Administration. Students could move easily from work in
nearby banks to the college classroom and back to work. But other
professional schools were added; Allied Health Sciences and Education
were two such additions. Currently, the School of Education enrolls
about 5,200 students and is now the largest. Business Administration
has dropped from first to third, behind Arts and Sciences, with 4,700.
Allied Health enrolls about 1,100 students.

The desire for instructional quality in professional programs,
then, is an increasing pressure to move away from the city-center
campus.

Political and Legal Pressures

In an era of increasing competition for tax dollars, the university
needs to be sensitive to its service obligations. In the city, which is
both the state capital and the largest metropolitan center in the region,
this sensitivity is especially important. While the needs of all professions and industries should be attended to, those in positions to exert

the greatest influence on dollar allocations receive priority. Indeed, the addition of a law school is contemplated. This tends to reinforce the central location of the university's campus because the economic and political power still reside, largely, in the center-city businesses.

The problem, thus, became clear. The university had to relocate some professionally-directed services to locations more convenient to the students. This made sense educationally, economically, and politically. However, the university had to maintain the vitality and integrity of the downtown campus. This had to be done to ensure degree integrity and to maintain the relationship with the city and its business heart. The solution, in concept, also became clear: restructure the university so that a single institution could operate one integrated set of programs with parts located at many sites.

DEVELOPMENT PROGRAM

At the time this outward shift began, the development of a city block of the university's property was being planned. The first phase of this building program was to be an $11 million, 12-story structure planned to focus on the School of Urban Life. It was to house the laboratories, data banks, personnel, and other facilities needed for the university to contribute to the city's development by strengthening its governmental services. The School of Urban Life was created at the same time as the Schools of Education and Allied Health Sciences. The university adopted an urban thrust in program planning and the president began referring to the institution as "the urban university."

This movement prompted the state-coordinated designation of a Rural Life Center at another college and the construction of several Regional Education Centers on the campuses of strategically located state colleges. The building being planned for the GSU campus thus became the Urban Life Center and the Metropolitan Education Center.

The initial building concept was essentially that of a conference or continuing education facility on the model of the Kellogg centers. The center would expect people to come to it to receive the desired university services. The center would contain all of the facilities, except overnight accommodations, necessary for the efficient providing of service to groups of metropolitan citizens.

The broadening of this building concept was the first tangible move toward the geographic broadening of the university. The percentage of the building's space designed for conferences was reduced; the percentage given to the housing of the administration of service provided elsewhere was increased. Space for the faculty of the other two new schools (mentioned above) was included, but no space was designed for clinical classrooms or for the duplication of existing field laboratories. In short, the building concept became more a management center and, relatively, less a self-contained public service center. It was at this time that the university officially described its campus as the entire metropolitan area.

The past experiences of three groups were also important in contributing to the resolution of the geographic dilemma. Faculty members in the School of Education brought with them a good deal of experience operating student teaching programs and other instructional plans which used public schools as sites. The faculty of Allied Health brought experience in the teaching of clinical courses in hospitals and other noncampus health agencies. And, third, in the university's metropolitan area the public schools had, 25 years ago, formed a consortium with three universities to offer, in public school classrooms, graduate extension courses for local teachers.

These experiences were of mixed benefit. They did provide a measure of confidence in the ability of the people to manage decentralized operations; but, at the same time, they provided a built-in set of biases about the best form and procedures for such operations. To many the design was patently simple; all that was needed was to recreate the administrative structure and republish the policies already governing the student teaching program at the university from which they came.

One of the first people outside these two schools to become a convert was one of the most significant: the chancellor of the state's university system informed the university president that the decentralization of some instructional services seemed to be an economically sound alternative to the continued construction of downtown classrooms. The president readily grasped the many advantages, including economics, commuter student satisfaction, and wider visibility.

The administrations in the arts, humanities, and sciences changed next. The logic of their support is fairly complex. Professional schools are usually viewed, and they often view themselves, as academically inferior to arts college disciplines. As a result, professional schools have often tried to become reactionarily isolated within the sanctum of the university—modern jargon would give them a low profile. But at this university, two professional schools began to operate on a different model and announced publicly, and perhaps audaciously, that what they were doing represented an educational improvement. This caused thought. The dean of Arts and Sciences gathered data and saw that students in his classes did not come to class and stay to use the library and other facilities; they made special trips to the university for these. He finally said publicly, "When the classroom door is closed, it doesn't much matter where the classroom is located." His feeling became the position of many of his faculty.

Two changes resulted from this movement of some instruction away from the central campus: first, courses can't simply be transported—they change when they are taught to specific groups of professionals at sites close to the professional operation; and, second, the character and the number of administrative problems have changed markedly.

Three characteristically different forms of instruction have emerged which seem related to geography. In opposition to the dean's statement (noted above), location does seem to make a difference. Courses dealing largely with abstract principles and theories seem to be enhanced by distance from the student-professional's base of operations. Abstract content is difficult to deal with close to the operation base because there is pressure on both students and the instructor to make quick, specific, and continual applications. Students find it difficult, in these locations, to keep an idea abstract long enough to thoroughly examine the logic and form of the idea itself.

A clinical form of instruction was apparent from the outset. And between the theoretical and the clinical forms has come a third— a translation—form of instruction. In such courses students can avoid focusing on single specific problems and can relate groups of similar problems or generalizable characteristics of problems to relevant disciplinary theory. Both clinical and translation instruction forms improve when taught in the field.

The changes in administration came primarily from the need to coordinate the provision of facilities on an interagency basis. Classrooms, security, instructional materials, etc., are usually provided by units within the university's administrative structure. With the change in site, these same services have to be arranged, scheduled, or purchased using both the university's policies and those of another institution. It is surprisingly difficult, it seems, for an administrator who finds it easy to schedule on-campus classrooms to arrange, instead, for classroom spaces through a school system or hospital. Registrars deal most easily, also, with students who appear in person for registration, fee payment, and problem resolution. But they, too, can adjust their procedures to deal effectively with students who do not come to the campus on any regular, scheduled basis.

No new titles were created; however, job descriptions and the necessary characteristics of the people to fill them have been changed. The university has been slow to treat this change and barriers remain where there is an administrator who can manage only what he can totally control.

CURRENT STATUS

Several difficulties remain; some are currently receiving attention.

As this university has changed over the years, university structures and the patterns of educating professionals also have been changing throughout the country. The coining of the term "external degree" signifies that universities are becoming alert to their responsibilities to provide academic service apart from on-campus courses. While the soundness of such programs is debated, the fact that the discussion is occurring is, itself, evidence of change in university thinking. The shift in thrust seen initially at this university as a radical departure from tradition, is now viewed as essential to the economic and educational health of the university.

One totally peripheral problem continues: The emphasis placed on urban programming is now being used to reinforce the center-city focus. The word "urban," which was meant initially to include the entire metropolitan community, is now being interpreted narrowly to mean only the center-city area. What was at first an expansive term is now the basis for arguing the restriction of the university's operation.

A total redefinition of faculty work expectations is still largely undone. Faculty members who teach clinical or translation courses tend to follow their students into daily situations to advise and assist. They thus tend to do less published research. Faculty teaching theoretical courses appear, to students, remote and removed from reality. The bases for the evaluation and reward of faculty need realigning to make them more consistent with the changes in role expectations.

The decentralized operation is consistent with national energy consumption problems. Fewer people move shorter distances. But here people must move in directions unsupported by the mass transportation system. It is still easier to get a bus going all the way downtown than to go a couple of miles around the perimeter.

Since not all of the students come, all of the time, to one location, the impact of the university as a racial, economic, or social integrator has been reduced. Following students to where they live or work tends to place the responsibility for social integration onto the professions themselves. This has not been a problem for the university, but it is a concomitant of the revised operational structure. The location of most of the shift at the graduate level has minimized this effect. At the undergraduate level the university does, still, attempt to expose students to situations different from those which they have already experienced.

A serious problem is growing, though, and will have to be faced: Some basic discipline departments believe they should become more oriented toward immediate field applications. The English Department might, for example, try to replace a retiring Victorian prose scholar with a specialist in the teaching of middle school grammar. Or the Biology Department might add an additional human physiologist to the faculty to teach basic biology rather than employing a plant physiologist. If unchecked this movement could produce a narrowness which would reduce the quality of the very support which the professional schools depend on. Professional education demands strength which disciplines can achieve only through pluralism.

SIGNIFICANCE

The operational changes described in this study were difficult, substantial, and, therefore, gradual. Much remains yet to be begun. So far the evidence is that change in intended directions is going on and that continuation in similar directions is appropriate.

The entire thrust could be lost, though, if external forces shift dramatically. If business growth slows enough that office shifts from downtown to the perimeter are uncompensated for by additional center-city growth, the center could lose its vitality. This would destroy the centralized-decentralized balance which the university is trying to maintain.

The political power of some community group could grow sufficiently for another state college to be built in the metropolitan area to serve the people of one suburban direction. This, too, would upset the balance being maintained. The imponderables of the future seem still to be potentially more powerful than the predictable forces.

What has been demonstrated, though, is still useful. It is possible for a university to grow and improve without leaping to a new structural orthodoxy. This university is beginning to sort out decisions so that neither habit nor immediate need dictate the directions for change. By viewing itself more as a center for managing learning rather than as a center for providing teaching, the metropolitan university has been able to follow people to the periphery without destroyin its center-city foundation.

5

INTERCAMPUS RELATIONS IN
MULTICAMPUS UNIVERSITIES
Leonard E. Goodall

One of the most notable trends in higher education in the 1960s and 1970s has been the development of the multicampus university. As population has expanded generally and higher education enrollments have experienced extraordinary growth, many states have responded by expanding one or more state universities to new campuses. In fact, in some parts of the country this trend is not particularly new. The University of California, for example, had campuses in Berkeley, Los Angeles, San Francisco, and Davis for many years, but then expanded to new locations, establishing campuses in Irvine, Santa Barbara, Riverside, Santa Cruz, and San Diego.

The trend to multicampus universities has been especially significant among the major state universities in the midwestern region of the United States. The major state universities in Michigan, Indiana, Illinois, Wisconsin, Minnesota, Missouri, Nebraska, and Arkansas are all multicampus universities today. In other parts of the country the trend is well represented by universities in Louisiana, Alabama, Massachusetts, and Maine. Some states such as Wisconsin, North Carolina, and New York have consolidated virtually all of their public university campuses into a single statewide university.

One important aspect of the trend has been the tendency for the major new campuses to be located in urban population centers. An obvious reason for this is that many of our great public universities were located, either by accident or by design, at some distance from the major urban areas of their states; the well-known names of

Leonard E. Goodall, Chancellor, University of Michigan at Dearborn.

university towns like Ann Arbor, Urbana, Madison, Columbia, Lincoln, and Boulder are illustrative because in each case they do not represent the major urban area of their respective states. Thus there has been the shift to the urban centers, with the development of the University of Michigan at Dearborn (in metropolitan Detroit), the University of Illinois at Chicago Circle, the University of Wisconsin at Milwaukee, the University of Missouri at St. Louis, the University of Missouri at Kansas City, the University of Nebraska at Omaha, and the University of Colorado at Denver.

The purpose of this study is to explore some of the problems and issues which arise in major universities as they become multi-campus institutions. The information presented is based primarily on the experience of the author as a member of the faculty and administration at two such institutions, the University of Illinois at Chicago Circle and the University of Michigan—Dearborn, but some information from other institutions is also included where appropriate. It should be emphasized that, while this presentation deals mostly with the tensions and conflicts which occur in such institutions, it would be very incorrect to assume that most of the intercampus relationships are in the nature of conflict. It is the author's firm conviction that most are mutually supportive and grow out of a spirit of cooperation and a commitment to making the institution a truly integrated university depite being located on more than one campus.

NEW CAMPUSES

New campuses of state universities commonly come into being because of the recognition by the university of needs which are currently unmet. Where the new campus is established in a populous metropolitan area, the need perceived is often that of large numbers of students who have the desire and the competence to be educated at the major state university, but who find it impossible because of finances, family commitments, job requirements, or other reasons to leave the metropolitan area and become full-time students on the older established campus. This was the primary motivation for the establishment of the University of Illinois at Chicago Circle. This campus originated as a two-year academic program opened on Navy Pier in 1946 to accommodate the large influx of veterans returning from World War II. As population grew and enrollments continued to climb, University of Illinois officials saw the need for a fully developed undergraduate and graduate public institution of higher learning in the Chicago metropolitan area. The result was the creation of the Chicago Circle campus, which now serves 20,000 students. The facts would

be similar if one were to review the history of the establishment of
state university campuses in Boston, Milwaukee, St. Louis, or
Kansas City.

The University of Michigan-Dearborn was created as a result
of the same kind of general need to serve increasing enrollments, but
its origins were also based on a perception of special needs for
increased opportunities for students in particular fields. Since the
campus was created originally through a gift of land and funds from
the Ford Motor Company, negotiations relating to the gift dealt with
the needs of the auto industry for additional graduates in business and
engineering. The desire to establish cooperative education programs,
in which the students would actually spend part of their academic
careers working in a commercial or industrial setting, was seen as
a major thrust of the campus from the beginning. While business and
engineering students have been a minority on campus numerically
since the early years, the establishment of the business and engineering programs was of great importance to the corporate donors in
the planning for the new campus.

While this specific interest in professional programs was quite
explicit in the early planning at Dearborn, it is one of the factors seen
as important in the establishment of most such urban campuses. A
survey of students on such campuses would show in all likelihood a
somewhat higher interest in professional education and preparation
specifically for employment than would be found among the students
on the older, more established campuses of these universities.

It is worth noting that new campuses of this type have not come
into being because of the complete absence of higher education in the
urban areas involved. Boston, Detroit, Milwaukee, Chicago, and
St. Louis all have highly reputable private institutions of higher
learning. In most cases, however, the tuition level at these institutions is beyond the reach of many urban students. Many private
universities, moreover, place a heavy emphasis on graduate and
professional programs and recruit from a nationwide pool of students,
with less direct orientation toward the specific educational needs of
the urban area in which they are located. Urban Catholic universities
such as St. Louis University and the University of Detroit are notable
exceptions.

Most of these urban areas also had existing public institutions
of higher education at the time of the establishment of the new state
university campus. Examples of such previously existing institutions
are Wayne State, in Detroit, and Eastern Michigan University, serving
the western Detroit suburbs; Chicago State and Northeastern Illinois
State, in Chicago, and Northern Illinois University, serving the
northern and western Chicago suburbs; and Harris Teachers College
(a municipal institution) in St. Louis. In some cities community

college systems also existed. For many students in the urban areas, however, the establishment of these new campuses met certain additional needs that could not be satisfied elsewhere. It was clear that these students did not want just a college education or just a state university education. They specifically wanted a "University of Illinois (Michigan, Wisconsin, etc.) education," with the history, tradition, quality, and opportunities associated with an education and degree obtained from the major public university in the state. These were students who had the competence and the commitment necessary for such an education. What they did not have was the flexibility of life style to move to a distant college town and become traditional full-time students.

There have been cases where community leaders and their representatives in the state legislatures saw private institutions in danger of closing down and thus no longer available to serve their urban clientele. The taking over of these institutions by state universities seemed to solve several problems at once. The continued existence of the institution was insured, and the opportunities for a low-cost state university education were extended to new areas. The establishment of the University of Missouri at Kansas City, which was formerly the privately supported University of Kansas City, is an example of this progress.

Usually there were also somewhat less idealistic and more pragmatic reasons involved in the establishment of new campuses. In many cases, university officials recognized the growing public pressures for creation of a new campus, and they preferred that it be a campus of their university rather than a separate institution which might be placed in a somewhat more competitive role in regard to the established state university. The universities sometimes perceived that this was the only way to achieve additional growth. Legislators and other state officials became concerned in the 1960s that some universities were getting "too big." There was little agreement on what "too big" meant—20,000 students or 30,000 or 40,000—but concern was widespread. Thus, as pressures grew to limit the size of a particular campus, the establishment of new campuses offered an opportunity for continued growth.

The desire to widen the university's political base and establish a presence in the major urban areas of the state has sometimes been a consideration. There is probably no scientific way to establish a relationship, but it may be significant that the development of multi-campus universities took place simultaneously with a dynamic growth of the nation's metropolitan areas and increasing pressure by the courts for state legislative systems based more nearly on a one-man, one-vote system of representation.

This point is illustrated by a conversation several years ago among University of Illinois officials about whether Chicago Circle would ever spin off and become a separate university. An Urbana faculty member was suggesting that as a campus matures and develops its own programs it may arrive at a point at which it is sufficiently strong to spin off and become an independent institution. At that point, a Chicago Circle faculty member noted that if any campus in the University of Illinois system were sufficiently mature and well developed to spin off, it was certainly the Urbana campus. He suggested that perhaps the Urbana campus should spin off and become Central Illinois State while Chicago Circle continued as a major campus of the University of Illinois. The Urbana faculty member quickly replied that, in addition to all other considerations, he could read census tracts and count votes in the legislature too well to be very interested in such an arrangement!

The trend toward the creation of new campuses by the state university has not proceeded without concern and opposition. Other universities in the urban area, both public and private, may view with alarm the possibility of the major state university establishing a campus nearby. Private universities in Chicago were a major political impediment to the establishment of Chicago Circle, and are still active in attempting to stop or slow down the creation of certain programs (such as the master of business administration degree) on that campus. Following the movement of the University of Massachusetts into Boston the strong disagreements between President John Silbur of Boston University and President Robert Wood of the University of Massachusetts were well publicized in the national news media.

Other state universities, even though not located in the urban area, may view the development of new urban campuses with concern if they feel it will strengthen the major state university vis-a-vis their own position in the state system of higher education. Southern Illinois University watched the movement of the University of Illinois into Chicago very carefully, and it was not long afterwards that a campus of Southern Illinois University was established in the metropolitan St. Louis area.

The character of the new campus may become an issue. Some citizens have been concerned that the new campuses are being created only to serve blacks. Conversely, others have been concerned that they are not being created to serve blacks. The issue of whether standards are lowered on the urban campus has sometimes been raised while others have argued specifically that standards should be lowered and the urban campus should implement some form of an open admissions policy.

THE CAMPUSES VIEW EACH OTHER

The concern or skepticism shown by other institutions when a new campus is established is sometimes no greater than the concern that the campuses within the university have about each other. The central administration of the university can usually be expected to support the establishment of the new campus and in many cases it is the source of the original impetus behind the new campus movement. That view is less likely to be shared by the faculty and those at lower administrative levels on the established campus of the system. The faculty of the Madison campus of the University of Wisconsin has shown continual concern about the expansion of the university to include other campuses throughout the state. The view has been expressed quite well by Professor Clara Pennimen of the Madison Political Science Department, who said, according to an article in the April 1973 issue of College and University Business: "The fundamental question is whether you can have a multicampus system with a substantial administration above the campus level and maintain the kind of quality university that Madison has represented."

Concern about the central administration can be exacerbated if the administrative offices are actually removed from the established campus. The University of Massachusetts moved its university system offices from its Amherst campus to Boston, and this has been a subject of much uneasiness among Amherst faculty. This new geographic distance of the central administration was at least a peripheral issue in the campus debate over collective bargaining in 1973.

Much of the apprehension about new campuses reflects concern about the dilution of university resources. If there is some finite amount of funds which the state is willing to invest in higher education, according to this reasoning, then any resources used to develop a new campus are necessarily unavailable for the older established one. Closely associated with the issue of financial resources is a subtle but seldom expressed fear of dilution of reputation. The established campuses by their nature have well-known national reputations. It says something about one to be identified as a faculty member of a particular established university. If there are now new groups of people identifying themselves as faculty of that university, there is the danger that the reputation associated with the university name may gradually become eroded.

The feeling may develop at the older campus that the new institution mistakenly thinks it can become an "instant university." New institutions seem to want immediate response to their demands for graduate programs, professional programs, massive facilities, and other resources which it took the senior campus a century or more to develop. Fortunately, the rapid growth of the 1960s enabled many states to respond favorably to these "instant university" demands without diminishing the growth and support of the established campus, and this served to minimize the concerns expressed about the rapid growth and development at the new location.

It seems inevitable that newer campuses also develop a rather standard set of fears and concerns about the established campus of the system. Regardless of how fast the growth, development, new facilities, and new programs are forthcoming, this will not be fast enough in the eyes of those on the new campus, and some blame for this inevitably will be directed toward the senior campus. There will be a feeling that people there are somehow trying to hold back or suppress the development of the new campus.

This is especially true among those on the new campus who do not understand the difference between campus administration and system administration. The expression "clear it with Urbana" always evoked strong reactions of resentment at Chicago Circle in the early years of the new campus system. In reality it generally meant that after an item had completed the review process on the Chicago Circle campus it had to be forwarded for review by the system administration, which happened to be located in Urbana. The system worked exactly the same for an item completing the review process on the Urbana campus, but it was often difficult on the developing campus to differentiate between review by individuals or units at the senior campus and review by a system administration which happened to be located in the same community as the senior campus. It will be interesting to see how a development such as the move of the University of Massachusetts system offices to Boston will affect this problem.

Though somewhat paradoxical, feelings of resentment which develop on the newer campus from a feeling of being suppressed or held back may not be as great as the resentment which grows out of a feeling of being ignored. It is natural enough that the state's major newspapers, the alumni association publications, the personnel officers of major corporations, the boards of foundations, and a multitude of other individuals and media will devote primary attention to the established campus. When this occurs, some on the newer campus will view it as oversight and others will consider it conspiracy, but whatever motive is ascribed to it, the "ignoring" of the newer campus will be a subject of much concern among faculty and staff there.

How Unique, How Traditional?

The creation of a new campus is commonly accompanied by much discussion about what its role will be within the university and the state. It may be cited as an experimenting campus, free from the traditions and mores that limit the older institution. If it is in a large urban area, it is often stressed as that part of the university which will be uniquely oriented toward serving the urban needs of the city in which it is located.

These statements of goals are generally espoused by faculty and staff on the campus as well as by those in the central administration. The exact meaning of such goal statements will often be difficult to determine, and they may lead to debate about the long-range goals of the campus. For example, if in fact the goal is to serve urban needs and not, for example, to develop graduate programs, the natural desires and tendencies of faculty members will cause them to question the so-called unique role of the urban campus. On the established campus, faculty will also express concern if they view the unique urban mission of the newer campus as implying that all funds for urban research will be channeled to the new location. The simple fact is that most schools have not done a very good job of moving beyond the rhetoric to define exactly what it means to be an experimental campus or to have a unique urban mission in higher education.

The problem is well illustrated by an editorial in Chicago Sun Times of June 22, 1971:

> Circle campus is becoming a carbon copy of the mother
> school at Urbana. It should instead be evolving into an
> urban institution dynamically concerned with the city,
> its people and its problems.
>   Chicago has great schools now. It doesn't need
> copies of any that exist now. It needs, in the words of
> a committee of the State Board of Higher Education, a
> "truly urban and core-city oriented higher institution
> devoted to social problem solving and public service."

This editorial raises precisely the kinds of issues that make some faculty members uneasy. What does it mean that Chicago Circle should not become a "carbon copy" of Urbana or that it should not attempt to be like other "great schools" in Chicago? Does it mean that Chicago Circle should not attempt to have graduate programs like Urbana? Does it mean that it should not attempt to achieve the quality of Northwestern or Chicago? Does it mean that it should not have the research facilities of such institutions? These issues were discussed in a 1971 position paper, "The Challenge of the University in a World of Flames," issued by a group of Chicago Circle faculty:

> The university thrives in an urban setting. Here is where scholars can fraternize because they come here in larger numbers than almost any place in the world. The urban university is not a peculiar institution. It is simply a university, urbanly located, and hence, most favorably ready to achieve excellence. We must not forget that the first and foremost function of the university is to replace ignorance with understanding. It does this at the under-graduate level by providing a program of quality and the accumulated knowledge and wisdom. It does this at the graduate level by expanding the boundaries of knowledge.

One can see in these comments the implied fear that when a new campus is called upon to be a uniquely urban institution it is being called upon to do so instead of performing the traditional university functions rather than in addition to performing them. Chicago Circle faculty holding this view often suggest that their campus should be developing along the lines of UCLA which, while not having quite the international prestige and reputation of Berkeley, is nevertheless a large, well-developed multiversity with a wide range of graduate programs and professional schools.

There are, of course, some faculty at Chicago Circle who would be more in agreement with the above editorial than with the state-ments of their colleagues. On developing campuses, urban or other-wise, the process of defining campus missions may evoke almost as broad a spectrum of opinion within the campus as among those outside.

Personnel Issues and Problems

The conditions of stable or declining enrollments characteristic of the 1970s are likely to create new kinds of issues for multicampus universities. The increasing interest in collective bargaining in higher education will raise new issues. Should the faculty on each campus be a separate bargaining unit or should there be a single bar-gaining unit for all campuses? The limited experience so far shows some institutions going in one of these directions and some in the other.

Closely related is the sensitive issue of whether there should be established salary differentials among the campuses. The Uni-versity of Wisconsin has moved in the direction of differentiation by campus function. The more complex campuses at Madison and Milwaukee, with their large numbers of graduate and professional programs, have a salary schedule which is differentiated from that of other segments of the university. Such a policy is bound, of course, to lead to some resentment among the "have-not" campuses of the university. Some Chicago Circle administrators, in contrast, will say that, compared on a person-by-person basis, faculty salaries are somewhat higher at Chicago Circle than at Urbana, and that this is justifiable in light of Chicago living costs.

As enrollments stabilize, promotion and tenure questions are becoming much more controversial than in the past. The issue of whether tenure is with a particular department or campus or with the system will undoubtedly be raised with increasing frequency. If the number of faculty positions is reduced on a campus because of declining enrollments, the question of whether the individuals released have first claim on positions elsewhere in the system will inevitably be raised by faculty groups. If the answer is in the affirmative, departments with declining enrollment may find it less difficult to make the necessary faculty reductions where the individuals can be placed on some other campus within the university. The receiving campus, on the other hand, is likely to resent a policy which, in its view, forces it to take the castoffs from elsewhere within the university. This issue will become especially difficult if the more prestigious campus is the growing one and the newer campuses are declining. Departments on the established campus would undoubtedly resist vigorously any policy which required them to accept faculty members who had been released from positions on the newer developing campuses.

The Stakes Are Low

It has been observed, somewhat cynically, that the reason academic battles are fought so fiercely is that the stakes are so low. This wisdom is not lost on multicampus universities. With all of the major issues concerning intercampus administration and relationships, small and seemingly trivial issues often create much irritation and aggravation on a day-to-day basis.

When a university system moves to designate each campus with a specific name, this inevitably causes some grumbling and discontent on the established campus. There was much uneasiness among University of Illinois faculty members when they were told that they must include in their university identification the suffix "at Urbana-Champaign." In the two or three years immediately following the transition to campus designations at the University of Illinois, Chicago Circle faculty were extremely sensitive on this point. It was quite common then for a faculty member to see an article in a professional journal or a badge at a convention in which one of his Urbana colleagues had not included the suffix in his university identification. The faculty member would complain to his department chairman who would in turn pass the complaint on to Urbana and eventually the "offender" would receive a rather perfunctory form letter reminding him gently of university policy concerning campus designation.

This issue sometimes works in just the opposite way. Faculty members at the established campus may be the most sensitive if faculty at the newer campuses identify themselves only with the university and not with the particular campus.

Another sensitive issue is how to refer to the status of the various campuses. Faculty on the newer campuses are often offended if the terms "main campus" and "branch campus" are used. It would be acceptable to suggest that the University of Illinois has three "branches"—Urbana, Chicago Circle, and the Medical Center—but to refer to the "main campus" in Urbana and two "branches" would be offensive to many in Chicago.

A 1971 study on multicampus universities, done by the Carnegie Commission on Higher Education, used the term "flagship campus" in referring to the older, established campus in a system. The term may be especially appropriate. The chancellor of the "flagship campus" in a system once remarked to the author that being chancellor of the campus on which the president has his system offices is like being captain of a ship with the fleet commander on board.

At the University of Michigan, the term "regional campuses" is often used to refer to the Dearborn and Flint campuses. This seems to be acceptable to almost everyone, although even the term "branch campus" seems to be more acceptable in Michigan than most other states. Dearborn faculty do prefer the term "Ann Arbor campus" to "main campus," and they are most offended by the term "mother campus," which is sometimes used in the media.

The matter of where faculty live has been an issue in Michigan and Wisconsin. In both states, there are newer campuses located near enough to the established campus for some faculty to live in Ann Arbor or Madison and commute to newer campuses. This has been a topic of discussion among faculty (and students) who live near the new campus and believe that a "university community" can exist only when people live in proximity to the campus and to each other. More vigorous critics will refer to the commuting faculty as "carpetbaggers." These faculty are likely to respond that the university research facilities and cultural opportunities are strong attractions in influencing their decision on place of residence.

Intercampus issues can also become very important to students. At the University of Michigan-Dearborn, students on several occasions have been quite interested in being assured that their diploma will look exactly like the diploma for the Ann Arbor campus. They are pursuing a University of Michigan degree, and they are quite concerned that the diploma which they receive reflect precisely that. Although this is in fact what happens, a rumor that this policy might be changed created sufficient excitement among the student body to evoke a series of articles in the campus newspaper and become an issue in an election for student government president.

There are numerous other day-to-day practical operating problems. Should students on one campus be eligible to get student tickets for athletic events at another campus (another major issue at Dearborn)? Should students transferring from campus to campus in a university have preference over students transferring from outside the institution to a given campus within it? Should there be one alumni association for the university or one for each campus? Should the university's endowment be available to all campuses or only the older, established campus (a major issue at Madison)? After the new campuses are created and the system is established these are the kinds of day-to-day questions that must be worked out, often in a pragmatic way that is most suitable for each particular situation.

THE STRENGTH OF THE MULTI-
CAMPUS UNIVERSITY

As was pointed out above, the fact that there are strains and problems within a multicampus university should not be interpreted as an indication that the problems are greater than the benefits of such a system. New campuses undoubtedly profit greatly from the experience and expertise which an established university can provide in planning and developing at a new location. There is no question that the quality of faculty and students which can be attracted to a campus is enhanced if it is a part of a major state university. To say that a student at Milwaukee gets an education of the quality maintained by the University of Wisconsin is not just an exercise in semantics. Precisely because it is the University of Wisconsin, it can attract the kind of faculty and students which will enable the high quality of education commonly associated with the University of Wisconsin to be maintained.

There may well be some financial savings if duplication of certain administrative and service functions can be reduced or eliminated. On the other hand, it is doubtful that these savings are so

great as to be a major factor. It is very likely, though, that careful
planning and coordination of the use of resources will increase the
quality of computer, library, laboratory, and other facilities available within the system.

The established campus can benefit through an extension of the
university services throughout the state. It is very easy for a prestigious state university to get a reputation for elitism and aloofness
if it is oriented toward the national academic community, is located
somewhat distant from the state's major metropolitan areas, and is
serving only a relatively small portion of the students desiring to
attend that university. It can enhance the entire university's image
within a state if its services are made available to more people in
more locations and to more diverse populations. The established
campus can benefit if it not only accepts but actively encourages the
role of the new campus as an experimenting and unique institution and
as an instrument for extending the university's services.

The people of the state benefit if the educational opportunities
of the major state university are now available to more people in
more places. The established campus in a nonurban area of necessity
serves primarily a resident student body made up mostly of full-time
undergraduates in the eighteen to twenty-four age category and graduate and professional students pursuing specialized educational goals.
The newer campuses bring the educational opportunities of the major
state university not only to students in the urban area but also to new
categories of students—part-time students, returning students, and
nondegree students, to mention only a few.

Finally, it should be emphasized that internal strains are not
new to universities. Our great universities have attained their reputations through constructive competition and give-and-take among
their various departments, research centers, and other administrative
units. Given the new needs of a new time it is to be expected that our
great multicampus universities will develop in the same manner.

Although it is understood that each of the foregoing commentaries on problems of universities in transition will evoke much independent thought, it is the intent of this followup to urge the reader's attention to some of the controversial byproducts of the questions raised by the authors. Prefatory thereto one may profit by considering to what extent these essays are interrelated and to what degree their messages hold some things in common. Conversely, it may be instructive to explore any factual inconsistencies in their testimony.

Given the data regarding recent and projected trends in higher education in the Hanson study, especially with reference to financial support and enrollment figures, what are the foreseeable implications for most campuses? What can or should a college or university do about these developments, be it public or private in nature? Precisely how has policy been affected at your particular academic institution as a result of the transition from the expanding to the steady state? Has administrative behavior been more or less vigorous or visionary as a result? If so, toward what specific ends? Do you now anticipate that solutions to problems will more greatly affect the faculty, the operating funds, the equipment or capital improvements, or some combination of these and other resources? Are overall academic emphases in proper order of priority? Is the decision-making process at your college or university sufficiently mature to bring about appropriate reforms without crisis? What impediments or forces, internally and externally, may prevent or complicate the pursuit of viable alternatives to current courses of action? Isolate those forces and outline a plan of action whereby they may be coopted in the general interest of your campus community.

The study by Case causes us to consider the rationality of our academic organizational life. Are departments basically tribal, or rather functional, at your institution of higher learning and at its various colleges and divisions? Might some good words be offered in defense of your institution's announced mission? Are its goals sound and to the point, realistic and generally understood? As for the normal routine of collegiate affairs, do they tend to be handled in a parochial manner or are most colleagues rather sophisticated in interpersonal relations? Is efficiency a principle of organizational behavior up and down your institutional hierarchy, or is duplication of effort and misuse of space a part of the standard operational procedure? Could reorganization improve the present conditions, particularly in terms of making more effective the efforts of all concerned on the campus? If not, why not; and if so, why so? Given the need, how would you go about the task of appointing a committee to study the prospect of reorganization? How many members should be on such a task force? Who would serve on it? Why? How much time would you give the group to complete its final report? Upon completion of the study, who would you permit to review it? Would those persons have the right to edit the contents? How about the higher administrators? To what extent is politics involved in such deliberations? Does the student body, the faculty, or the public have a right to know those findings prior to their implementation?

Regarding the Barbe and Hall analysis, how does one determine if and when one's academic institution is meeting the educational needs of its community, however those terms may be defined? Does it matter what the institutional leadership thinks, if the local or state community thinks otherwise? Would decisions be different for a private versus a public college or university considering an extension of its services? Assuming that decentralization is in order, whether elsewhere in the state or at the fringe of the metropolitan area, what positive and negative results can you visualize for the faculty, students, and administrators on each of the affected campuses? Would the positive effects generally outweigh the negative? If there a particular point, or a specific set of conditions, to which you might normally refer to justify the decision to decentralize? Would that judgment be rationalized on the grounds of making more effective use of existing resources, of enlisting or enrolling a significantly larger number of students, of better interrelating theory and practice for the benefit of the learner, or do some other criteria come to mind, singularly or in combination? Might the decentralization of your academic institution be justified primarily on the premise that it recognizes the need today to be a center for managing learning rather than a campus for managing teaching?

Last but not least, the Goodall study will prompt many of us to attempt to distinguish rhetoric from reality. For those who have wondered about the goals of their college or university, has the catalog statement thereon become a reasonable guideline for daily performance? Has the comparable statement on the objectives of the statewide system been reflected in the achievements on individual campuses? Moreover, to what extent does a centralized public statewide system of higher education actually serve the public better than the alternative of autonomous colleges and universities? Conversely, what is the substance of the argument in favor of the current trend? Under what circumstances would you support branches of a flagship campus? Is size of the student-faculty body on the main campus the major consideration? Why not solely to broaden the political base of the public

educational institution? Would competition at the site, such as a
private university or a municipal junior college, affect this decision?
What if the proposed expansion would negatively affect the prestige of
the mother campus? Should the satellite school therefore be treated
differently, or should the members of its faculty and student body be
entitled to the same privileges as their peers on the main campus?
And should the system administrators be based on the original campus,
at the new locale, at a site equally accessible to all of the satellites
of the multiversity, or at the state capital if at none of the foregoing?
With all of those answers fresh in mind, perhaps it is now timely to
consider in retrospect the validity of the experiences that have led
to them!

Generalizations on the transitions in higher education are meaningful to the extent that they offer an overview or macroanalysis of the major forces affecting the destiny of postsecondary learning. They are also helpful if they have managed to communicate some of the specific consequences on the campuses, toward a view of the collegiate scene in microcosm. In either event, causes have their effects, and the impact for educational programs is no exception to the rule. Policy and process in academe are affected by the external winds of change, and a toll is taken among systems unable or unwilling to cope with the new realities or their consequences. It is appropriate, therefore, that a series of our case studies is geared to the consideration of the organization and methods of decision making, and in particular to an assessment of the strategies and results thereof.

How better could we proceed to seek to grasp the nature and effect of human behavior in large organizations than to ponder at the outset the impact of an impending revolutionary change? Although panic or program dysfunction might as well follow, George A. Drake, leading off Part III, advises that successful curriculum innovation seems to rest in the art of calm persuasiveness. Yet institutional policy development, regardless of political acumen, is not always in accord with stated purposes, as shown by Charles E. Martin in the subsequent study. Programs are seldom effectual under such circumstances, and the case in point should serve to caution the administrator that there is more to decision making than the mere act of making a decision.

An integral part of the decision-making process and governance of progressive academic communities are the multitude of faculty-student committees. As suggested in the article by Mary K. Carl, the committees can be structured and encouraged to be both viable and productive; as admitted and well known by veteran participants and observers, they tend more often to fall short of those ideals. Committees need not always be internal to be influential, as state legislators are prone to make clear, and F. C. Fitchen's analysis of an experience in academic accreditation is a pointed reminder of the dependency that is fostered by lack of self-adjustment.

The manner in which members of organizations go about the task of choosing among alternative courses of action is not generally well documented; it is even less understood by scholar-participants in the halls of ivy. Therefore, it is particularly worthwhile that care

be taken to read out of and in to the following studies as much as one's
mind can deduce and conjecture. Relatively new ground in academic
organizational inquiry is being broken, and it will remain for others
to build the models for theories that can better serve to conceptualize
and explain the structure and management of our institutions of higher
learning.

6

THE POLITICS
OF REFORM
George A. Drake

The question I most frequently have been asked by those interested in the Colorado College Plan is, "How did your faculty ever agree on such a revolutionary change?" I hope in this study to provide the answer. The story is one of good fortune with a blend of intelligent planning and a remarkably open political process.

The decision to adopt the new plan was made in the fall of 1969. The executive committee of the faculty, a year and a half earlier, had asked a colleague to superintend a study to determine if the college ought to enter the decade of its centennial (to be celebrated in 1974) with a significantly altered curriculum. It is, by the way, important to the analysis of subsequent developments to understand that this request was grounded in self-confidence rather than its opposite.

The result of this study was the Colorado College Plan, inaugurated in September 1970. The plan is a structural change from the traditional semester system to a pattern in which courses are taught one at a time in $3\frac{1}{2}$-week blocks. Faculty teach one course per block while students take but one course. Courses normally are offered for a single block, though some two-block (seven-week) courses are available. Each block is separated by a $4\frac{1}{2}$-day "break," and there are nine blocks in the academic year. Study in an intensive course plan successfully invites student involvement and commitment, holding the promise of improved undergraduate general as well as preprofessional education. Obviously, a conscientious faculty would ignore such promise at its peril.

George A. Drake, former Dean, Colorado College.

One would like to believe that major academic reform results primarily from the best of motives guided by rational judgment. I know that I am open to the suspicion of naivete in stating that the events which produced the Colorado College Plan contained a gratifying measure of these qualities. Little would have happened without them. However, of equal importance was the political process.

Glenn Brooks, Professor of Political Science at the college, was asked by the president and faculty executive committee to direct the planning effort. The choice could not have been better: Professor Brooks enjoys unusual respect from colleagues, has a keen political sensitivity, is a man of ideas, and has professional interests and publications in the fields of public and university administration.

He was given a free hand. No timetable was set, nor was he asked to follow a prescribed pattern. Typically, the academic planner will begin by placing himself at the head of a committee of colleagues, administrators, and students. Brooks chose not to do this. He worked independently, meeting with each department, individual faculty members, committees, administrators, and students as the occasion required. His strategy was to begin without preconceptions, instead asking the constituencies to identify the strengths and weaknesses of the college as well as their particular bailiwicks. He then asked what each would do to overcome the deficiencies while preserving the strengths? These formal reviews by academic and nonacademic departments, including students as well as faculty, occupied about six months. They led to two clear conclusions: (1) Colorado College already possessed the basic ingredients for sound liberal education— a strong student body, a good faculty, and adequate facilities; and (2) the ingredients weren't meshing properly, primarily due to inefficient use of time.

Listening to the college's constituencies while scrupulously avoiding the pitfall of advancing his pet notions, Professor Brooks was able to say to the faculty, following the departmental reviews, "You have told me about our strengths and weaknesses, and I believe that I have a proposal which is addressed to your evaluation." The germ of his proposal was known to be the idea of another colleague and not Brooks's brainchild. Given the nature of academic politics, this was a distinct advantage.

Professor Brooks had the foresight and energy to meet individually, or in groups no larger than two or three, with virtually all of the 135-member faculty and most of the administration, as well as large numbers of students and staff (for example, the secretaries) to explain his ideas. These meetings were invaluable as they gave individuals and groups a chance to explore the planner's ideas and to contribute their own views. In addition—a truly rare experience— almost no one felt excluded. These meetings may have been the most important part of the political process. This is the kind of step which almost without exception is left out of academic planning ventures, because it is so time consuming. Each session with a member of the faculty took from one to two hours, which means that Brooks spent between 200 and 250 hours in this process alone. Add to this the meetings with other constituencies, and the figure rises to at least 350 hours. Exhausting as it was, all now agree that this was a crucial aspect of the planning process. In addition to the advantages already mentioned, the plan emerged tempered by its severest critics. Most conceivable criticisms had been raised, and those which did not spawn modifications at least were met forthrightly in private as well as public discussion.

The care with which each faculty member had been approached was influential in keeping the debate focussed on issues rather than personalities. Traditional alignments were of diminished importance; ad hominem, the bane of academic politics, was, for the time being, disarmed.

Simultaneously with the faculty and staff consultations, the planning office undertook important research and simulations. For example, the block plan requires the exclusive use of one classroom for each course. Since the college used the same room for several courses under the semester system, it was important to know if there would be enough new classroom space to accommodate the change. Planning office surveys unearthed the requisite space—provided some faculty would be willing to teach in dormitory and fraternity lounges. Another pressing question was whether it would be possible to piece together a workable course schedule under the block plan? This question was particularly pressing since a 25-student maximum per course was to be imposed. The answer was provided by a simulated course schedule produced by all the departments and tested by scores of student volunteers. These and other crucial questions of mechanics were laid to rest by such carefully conceived and executed planning office efforts.

Upon completion of the personal consultations with faculty, as well as the research and simulation necessary to provide a satisfactory answer to the most basic of all questions—is the block plan mechanically possible—Professor Brooks used the summer of 1969 to issue three papers which contained the rationale as well as the content of the plan. These papers were debated at a fall conference which traditionally opens the academic year for the faculty. Seldom has a debate been more instrumental for our college. Particularly memorable was the statement of a highly respected colleague, not marked as a supporter of the plan, that in summer session institutes he had taught intensive courses which, though exhausting, clearly were superior to almost all his teaching experiences in the traditional semester course format.

Following the fall conference, the planning office, its proposal formally having been presented, yielded the initiative to the regular academic processes. The dean began to assume a more active role as did the faculty's academic program committee. It was decided that the final vote would be sought at a faculty meeting in late October. Thus, there were to be only two months between the fall conference and the final vote. This surprised many who were accustomed to a more leisurely pace of academic change. However, the planning office and the administration could see no good reason why the already well-understood proposal should not be decided on in October, and they feared that prolonged consideration would end in talking the plan to death. An additional imperative was that if the plan were to be implemented in the following academic year, late October was nearly the last possible date for adoption, since much lead time would be required to effect major curricular and procedural changes. (For example, each department changed its entire course offerings, and these had to be reconstituted in a workable pattern.)

Realizing that indeed the decisive vote was upon them, the faculty set to work. The planning office agreed to help the opponents of the plan to refine counterproposals, while the academic program committee began to put the plan into its final form. Of course, Brooks worked closely with this committee as well as the opposition. At this stage some of the more cogent criticisms were incorporated into the plan as modifications. For example, the proposed block length was reduced from 4 to $3\frac{1}{2}$ weeks. This change recognized the objection that to move immediately from one block to the next would not provide sufficient time to faculty for grading and last-minute preparations for the next course. In another refinement, an alternative track was inserted, permitting some faculty and students to carry two courses at a time over three blocks. Formulation of these "extended half-courses" acknowledged the claim that not all subjects are suitable to the intensive course pattern.

Early in September, Professor Brooks presented the plan to the entire student body in a formal convocation. Some faculty objected to the use of this forum, claiming that it invited student pressures on faculty. This was one of the few occasions when faculty bitterness surfaced. The risk of losing some ground with the faculty was a necessary one, however, as the danger of not bringing the proposal before the student body prior to a faculty vote outweighed all other considerations.

Fortunately for the prospect of adoption, the question of who should decide on the plan never formally was advanced by the students. Keep in mind that this was 1969 in a college with an active student body. It was a minor miracle that students did not push this issue. A quarrel between faculty and students over the former's exclusive

right to pass on the plan probably would have diverted the college into
a procedural morass from which little but frustration would have
emerged. A prime factor in forestalling this issue was the extent to
which large numbers of students already had been instrumental in the
planning process. Well over 100 students had worked as volunteers
for the planning office, and one of their roles had been to explain the
plan to students in informal meetings in the dormitories. Deep involvement of many of the most active students as well as the care with
which other students were kept informed seem to have disarmed any
serious student efforts to make an issue out of their exclusion from
the final decision.

A spirit of accommodation marked the last month of deliberation.
The final vote was, in consequence, a remarkable experience. In the
days immediately before the October faculty meeting, the academic
program committee discussed the voting procedure. The question,
above all, was what vote would constitute an appropriate mandate.
All agreed that a simple majority would not suffice in a matter of
such importance. The suggestion of a two-thirds majority was
rejected on the ground that, in academic politics, no major change
would be possible if so large a majority were required. With considerable uneasiness it finally was agreed that no figure would be set.
Rather, a substantial majority was called for, without defining what
was meant by "substantial."

On the president's initiative, it was agreed that certain administrators who legally have a vote in faculty meetings would be disfran-
chised in this case. This was done to neutralize the threat of a
significant "city hall" vote which certainly could have been rallied in
support of the plan. As it turned out, every possible opposition vote
was mustered (including that of the six-man coaching staff), but the
plan passed with a 58 percent majority. Immediately following the
tally of written ballots, one of the principal opponents moved that the
plan be implemented, and only one vote was cast against his motion.
This particular solution to the question of the mandate was, as far as I
know, spontaneous. It bespoke the trust which prevailed after months
of intensive planning and discussion. Those who opposed the plan felt
that they had had every opportunity to air their views and to win adher-
ents. Their ideas had been taken seriously enough to be incorporated
in part into the final proposal; and they realized that they had had a
fair chance to win the vote in a faculty meeting in which the president
had made rulings which cut into the potential votes in favor of the plan.

This spirit of trust produced a remarkably high morale which
was instrumental in the college's ability to implement the plan in the
following academic year, as well as an atmosphere where proponents
and opponents have worked equally effectively for the striking success
it has enjoyed.

CONFLICT BETWEEN POLICY
AND INSTITUTIONAL PURPOSE
Charles E. Martin

State University was established by the state legislature in 1956 in order to bring public-supported higher education to the state's largest urban complex. The board of the parent institution, the nationally and internationally recognized State University, was authorized to acquire the land and buildings for the new campus and to exercise subsequent control of its operations.

In September 1958, State University opened with 1,500 freshman students. During the first year only a freshman curriculum was offered. In succeeding years additional class levels were added, and by the academic year 1973-74, State University was operating a full undergraduate degree program and graduate degree programs terminating at the masters and doctoral levels.

The academic segments of State University were organized into the College of Business Administration, the College of Liberal Arts, the College of Sciences, the College of Education, the Junior Division, the Graduate School, the School of Engineering, the Urban Studies Institute, and the Division of Continuing Education.

State University, a campus of the State University System, shar in the purposes for which the State University System was organized and which are shared in the revised statutes of the state:

> The university is established and maintained to serve the
> needs of the people of the state. It shall seek to expand
> the areas of knowledge and understanding through scien-

Charles E. Martin, Chairman, Louisiana State University at New Orleans.

tific and speculative inquiry and in various ways shall
encourage and assist the people of the state to fuller
development of their resources. With these ends in
view, an adequate program of studies shall be provided
in the liberal arts and sciences, in the important vocational and professional subjects, including agriculture,
commerce and business, education, engineering, law,
medicine, and military science and tactics; and any
additional courses may be provided in such other subjects as shall appear to be worthy of inclusion in the
program of the university. Libraries and laboratories
adequate for important and effective research and
investigation shall be provided and maintained.

Though the primary purpose of the university is
to provide and maintain the highest type of instruction
in the various important branches of knowledge for
graduates of the high school course of study, it shall
also offer such opportunities for instruction as may be
practicable to persons in the state who are not in residence on any of its campuses.

THE DEPARTMENT OF ELEMENTARY AND SECONDARY EDUCATION

The Department of Elementary and Secondary Education is one
of several departments within the College of Education at State University. The department administers programs in the areas of curriculum and instruction, counselor education, educational foundations
and research, and educational administration. A division of student
teaching is administered under the auspices of the department. Programs and curricula are administered at both the undergraduate and
graduate levels.

The department assumes as its primary role those imperatives
defined by the purposes of the College of Education, as stated in the
General Catalog of State University. This role is to prepare teachers
and educational leaders who will render professional service of a high
quality in the elementary and secondary schools. Attending this
principal purpose are the corollary functions of promoting independent
and contract research and providing consultative and advisory services
to the educational community.

The faculty of the department is rather typical in terms of competency, interests, and philosophy. Some members of the faculty are
interested primarily in teaching, others in research, and still others

in the service role. The department, due to the relative infancy of the
institution and somewhat limited staffing, can meet the diversified
interests of the faculty only to a limited degree.

Criteria established by the university mandate a teaching load
of nine semester hours per semester for associate and full professors,
and twelve semester hours for assistant professors and below. Released time for research and service is not permitted under university
funding.

The criteria for each promotion in rank are the traditional ones
which are as old as universities. They are the types of criteria which
force the faculty member to continue to turn inward to personal considerations. Only incidental treatment is given to the necessity for
assisting people and agencies to implement theoretical concepts and
knowledge.

The expectation of State University, the College of Education,
and the Department of Elementary and Secondary Education is that all
faculty members become involved in the three basic functions, namely
instruction, research, and service.

THE POLICY CONFLICT AND INSTITUTIONAL PURPOSE

Departmental Purpose

The Department of Elementary and Secondary Education has
postulated its own statements of purpose and has reflected the State
University and College of Education statements as previously identified.
The three areas within which the department's activities fall are indicated by the following stated goals of the department:

1. Provide and maintain the highest type of instruction in various
important branches of knowledge for graduates of the high school
course of study.

2. Seek to expand the areas of knowledge and understanding
through specific and speculative inquiry and in various ways—encourage
and assist people of the state to further development of their intellectual capacities and a greater enjoyment of their resources.

3. Offer to individuals, groups, organizations, and agencies the
resources of the department for the general development of a delivery
system attuned to the needs and betterment of society. Resources
may be identified in areas of consultative services, advisory services,
research and development projects, school support services, etc.

The University Policy

Outside Activities of University Employees

The University recognizes the rights of employees to serve as expert witnesses and consultants and to engage in other outside activities consistent with their university connections.

This policy relates to activities directly undertaken by members of the university academic and nonacademic staff with outside individuals, groups, organizations, and agencies and does not relate to activities in which arrangements are made officially through the university by contracts with or grants to the university.

Statement of Policy on Outside Activities

1. A member of the faculty or staff may engage in outside activities, paid or unpaid, which do not interfere with instructional, scholarly, and/or other services he must render in the nature of his university employment. Outside activities of members of the faculty or staff of the university should give promise of contributing to the competence or professional stature of the university employee concerned.

2. A full-time member of the faculty or staff who is presently engaged, or who plans to engage, in gainful activities of an extensive, recurring, or continuing nature outside of his broad institutional responsibilities during any period of full-time employment by the university should report in writing the nature and extent of such activities for the recommendation of the chairman or head of his department and for the approval of the appropriate deans or administrative officers. These officers may wish to consult the chancellor in certain cases.

3. Prior approval of the president of the university should be obtained in all cases of outside activities involving matters of public interest or policy.

4. A university employee may be engaged as a consultant on a research project or projects conducted by an outside agency. However, if the university employee has responsibility for the conduct of the research, he is considered a participant or a part of the research team rather than a consultant. In cases of this sort the outside agency must have a contract or specific written agreement with the university regarding the employee's participating in the research. For example, if a university employee is listed as a participant in a grant or contract proposal by an organization other than State University, he is assumed to have some responsibility for the research; accordingly, the

university will require a subcontract or agreement to cover the employee's participation. Any exceptions to this provision require written approval of the dean or director of the appropriate college or school and of the chancellor.

5. It is the responsibility of the university employee to make clear to any outside agency that in accepting such employment he does so as an individual independent of his capacity as a member of the staff of the university. It is felt that this can best be accomplished in oral testimony or written reports by including a statement that the views expressed are those of the speaker or writer and do not necessarily reflect the views of the university. In no case should the individual concerned identify himself by his university title nor use the name of the university.

6. The university recognizes the fact that a person qualifies as an expert because of his training and experience. Therefore, biographical data, including a statement of employment by State University, may be included as introductory material to written reports (but not incorporated in the body of the written report) by the outside agency by way of establishing the writer as a qualified expert.

7. Department heads and deans shall assume the responsibility for determining that university laboratories, services, and equipment are not used in connection with outside activities.

The stated problem regarding outside activities is the propriety of a university professor engaging in outside activities during the regular academic day and under circumstances that would conflict with the professor's duties and responsibilities to his appointing authority.

During the 1973 spring semester, the State Commission on Governmental Ethics received a request from the legislative auditor requesting an advisory opinion as to the following described activity:

> The legislative auditor's examinations of the records of colleges and universities of the state revealed that many full-time academic personnel are rendering services during the normal academic day to private and other public agencies for which the personnel are being compensated. During the employee's absence from their respective posts of duty, the instructional and other academic work which the employee is required to perform for his appointing authority either goes undone or is done by graduate assistants or other university personnel.

On July 3, 1973, the State Commission on Governmental Ethics responded with the following advisory opinion:

At the outset, the Commission anticipates the argument that academic personnel who are the subject of this advisory opinion may be exempt from this Commission's jurisdiction pursuant to the authority of Section 1111 (4) (f) of the Code of Ethics which proviso states, in part, that:

> "Notwithstanding the foregoing, the term 'state employee' shall not include, while acting in their official capacities . . . the teaching, professional and administrative officers of all schools, colleges and universities of the state."

At first blush, this exception would appear to deny this Commission supervisory jurisdiction over college professors and other administrative personnel of public institutions of higher education. However, the Commission must read the above proviso in its entirety and give credence to every phrase contained therein; specifically, the Commission is mindful of the language that the exclusion applies to professors and other administrative personnel only "while acting in their official capacity." And, it is patent that a college professor or other academic personnel most certainly is <u>not</u> acting "within his official capacity" as a college professor or administrative personnel while he is engaged in outside employment in violation of pertinent provisions of the Code of Ethics. Accordingly, it is the opinion of this Commission that such employees of public institutions of higher education most certainly are subject to this Commission's jurisdiction while engaged in outside employment activities in violation of the Code of Ethics.

Turning now to the substance of this opinion, the Commission is, of course, mindful of the provisions of Section 1101 (B) which provide in part as follows:

> An essential principle underlying the staffing of our government structure is that its elected officials and employees should not be denied the opportunity, available to all other citizens, to acquire and retain private economic and other interests, except where conflicts with the responsibility of such elected officials and employees to the public cannot be avoided.

However, the Commission is equally cognizant of
the provisions of Code of Ethics Section 1113 which provides as follows:

a. Payments for Services to the State. No
state employee shall receive any thing of
economic value, other than his compensation
from the state, and other normal employee
benefits provided by the state, for or in consideration of personal services rendered or
to be rendered to or for the state. Any thing
of economic value received by a state employee
prior to or subsequent to his state employment
shall be presumed, in the absence of a showing
to the contrary by a clear preponderance of
evidence, not to be for, or in consideration of,
personal services rendered or to be rendered
to or for the state.

b. Compensation for Service to Others. No
state employee shall receive any thing of
economic value for or in consideration of
personal services rendered, or to be rendered, to or for any person during the term
of his state employment unless such services
meet each of the following qualifications:
(1) The services are bona fide and are actually
performed by such employee; and
(2) The services are not within the course of
his official duties; and
(3) The services are not prohibited by R.S.
42:1112 or by applicable laws or regulations
governing non-state employment for such
employee; and
(4) The services are neither performed for
nor compensated by any person from whom
such employee would be prohibited by R.S.
42:1114 from receiving a gift; unless the
services and compensation are fully disclosed in writing to the head of the employee's
agency.

Professors (and other academic personnel) of public
educational institutions are, of course, employed to dis-
charge certain instructional, educational, other academic

or administrative duties. In exchange for these duties, the employees are compensated with public funds. These duties and responsibilities are to be discharged, to the extent possible, during the regular academic day. For employees of institutions of higher education to subvert or otherwise put aside the functions and responsibilities for which they are being paid with public funds in favor of private vocational pursuits—regardless of how noble such private pursuits might be—does in the opinion of this Commission constitute a clear abridgement of the employee's obligation to his appointing authority and does moreover constitute a violation of Section 1113 of the Code of Ethics.

College and university professors and other academic personnel hold positions of employment in public trust with the State for the purpose of rendering instructional or other educational services at their respective public institutions of higher education. Their positions are not to be used as a springboard to engage in outside employment during the regular course and scope of their public employment and in a fashion that would necessarily interfere with, subvert, or otherwise postpone their primary duties and responsibilities.

Likewise, the provisions of Code of Ethics 1120 (F) are apropos. It is here provided, in part, that "Knowingly having one or more employees on the payroll who are not rendering service for which they are being paid shall subject the agency head as well as such employee to the disciplinary action and penalties provided by this Part." In view of this admonition, those charged with the responsibility of regulating the activities of full-time academic personnel are themselves admonished to ensure that these full-time employees of the State do in fact devote to the State services "for which they are being paid" and that they conduct their outside employment activities in such a fashion as would not interfere with their obligations and responsibilities to their appointing authority and that they refrain from systematically engaging in extracurricular activities during the normal academic day.

s/ John Certain   s/ Bill Know
s/ Mary Sure   s/ Joe Competent

COMMISSIONER SAM AGAINST DISSENTING:

I dissent from the conclusion that the Commission
has jurisdiction over the alleged activity of the college
professor in their advisory opinion.

To conclude that a college professor or any other
excluded "state employee" is not acting in his official
capacity when engaged in an activity which violates his
duty so as to make him amenable to the regulations of
the ethics law he is outside his official capacity and is
therefore within our jurisdiction.

It is only when one violates his duty in some way
related to state employment that the ethical merits of
his conduct is of substantive concern to the commission.
It therefore follows from the majority reasoning herein
that violations of duty by excluded employees remove
them from their "official capacity" and make them subject to our jurisdiction so that we have jurisdiction
whenever we find that the excluded employee has vio-
lated his duty in a manner which also violates the
ethics code. We thus put first things last. This is
inconsistent with the concept and purpose of jurisdictional limitations.

The strained "logic" of the rationale employed
by the majority in this opinion leads to the absurdity
that it is because the college professor is violating his
official duty to teach and attend to other academic
duties that his conduct is unethical; yet he is within
our jurisdiction because such violation of duty removes
him from acting within his official capacity.

Perhaps the question is asked: Why did the
legislature qualify the limitation of jurisdiction over
certain state employees "WHILE ACTING IN HIS
OFFICIAL CAPACITY"? The answer comes to light
when it is realized that one may hold a position in an
excluded employment and at the same time be a state
employee in an included employment. For example,
college professors and teachers serve on the Ethics
Commission. Their role as Commissioners make
them state employees within the jurisdiction of the
Commission and they are not made immune by reason
of being a professor or teacher because their function as
Commissioners is outside their function as college
professor or teacher.

In final analysis, an excepted employee is not excluded from our jurisdiction when he acts in a role independent of and unrelated to the excluded category. It seems absurd, however, to say that conduct arising out of and related to an excluded position falls outside the scope and purview of the excluded job category and position and falls outside the "official capacity" of the employee merely because it violates the duty of the job or position.

In the instant case it is precisely because the employee is a college professor working for a college or university of the state (which are excluded from our jurisdiction) that the ethical propriety of his conduct is brought before us.

When the reasons for limitation of jurisdiction are viewed seriously and deeply within the context of sound political theory and governmental policy, it is realized that jurisdictional issues should be weighed and considered cautiously and certainly without whimsical interpretation so as to expand the reach of the interpreter whose jurisdiction is in question.

A quick glance at the list of those excluded from our jurisdiction—judges, elected officials, pensioners, inmate employees of penal institutions, teachers and administrative officers of schools, colleges and universities—brings into focus the policy reasons underlying and permeating the legislative intent. The excluded categories are those which either have their own ethical standards of self-policing or must be left independent of external administrative supervision or are independently elected so that they should not be subject to the regulations of an appointed agency.

College professors in our state system are self-policing by faculty peers. They are subject to the immediate supervision of their department heads, deans and college presidents. The whole system is subject to the authority of an elected Board of Education which makes policy and rules for the regulation of the college and university personnel. There is ample power and authority in the Board to control corruption in the ranks of college and school personnel under the Board's jurisdiction.

Furthermore, rules and regulations of schools and colleges are interwoven with a plethora of standards

and rules of rating and accrediting association. For the
Ethics Commission to set piecemeal standards by ad hoc
consideration of isolated problems of college personnel
is to invade dark thickets without a light, whereas
Aladdin's lamp is needed. Indeed our well meaning in-
cursion may constitute a violation of principles of academic freedom and independence from external political
intermeddling and control which is a prime requisite of
academic rating.

For the above reasons, and for other reasons of
policy discernible in legislative intent, I respectfully
maintain that we have no jurisdiction in the matter
involved in the Advisory Opinion.

s/ Sam Against

On August 29, 1973, Ima Leader, President of the State University System, responded to the legislative auditor with a revised policy
on outside activities of university employees. The revised policy
stated:

This policy relates to activities directly undertaken by
members of the University academic and nonacademic
staff with outside agencies and does not relate to activities in which arrangements are made officially through
the University by contracts with or grants to the University. The policy outlined below relating to outside
activities should be brought to the attention of all
employees.

Statement of Policy on Outside Activities

1. A member of the faculty or staff may engage
in outside activities, paid or unpaid, which do not conflict, delay or in any manner interfere with instructional,
scholarly, and/or other services he must render in the
nature of his University employment.

2. A full-time member of the faculty or staff who
is presently engaged, or who plans to engage, in such
activities outside of his broad institutional responsibilities, during any period of full-time employment by
the University, shall report to the chairman or head of
his department of the amount of compensation to be
received and the amount of time the work will require.
In all such instances, the department head or chairman
shall forward the report to his administrative superior

who will make a complete disclosure of these facts to the campus head.

3. No full-time member of the faculty or staff shall engage in such outside activities (or continue such activity if already so engaged) without the written approval of the department head and dean. In the event that either the department head or the dean believes that such outside activity involves, or may involve, a matter of public interest or policy, the matter shall be referred through the appropriate channels to the President of the University for approval.

4. With such written approval of the department head and the dean, a University employee may be engaged as a consultant on a research project or projects conducted by an outside employer. However, if the University employee has responsibility for the conduct of the research or is in fact performing or is to perform the research, he is considered a participant or a part of the research team rather than a consultant. In such instances the outside agency must have a contract or specific written agreement with the University regarding the employee's participation in the research. For example, if a University employee is listed as a participant in a grant or contract proposal by an organization other than State University, he is assumed to have some responsibility for the research; accordingly, the University will require a subcontract or agreement to cover the employee's participation.

5. It is the responsibility of the University employee to make clear to any outside agency that in accepting such activity he does so as an individual independent of his capacity as a member of the staff of the University. This might best be accomplished by providing with oral testimony or written reports a statement to the effect that the views expressed are those of the employee and do not necessarily reflect the views of the University. In no case should the individual concerned use the name of the University or his University title officially or in any way in support of any position he may take.

6. The University recognizes the fact that a person qualifies as an expert because of his training and experience. Therefore, biographical data, including a statement of employment by State University may be included as introductory material to written reports (but

not incorporated in the body of the written report) by the
outside agency, or orally in the case of expert witness,
by way of establishing the writer as a qualified expert.

7. Campus heads, through their department heads
and chairmen, deans, or other appropriate administrators,
shall assume the responsibility for determining that University personnel, laboratories, services and equipment
are not used without authorization in connection with outside activities of University employees.

8. These policy provisions are applicable in nonacademic as well as academic departments and divisions
of the University.

This policy was devised and revised without input from the
various segments of the university family and without regard for the
diversified functions and obligations of the several departments of
the university.

IMPLICATIONS FOR ACTION

On September 6, 1973, the chancellor of State University notified,
by memo, the deans and chairpersons of the several colleges, departments, and divisions to implement the revised policy submitted by the
president to the legislative auditor. Immediate problems began to
emerge, faculties became restless, and commitments became questionable. The chairman of the Department of Elementary and Secondary
Education encountered many difficulties in implementing the new
policy. Interviews were conducted with chairpersons in other departments of the university, with faculty representatives, and with university and systemwide administrators.

Initial concerns and questions to be resolved include the
following:

1. Is the position stated by the Commission on Governmental
Ethics consistent with the stated expectation, function, and purpose of
the Department of Elementary and Secondary Education? Is this
within the purview of the Commission on Governmental Ethics?

2. Is the revised policy of the University System, a result of
the report of the Commission on Governmental Ethics, consistent with
the stated expectation, function, and purpose of the Department of
Elementary and Secondary Education?

3. Does the revised policy consider the unique and diversified
responsibility of the several departments within State University?

Is there a need to consider the uniqueness of a particular department?

4. What value is scholarly work in professional areas unless it can be implemented? Is professional implementation as important as discovery or proposals of scholarly concepts? Will the policy tend to turn the faculty inward rather than outward?

5. Should faculty members be permitted to engage in outside activities for compensation if this is an expectation and released time is not available for this involvement? Should this participation be on an unpaid basis?

6. Is there a need for a new procedure in policy development? Should policy development be accomplished by unilateral action?

7. What constitutes a "normal" academic day?

8. Is the policy consistent with university criteria and expectations for promotion?

Many additional concerns and questions were raised, but those enumerated here deal with the central issues involved in the implementation of the new policy. Suffice it to conclude that the answers strike at the heart of the faculty role in the academic community. And conceptually as well as pragmatically this case study offers an opportunity for reflection on many facets of an institutional policy that is in apparent conflict with its stated purposes.

8

RESPONSIVE AND RESPONSIBLE
FACULTY COMMITTEES AS A
MEANS OF PARTICIPATION
IN COLLEGE GOVERNANCE
WITHIN A UNIVERSITY
Mary K. Carl

The assumption has been made that faculty committees are a meaningful tool in bringing about interaction between administrations, the faculty, and students in areas of concern to all in the academic community. In most instances, however, the fact remains that this mechanism has not reached its potential in actual implementation. Some of the problems which have surfaced can be attributed to lack of clarity on the part of the participants with regard to roles, responsibilities, and functions. The symptoms which have resulted run the gamut of inadequate and sparse participation, inefficiency, little or no productivity, and absence of responsiveness in meeting the needs of the academic unit. This study is a description of the sequential development of the viable and productive committee structure within a college of a major university, which may prove equally as applicable and fruitful elsewhere.

To begin, it is essential that an important committee structure be established within the framework of a climate which is conducive to mutual interaction and respect among all members of the college. The philosophy and rationale for this structure implies a demonstrated attitude of respect by administration for the capacities of both faculty and students to give thoughtful consideration to the issues involved, and to evolve solutions to problems which embrace options for progress. Administration must be capable of (1) requiring that the reports and recommendations of the committees are responsive and responsible; (2) giving all faculty and students the opportunity to discuss and sanction the recommendations; (3) providing administrative mechanisms to

---

Mary K. Carl, Dean, University of Delaware.

facilitate progress toward meeting the recommendations; and (4) communicating with committee chairmen for input by committees when consultation is necessary in specific areas of interest to specific committees. Faculty must respect the integrity of administration and be capable of (1) producing responsible reports and recommendations which embrace the well-being of the entire academic unit; (2) keeping abreast of the scope and functions of the committee(s) on which they hold membership; (3) communicating their recommendations through open forum to all members of the academic unit, and reworking their recommendations when appropriate; and (4) respecting the contributions of students in areas where their input is essential.

Within this atmosphere of mutual respect for each other's responsibilities and capabilities, the college within a university described here designed its committee structure and operations.

COMMITTEE STRUCTURE

Prior to the fall of 1971, the college had designed a committee structure which anticipated the structure that would possibly develop in the University Faculty Senate. College administration believed that it was important to anticipate the design which the senate may adopt for several reasons. First, this would provide opportunity for the faculty of the college to test out various functions of the committees, to set goals for definite periods of time, and to evaluate the outcomes of committee decisions and their value to the overall academic unit. Second, this would provide ample time to explore the various parameters of each committee to ascertain their boundaries and interaction. Third, there would be opportunity to identify areas where committee activity was needed or major gaps existed. This lead time of approximately two years was of definite value, for, in addition to the above, it permitted administration, faculty, and students to become accustomed to a meaningful and responsible mode of interaction and to identify unique and collaborative roles.

In the spring of 1972, with the described prior experience, the faculty of the college adopted a constitution which established the faculty as the official channel of faculty recommendations on all matters which bear upon the academic programs of the college. Article 2 of the constitution deals with the committees of the college (and it is to this article that references will be made below).

The general functions of the committees of the college are (1) to investigate, advise, and recommend regarding designated areas, and (2) to carry out assigned duties.

Each full-time member of the faculty of the college is eligible for membership, with power to vote, on faculty-student standing committees of the college. The Organization and Rules Committee of the college canvasses the faculty and in consultation with the dean makes its appointments to the standing committees. The Organization and Rules Committee consults with the advisor for and the officers of the Student Council for appointments to the standing committees.

To provide continuity to the committees, members are appointed for two years, with one-half of each committee retiring from office each year.

The chairman of each committee is appointed by the Organization and Rules Committee in consultation with the dean, and when possible, is chosen from those members on each committee for at least one academic year.

In order that adequate communication is possible among standing committees and administration, faculty, and students, copies of minutes of these committees are sent to the administration, faculty, and student members of committees plus the president of the College Student Council. In addition, an annual report is prepared by the chairman of each committee for distribution to administration, faculty, and the Student Council. The annual report for each committee contains the following information: purpose of the committee; membership; number of meetings; actions taken; recommendations referred for faculty action; matters still under consideration; recommendations for future deliberations of the committee.

Hearings are encouraged for the discussion of committee proposals prior to presentation to the faculty for action. This is particularly the case when major or significant proposals are under consideration.

As described above, the manner in which members of standing committees are chosen, the activities of these committees, and the channels which are provided for in-depth and open interaction—all of these add up to a framework of communication which is conducive to responsible participation.

Without further elaboration as to the scope, role, and functions of these major standing committees, however, this study would not be complete; below is a brief description of the implementation aspects of these committees.

The standing committees as presently constituted are as follows:

1. Coordinating Council
2. Organization and Rules
3. Undergraduate Curriculum
   a. Winterim Subcommittee
   b. Evaluation Subcommittee
   c. Advisement Subcommittee

4. Student Affairs
5. Student Status and Progress
6. Graduate Program
7. Research
8. Publications
9. Instructional Resources
10. Community Programs
11. Continuing Education
12. Faculty Development
13. Faculty Promotions and Tenure

The functions of each committee and subcommittee is described below (according to the constitution and bylaws of the college).

The coordinating Council is a faculty committee consisting of the dean or assistant dean of the college plus four faculty coordinators. Its functions are—

1. to act in a consulting role to the dean of the college upon request by the dean;
2. to participate in the formulation of the agenda for all regular faculty meetings;
3. to collaborate with the dean of the college when immediate or emergency action is required and a special meeting of the faculty is not possible;
4. to collaborate with the dean in facility planning and development;
5. to disseminate pertinent information to the faculty members in their area;
6. to discuss matters which involve coordination and cooperation between faculty groups;
7. to appoint, in consultation with the dean, the chairman and members of the Organization and Rules Committee—appointments for the next academic year should be announced before the Organization and Rules Committee appoints other committees for the next year.

The Organization and Rules Committee is a faculty committee consisting of one member from each faculty discipline. Its functions are—

1. to review, revise, and recommend changes in the constitution and bylaws of the faculty as appropriate;
2. to conduct the nomination and election procedure for university senators and notify the college faculty and the secretary of the University senate of the results;

3. to appoint a member of the college faculty to serve as secretary for the faculty;
4. to consider carefully the equitable distribution of committee assignments among the full-time faculty and consult as necessary with faculty coordinators concerning the work loads of faculty members;
5. to solicit faculty members' interest in committee activity, select the members to serve on the standing committees and standing subcommittees, and designate the chairman of each standing committee and standing subcommittee;
6. to make appointments to fill unexpired terms of office of chairman or members of standing committees or standing subcommittees;
7. to contact the College Student Council for recommendations for student members to serve on student-faculty committees;
8. to circulate to each graduate student descriptions of committees with graduate student membership, and elicit preferences of graduate students for committee appointments;
9. to appoint task forces or study panels at the request of the faculty;
10. to consult with the college representative on the senate committee or committees regarding nominations of college faculty to senate committees;
11. to advise the dean, upon request, regarding appointments of college faculty to university, professional, or community committees;
12. to ascertain that official copies of annual reports and minutes of meetings of committees are on file in the Office of the Dean;
13. to solicit, receive, and hear faculty suggestions regarding college committees and their functions and act in a consultative role to promote committee effectiveness;
14. to prepare, distribute, collect, count, and report results of ballots presenting proposed amendments to the constitution or bylaws of the college;
15. to receive requests from the faculty for matters to be considered by a committee and refer them to appropriate committees.

The Undergraduate Curriculum Committee is composed of one faculty member from each curriculum level, one faculty member at large, the chairman of the Evaluation Subcommittee, the chairman of the Winterim Subcommittee, and the chairman of the Advisement Subcommittee. Its functions are—

1. to review continuously the planned undergraduate program of studies in light of stated philosophy and objectives and recommend to the faculty changes to enhance the effectiveness of the program;
2. to encourage, initiate, and recommend changes in the curriculum to meet present and future roles in society;
3. to study, report to, and recommend new, innovative teaching strategies which may be of value to the attainment of the stated objectives;
4. to review and recommend alterations or changes in course offerings;
5. to collaborate with other colleges in planning and arranging courses utilized by students in college;
6. to receive and review the recommendations of the Subcommittee on Evaluation;
7. to receive and review the recommendations of the Subcommittee on Winterim;
8. to arrange for hearings on any proposal for substantive change in the undergraduate curriculum prior to presenting recommendations to the faculty.

The Winterim Subcommittee of the Undergraduate Curriculum Committee is composed of one faculty member from each curriculum level, one faculty member from the graduate program, six students, one undergraduate student from each curriculum level, and two graduate students. Its functions are—

1. to develop a program of course offerings which will enhance the interest and goals of the overall educational offerings;
2. to encourage innovations, creativity, and independent study in development of the Winterim;
3. to encourage faculty to offer some Winterim activities for majors at all levels;
4. to encourage faculty to offer one or more related Winterim activities for nonmajor students.

The Evaluation Subcommittee of the Undergraduate Curriculum Committee is a student-faculty committee composed of one faculty member from each curriculum level, five students, one undergraduate student from each curriculum level, and one at large. Its functions are—

1. to develop a program of evaluation of the attainment of the objectives of the undergraduate curriculum which includes such indicators as course evaluation, standardized test

results, course grades, end-of-program achievement,
licensing examination results, and periodic review of the
status of the graduates of the baccalaureate program;
2. to implement, following acceptance by the Undergraduate
Curriculum Committee and the faculty of the protocol for
evaluation of the undergraduate curriculum, those aspects of
the protocol assigned to the Evaluation Subcommittee;
3. to periodically review the evaluation protocol and recommend
necessary revisions to the parent committee;
4. to promote evaluation as an integral part of program evolve-
ment;
5. to work upon request as consultants with individual faculty
members in developing tools of evaluation.

The Advisement Subcommittee of the Undergraduate Curriculum
Committee has four faculty and five student members. Its functions
are—

1. to plan, implement, and evaluate a program of academic
advisement for prospective and enrolled undergraduate students, with the approval of the Undergraduate Curriculum
Committee;
2. to collect data and report to the parent committee on the
problems encountered by students in selecting courses and
in registration;
3. to conduct an orientation program for new advisors in cooperation with the Faculty Development Committee;
4. to consult with the advisor to transfer students on the problems encountered in implementing the open curriculum
concept.

The Student Affairs Committee has four faculty and four student
members. Its functions are—

1. to consult with the advisor and officers of the College Student
Council on student-faculty activities;
2. to consider, upon request of individual students or the Student
Council, special problems affecting groups of students;
3. to consider, upon request of the Dean, special problems
affecting groups of students;
4. to review, revise, and recommend to the faculty policies
specific to majors;
5. to establish a procedure and assume responsibility for noti-
fying majors of policies specific to students in the college;

6. to make recommendations for and provide active support in recruiting majors;
7. to encourage and support student participation in the College Student Council;
8. to familiarize and encourage faculty and student awareness of the counseling, tutoring, and other supportive services in the university community.

The Student Status and Progress Committee has four faculty members, one from each undergraduate level. Its functions are—

1. to establish, review, and revise criteria for honors programs and awards of the college;
2. to make recommendations regarding students whose academic standing makes them eligible for various honor awards or honors programs of the college or the university;
3. to plan and implement Honors Day activities of the college, in consultation with the dean;
4. to consider and make recommendations on requests of undergraduate students with satisfactory academic standing to take a major course out of sequence;
5. to review and recommend policies regarding progression in the undergraduate program;
6. to review and recommend candidates to receive their baccalaureate degrees upon completion of the program;
7. to review the academic records of all undergraduate students in the college, advise faculty about the overall status of the students, and consult with the academic advisors of students on probation or in some other academic difficulty;
8. to encourage and support the honorary society in the college and, upon request of the faculty advisor, provide a list of students with the required academic standing;
9. to make recommendations on the program for the dean's scholars upon request of the dean.

The Graduate Program Committee has four faculty members and four students. Its functions are—

1. to review continuously the planned graduate program of studies in light of stated philosophy and objectives;
2. to encourage, initiate, and recommend changes in the curriculum to meet present and future roles in society;
3. to formulate policies for admission to graduate study in the college;

4. to recommend to the dean, for submission to the College of Graduate Studies, alterations, additions, or deletions of individual courses which have been approved by the graduate faculty in the college;

5. to review the academic standards of graduate study;

6. to recommend to the dean certification of students who have completed the requirements for advanced degrees;

7. to review and recommend changes in Graduate Program brochures and catalogues to the Publications Committee;

8. to conduct a periodic review of the status of graduates of the program;

9. to consider, upon request of the dean or committee members, special problems affecting groups of graduate students;

10. to make recommendations to the Winterim Subcommittee regarding graduate student activities during Winterim;

11. to make recommendations to the Research Committee regarding graduate student participation in research activities in the college;

12. to hold open hearings on all substantive changes in the graduate curriculum before making the recommendations to the graduate faculty;

13. to collaborate with other colleges in planning and arranging courses utilized by graduate students in the college.

The Research Committee has five faculty members and its functions are—

1. to provide leadership in defining and determining the research thrusts of the college and the strategies for implementing these thrusts;

2. to recommend policies and procedures related to research activities of faculty, graduate, and undergraduate students;

3. to stimulate individual faculty members to engage in research and serve as research consultants, upon request;

4. to consider and recommend faculty participation in outside research projects;

5. to collaborate with other colleges in research endeavors;

6. to encourage participation of graduate and undergraduate students in research activities in the college, when appropriate;

7. to recommend to the Faculty Development Committee educational programs related to research;

8. to recommend to the Graduate Program Committee and the Undergraduate Curriculum Committee changes in the research component in each program.

The Publications Committee has two faculty and three student members. Its functions are—

1. to review and revise Undergraduate Program flyers or brochures and catalogues as deemed appropriate;
2. to submit news releases on faculty activities to the university publications office;
3. to review and recommend news releases to local and state newspapers concerning faculty, students, programs, and activities of the college;
4. to receive and implement recommendations of the Graduate Program Committee for the revision of Graduate Program brochures and catalogues.

The Instructional Resources Committee has five faculty and five student members. Its functions are—

1. to assist faculty members in developing instructional resources;
2. to conduct educational programs and/or workshops to familiarize faculty members with instructional media;
3. to plan and implement an orientation for new faculty members on instructional resources, including library resources;
4. to promote effective utilization of various instructional media and strategies;
5. to recommend policies and procedures involving requests and utilization of instructional materials;
6. to review requests of faculty members, through the respective faculty coordinators, for purchase of instructional media and submit such requests to the instructional resources consultant for the faculty;
7. to recommend the policies for the operation of the instructional media and reading room facilities in the college for undergraduate and graduate students;
8. to conduct an annual review of the facilities and services in the college and make recommendations to the Coordinating Council;
9. to recommend policies and procedures for requesting book and periodicals acquisitions for the university library;
10. to consider and make recommendations regarding the utilization of the collection in the university library;
11. to supervise staff in the maintenance of an index of instructional resources available in the college and in the university library.

The Community Programs Committee has three faculty and four student members. Its functions are—

1. to recommend participation in new or ongoing projects or programs in the community;
2. to initiate and provide leadership for innovative or creative ideas, plans, and/or programs which are directed to needs in the community;
3. to recommend, upon request, consultants to service agencies needing a specific kind of expertise;
4. to encourage and support faculty participation in community programs.

The Faculty Development Committee has four faculty members and its functions are—

1. to conduct an orientation program for new members of the faculty of the college in collaboration with the dean, the chairmen of appropriate committees, and the faculty coordinators;
2. to maintain, review, and revise the faculty handbook;
3. to recommend policies specific to college faculty members;
4. to develop and implement a procedure for selecting faculty members for teaching excellency awards;
5. to serve as the social committee for the faculty—recommend a social program, recommend a dues system to support the program, and plan and conduct the program;
6. to recommend, plan, and implement an educational program for faculty members—receive and consider requests from the dean, faculty, and committee chairman on the content of the program;
7. to develop and recommend a grievance policy and procedure for faculty members;
8. to hear, investigate and mediate specific grievances of individual faculty members in matters of promotion, tenure, appointment, dismissal, sabbatical leave, and other conditions of employment.

The Faculty Promotions and Tenure Committee has four faculty members and its functions are—

1. to conduct periodic reviews of the qualifications of each faculty member for promotion and tenure, and submit recommendations to the dean;

2. to consider and make recommendations to the dean concerning the requests of faculty for sabbatical leave;
3. to review the policy and procedure for promotional review and recommend changes to the faculty.

EVALUATION OF A RESPONSIVE AND RESPONSIBLE FACULTY COMMITTEE STRUCTURE

The evaluation of this committee system is based upon several criteria, namely (1) satisfactory completion of most of the functions of the committee (quantitative aspects of productivity); (2) characteristics of the recommendations of the committee (qualitative agents of productivity); and (3) type and amount of academic community (college) participation in deliberations of the committee.

Since the constitution and bylaws of the faculty of the college were approved in 1972, an overall appraisal of the worth of the system has been made by the Coordinating Council.

SUMMARY

Considerable planning, development, and evaluation effort must occur before faculty committees can have significant impact upon the academic endeavors of a college. These committees can be a meaningful tool to improve the overall quality and integrity of a college. The success or failure of the mechanism depends in large part on the commitment of administrators, faculty, and students to participate in this responsive and responsible form of college governance.

9

Lake University is a state-supported institution granting degrees through a doctorate in some fields. It provides programs of study in the liberal arts, in the sciences, and in several professional areas. Because of a lack of opportunities for professionally trained persons to work in their home state, many of the graduates of Lake University emigrate to the large cities of nearby states in order to find employment. The low average income of the primarily agricultural work force in the region has contributed to low faculty salaries at Lake University. The consequences of this fact have been that the university functions with a small nucleus of highly dedicated instructors, and that the turnover is high among the more qualified faculty. The university experiences great difficulty in attracting trained faculty to positions in those professions where the supply of such persons is short nationally.

At the time of this case study, the College of Engineering at Lake University was one of the largest of its professional schools. The college is organized into six departments with a total of 65 full-time faculty members. The employment background of the dean of engineering is primarily industrial. This experience had its merit in the classroom and in industrial relations, but it did not give him a clear understanding of trends in engineering education. Never having been a faculty member, he was not cognizant of many of the problems that can exist at the grass-roots level. However, he was well aware that attracting qualified faculty was an almost impossible task. He

---

F. C. Fitchen, Dean, University of Bridgeport.

assisted to the best of his ability in recruiting staff, but, as often happens, he tended to grasp at straws upon encountering failure.

The chairman of X Department had been in the position for 30 years. He too had experienced many failures and had gravitated over a number of years toward an area of his personal interest where satisfaction and accomplishment was possible. That area was local government. Without adequate leadership, some of the faculty of X Department drifted toward technology and away from the highly challenging frontiers of sophisticated engineering. These problems tended to be further accentuated by the fact that industrial research and development (R & D) and design engineering were almost non-existent in the isolated geographic area of the campus of Lake University.

ENGINEERING ACCREDITATION

Engineering accreditation at the university is the function of the Engineers Council for Professional Development (ECPD). At regular time intervals a team is assembled consisting of one specialist for each program or department to be evaluated, plus a team chairman. Engineering accreditation is given to the program, not to the department. However, in most instances these are synonymous. The on-site portion of the inspection covers a one-to-three-day period depending upon the number of programs up for accreditation. The majority of team members are from academic institutions and are often deans of engineering. Every aspect of the educational situation, including all phases of budgeting, support services such as libraries and other academic departments, and administration, is evaluated. During the 1950s and 1960s, standards for accreditation advanced swiftly. The trends during those years were toward improved faculty credentials, particularly doctoral degrees and publications, solid scientific bases for engineering subjects, and design content in each curriculum. The trends were away from skill courses in any shape or form. While the accreditation is of undergraduate programs exclusively, the team is not blind to activities at the graduate level.

The Visit of the Accreditation Team

It was in the light of the conditions already mentioned that the accreditation team descended upon Lake University one year during the 1970s. The usual time for such a visit is late winter. The inspector of X Department was a highly progressive sixty-year-old educator. He did not like what he saw. Certain aspects of his dislike were made known verbally to the department chairman and the dean at the conclusion of the visit. The written report that forms the basis for the next accreditation visit was, as is the usual custom, not made available to the president of Lake University until the following fall. It awarded a two-year accreditation to X Department. Other departments fared better. A two-year accreditation represents the smallest number of years awarded to any accredited program, and implies that sincere and sweeping changes must be made before an extension can be given if warranted after the next accreditation.

The serious consequences of loss of accreditation were known to the dean. The group that suffers is primarily the graduating students who find few recruiters coming to campus after a loss of accreditation. Some loss in student body is also bound to occur.

The criticisms leveled against X Department covered the gamut. Salaries were criticized, the faculty was said to be provincial and the curriculum antiquated, and research space was virtually nonexistent. Perhaps the most important point was that the image of the department, as projected to the inspectors, was that of a typical engineering department of the 1930s and 1940s rather than of the 1970s. A further criticism of the staff centered upon the low level of research activity and of faculty publications. There were no graduate students studying in the department at the time.

The Response

In response the chairman of X Department tried to marshal his resources in order to satisfy the criticisms contained in the accreditation letter. However, he had neither the staff, the leadership ability, nor the insight to solve the problems facing the department. Some minor curriculum revisions were made.

Discussions between the dean and the chairman of X Department eventually resulted in the decision that the chairman would step down and that the dean would be free to seek another chairman who could revitalize the department and extend accreditation. Since there was no talent for this in his College of Engineering, the dean had to look elsewhere at a time when engineers were in short supply throughout the nation and Lake University was still paying well below the national average for experienced engineering educators.

Through a stroke of good fortune, the dean was able to find a man—Dr. Jones—to head X Department who perhaps could solve the problems. The initial contact was made through an advertisement in a professional journal. The dean hired Jones at a competitive salary from his previous academic position as associate professor. Jones had written a widely accepted textbook, had had a history of six years of industrial experience and ten years of academic experience, but had not been a principal investigator on any research grant or contract. He was the best-qualified applicant to respond to the announcement in the journal.

Jones viewed the position of chairman of X Department as a challenge of the highest magnitude in educational organization and leadership of people. He felt that he knew how to pull the department out of its dilemma. He had experienced the upgrading of an engineering faculty in his preceding assignment, and had a sleeveful of tricks.

Jones came on board on July 15. The two-year accreditation extension was up in March of the following year. This left only 8 months for Jones to make significant inroads in the problems of upgrading and updating the department and its activities. Including the chairmanship, the department had ten positions. However, two of the most promising faculty members were on leaves of absence, pursuing doctoral studies. The administration agreed that these persons could be replaced since their leaves would be at least two years in length. It was clearly obvious that any replacement could not be accomplished for the fall semester; but there was perhaps some hope to fill at least one of the positions for the forthcoming spring semester. The faculty improvement program envisioned by Jones certainly did take into account the addition of his own resume to the department's credentials. Of the eight faculty on board that fall, two held a doctorate, including Jones. All others had earned a master's degree. Doubling the number of doctors on the staff was not the only consequence of his employment. His publication record essentially doubled the number of publications of the faculty. In addition the second edition of his textbook was nearing completion and while it would not be available at inspection time, it would be useful to cite in his resume.

Positive Steps

Jones decided on a philosophy of upgrading that essentially by-passed many of the problems noted in the accreditation letter. Since accreditation team members almost always come from larger schools with well-established graduate programs, he made a special effort to "pump up" the research-graduate student posture of the department immediately. He found but one research-oriented professor, Mr. Blue, among the faculty, and a graduate student body that totaled one student!

As the result of some hard work, he successfully recruited a second graduate student before classes started in September. Thus a 100 percent increase was accomplished.

Jones spent the month of August writing research proposals. He had wrestled with the question of which comes first, the money or the students, and had concluded that money was the first necessity in recruiting graduate research assistants. Before the end of August, he had experienced a failure in getting financial support for transportation research from the state highway department. His other proposals were mailed for evaluations, and time would tell the eventual outcome.

Image is of primary importance. To recruit graduate students, it is necessary to present an image of interesting research activity. As a first step in this direction, Jones cleared out a large storage closet in a room, obtained laboratory tables for the room, and placed a sign on the door that read "Research Lab No. 3." This was more of a showplace than a genuine working area, for he hoped that most of the actual research activities in the department would be done by graduate students.

Dr. Green, the other Ph.D. on the department faculty, had not engaged in research since his own graduate work of two years previous. He was strongly encouraged "to get something going," and responded affirmatively, although his activities were ineffectual.

A biweekly seminar for faculty and graduate students was initiated in the hope that it would provide a stimulant for the department. Also, as was well known to Jones, this is an activity looked upon favorably by accreditors as a means of faculty development.

A set of ten modern graduate level courses were proposed and accepted, even though the department had only two graduate students at the time.

Undergraduate Activities

Thirsting for leadership, the department faculty underwrote Jones' suggestions for curriculum revision. The changes were essentially minor; those instituted during the preceding year didn't go quite far enough. The combination resulted in a modern program that would be hard to criticize.

Much of the undergraduate laboratory work was done in a huge, high-ceilinged room of about 4,000 square feet. Upon entering, the impression one received was that of a 40-year-old heavy equipment shop. To combat this image, Jones proposed partitioning the space into four laboratories. He won approval of this idea, and the work was completed during the Christmas vacation. Some modern equipment was moved in, including items purchased by a recently won grant of $1,200. Certain older equipment was junked, again to alter the image.

Two of the faculty were stimulated to plan new laboratory offerings, and were busy during the fall semester with this activity.

Winter Wonderland

Perhaps the greatest breakthrough occurred early one winter day when Jones was notified by mail that he would receive a $25,000 research grant for an 18-month experimental study. This would also involve Professor Brown, but the bulk of the funds would go for support of research assistants.

Jones's goal of having 50 percent of the faculty engaged in research was reached when the university research fund announced that it would fund Professor Red for the coming summer.

Recruiting of graduate students was beginning to pay off. Two January graduates agreed to continue their studies and a foreign student arrived in January. Thus the graduate program had five students during the all-important spring semester. With the research funds available, three additional students agreed to become research assistants after their graduation in June.

The problem of hiring faculty was nearly insolvable. There are few if any pioneers who will accept the challenge of working to upgrade a mediocre department in a university that has a bland reputation and is situated far from big-city lights. After many months without success, a Ph.D. candidate at a Canadian university finally responded affirmatively to an offer of employment from the department. While he would not join the staff until June, this acquisition could be pointed out to the accreditation team.

THE CRUCIAL VISIT

Time for development had run out. Jones's final check list took the following form:

Faculty
morale	good
number	eight plus one being hired
number holding Ph.D.	two plus one being hired
development	seminar series, summer institutes, two on leave
salaries	low, but being improved
publications	two with very good records

Students
    undergraduate numbers   adequate
    graduate numbers   five and rapidly growing
    quality   good
Curricula
    undergraduate   modern
    graduate   modern
Support
    number and type of
      personnel   adequate
    travel budget   adequate
Facilities
    teaching laboratories   good
    research space   adequate
    office space   adequate
    equipment acquisitions   good
Research
    activity   50 percent of faculty

A single inspector arrived in late March for a one-day visit. Jones was confident that all leaks had been plugged. What remained to be done was to communicate the essence of all changes to the accreditor. The inspector's initial request was for a one-half-hour interview with each member of the department. After two hours with Jones, the visitor went to Red's office. While the visit with Red was taking place, Jones clued in Brown on those items of importance that were not discussed in the two-hour meeting. Brown squeezed them into his conversation with the inspector.

The Outcome

The accreditation report contained praise for the department and its program. No serious criticisms resulted from the visit. However, because continued improvement was called for, a revisit in two years was scheduled. The corner had clearly been turned.

The next accreditation visit found the department with a staff of 12, half holding a doctorate. The graduate student body had grown to exceed 20, and the department had research support of about $100,000 per year. The publication record was greatly improved, with more than 50 percent of the staff engaged in research. Additional research space had been acquired and morale was excellent. The verdict was accreditation extension for the maximum length of time.

Academic programs and human needs and aspirations are interrelated, and the manner in which the college and university organizes
for their delivery is a subject inadequately explored in the literature
of higher education. Of course, organization charts and management
rationale are readily available in most institutions, but neither really
serve to communicate an understanding of the real process at work
nor do they depict the gap between administrative objectives and
achievements. We believe that the preceding studies can serve to
bridge that level of comprehension.

Relative to the Drake study on the sequence of decisional events
at one college, is it typical of that experienced at other academic institutions? Is revolutionary change revolutionary in fact, or is it an
expedient alternative to otherwise dire consequences? Will intelligent
planning and an open political process assure an affirmative result in
most instances? Must the clientele group, such as the faculty or students, be ready or conditioned for academic change before even the
most rational of alternative programs has a chance for success?
Surely none will contest the need of sponsorship and strategy to guide
an innovative effort, but is this to suggest that academe is inherently
opposed to nontraditional means of postsecondary education? Is alternative curricula feasible only if the change agent is politically astute,
suggesting that the merits of a proposal may not be as relevant? How
else might the revolution in this case study have been undertaken
with equal success, and what are the usual impediments thereto at
most institutions?

Revolutionary change, of a different order, might also characterize the Martin study on policy conflicting with institutional purpose.
What problems, common in academe, are represented by that case
study? What alternative courses of action were considered and how
applicable was the one chosen? Would your decision and approach
differ if you were viewing the problem as a member of the faculty as
opposed to an administrator? If so, what does that suggest in terms
of human values? If not, do you submit that all policies are perceived
in similar light? Given the outcome in this experience, what do you
surmise were the circumstances leading to the adoption of the stated
policy, and what good reasons can you offer in support of it?

Faculty committees and faculty-student committees are often
cited as evidence of democracy in corporate behavior, on campus
and elsewhere. In the Carl study we are presented with an overview
of what ought to exist in academic community decision-making against

111

a background of what already exists. Aside from our professional
interests and sympathy for one another, it is timely to question anew
some assumptions before reaching the substance in question. What
justifications exist for the inclusion of faculty, much less students,
in the policy-making process of academe? If historically, legally, or
collegially rationalized, who and how many of these beings are suitably
prepared for such responsibility? On what grounds do you defend that
judgement? Can all of the same be said for student participation in
the decisional process? Given some justification for committee
membership, how should the members be selected: by vote of peers,
by age or sex, by rank or seniority, or simply by the whim of
superiors? Likewise for the student representatives? Whatever that
determination, what authority should each committee be given? By
whom and with what ultimate effect? Can their recommendations be
subject to administrative review at all levels in the hierarchy? If so,
why so; if not, which levels would you exclude and why? Is this line
of thought helpful in ascertaining the pinnacles of power in institutions
of higher learning? Who does govern your academic community?

Governance in any large-scale organization is a fascinating
phenomena of human interaction, both within and outside the corporate
structure. In academe, the policy influences of alumni, wealthy
donors, sports fans, politicians, persons of the cloth, and other
friends of the intellectual community remain somewhat a mystery to
all but a few at most colleges and universities. Academic inquiries
into this enlightening and exciting field have led many researchers to
find greener pastures in a hurry, for there are some pursuits of
knowledge that are deemed inappropriate for the consideration of
learned men and women. It seems, therefore, that one does not become sufficiently wise to recognize the wisdom of these words until
he or she possesses the power that others might analyze.

Power and influence are convenient terms used to express the
ability of some to cause others to respect their wishes. The locus
may be external or internal for institutions, and exerted for the
common good more often than for special interests. The Fitchen
study of an accreditation experience is a case in point, as well as an
illustration of an ordeal or opportunity endured quite frequently each
year from coast to coast. Is the practice of accreditation a necessary
feature of academic certification? Why shouldn't the concerned faculty and students be left the privilege of self-assessment and remedial
action? Is accreditation an institutional admission of occasional deception in the purported pursuit of academic excellence? If not, why
is periodic investigation and evaluation necessary? And what about
those evaluators—are they specially qualified for such work or selected owing to their peculiar influence in the profession? Who rules
and operates the accrediting agencies, and why? Devise a schematic

of an alternative system and consider the conditions of membership, collective goals, and the responsibilities of the newly created accrediting authority. Compare and contrast those with an agency with which you are familiar. Whatever the differences be, they are likely to reflect your perception of the weaknesses real or imagined at your present or past college or university. Therein may lie the answer to the question of need.

Not unlike other large organizations, centers of higher learning are fraught with a wide array of institutional problems. Some of these concerns are common and routine; others are unexpected and infrequent. The former are usually considered an integral part of the normal housekeeping functions of any enterprise; the latter are often labeled as crises or unintended consequences. However defined or classified, the commonality and the anxieties in academe are not particularly out of harmony nor disproportionate with the reported experiences in most businesses and industries. Although material productivity as a standard is secondary to the expansion of awareness and human character development in most academic communities, the basics of entrepreneurial enterprise on campus differ little from those of other professional organizations, particularly in terms of in-house accountability.

Nevertheless, it remains unquestionable that in legal structure, in organization and purpose, in spirit and process, and in sources of support as well as nature of clientele, our colleges and universities the world over are intrinsically different from most other forms of collective endeavor. And it is equally clear that some peculiarities and expectations growing out of this institutional uniqueness, such as academic freedom and tenure, are responsible for special dilemmas in the higher learning professions. Such exceptions aside, one should not categorize as mundane the preponderance of staff and line work in support of teaching and research, for the effective functioning of administrative services is crucial to the very viability of the institution, on campus as well as elsewhere. Suffice it to observe that it is difficult, if not impossible, to find a significant organization that is not vitally concerned with the common denominators of policy or process, financial management, personnel administration, and client or product orientation. And in view of the rapidity of change in society and on the educational scene, it may soon become axiomatic that scholastic pursuits without sophisticated management is tantamount to exploratory rocketry without scientific instrumentation.

To return to the world of humanistic realities, we homo sapiens are properly inclined to seek solutions to our problems rather than to redress our successes. Thus it is fitting that this part of the book be dedicated to exploring some experienced anxieties in higher education rather than having it flaunt an equal number of accomplishments. Prefatory thereto it is worth asserting that most campus difficulties are immediately confronted and resolved, more often than not without fanfare or serious consequence. When unattended or avoided, the problems tend to result in a traumatic experience, with unpleasant ramifications or irreparable harm for all concerned. Whatever the outcome, or how well or poorly conceived the strategy for the solution to the problem, it is important to bear in mind the context of its evolution, the rationale of adversaries therein, and the lessons that all of us would better learn from the experience of others. These insights and more can be deduced from the following group of studies.

To lead off this set of problem-oriented case studies, the editor discusses some sources of personal and professional conflict and their planned as well as circumstantial development. His study relates to matters of importance at all levels of the administrative hierarchy of academe, and it also raises pointed questions regarding the propriety of decision making by faculty and students when directly affected. John B. Duff follows this by evoking additional thought on the decisional process in his analysis of complications inherent in treating the recalcitrant or otherwise unwelcome educators. In addition to presenting a forthright illustration of the agonies associated with policy change and efficacious management, he also offers the reader a good glimpse of the oft-ignored drama of human events in the seeming quietude of objective scholars at work.

John D. Williams concludes this series of studies with reflections that ought to be of considerable value within and outside the college or university. His experience should admonish all of us interested in education, higher through lower, to vigorously endorse its proven achievements, to defend its basic purposes, and equally importantly to denounce its false prophets and uninformed adversaries.

Hopefully it will become apparent that these case studies are reasoned and reasonable representations of the bevy of problems that have produced anxious moments on campuses across this country and abroad. Surely similar examples are not everywhere to be found, but situations comparable in form or substance are known to be plentiful. Perhaps it is well to note here again that our concern as educators and learners is that so relatively few academic administrators have evidenced the courage or conviction or stamina to give others the benefit of their wisdom borne of battle. The sheer number and kind of such episodes should attest to the dynamic nature of the educational enterprise; the turnover of administrative personnel up and down the academic ladder will advise of its inherent dangers and exciting opportunities.

10

THE CHAIRMANSHIP:
ONE INVITATION
TO DISASTER
George J. Mauer

Institutions of higher learning differ in scope and depth of purpose, but their administrative organizations hold much in common. Aside from distinctions owing to the varying size of institutions and the constituencies they serve, our colleges and universities are managed by a comparable hierarchy of superordinate and subordinate officers. For academic responsibilities, this framework depends greatly upon decentralized decision making to the operational level, and in particular upon the heads of the departments of the respective disciplines. This case study concerns an administrative experience relative to that position and some not infrequent conditions and circumstances that affect the selection of many who serve higher education in that capactiy.

THE SETTING OF YANKEE UNIVERSITY

Few urban universities are blessed with the historical and physical attributes of Yankee University (YU). Born in the outlying area of a large midwestern city soon after the turn of the century, it grew with the metropolitan area and in response to the area's higher educational needs. As a result, it numbers today among those relatively unique private institutions which enjoy a measure of stability in an era of increasing insecurity among its sister schools.

In large part, YU may be said to owe its good fortune to a combination of events, some influenced by it and others circumstantial to its location. Although it is legally categorized as a nondenominational and not-for-profit enterprise, the university was founded and

---

George Mauer, Research Associate and Visiting Scholar, University of California at Berkeley.

developed by the leadership of a Protestant church. Those roots are
not ignored, neither in appointments to its board of trustees nor in
the religious credentials of its highest administrative officer. But
far more important to the reputation of the institution is its unrelenting commitment to intercollegiate athletics, and in particular to two
sports in which it has gained and maintained regional if not national
prominence. Indeed, this extracurricular emphasis, rather than its
academic accomplishments, has been chiefly responsible for the recruitment of many of the school's 7,500 students and some of its 350
members of the faculty.

After an earlier and natural inclination toward the training of
ministers and both elementary and secondary teachers, YU elected
to systematically adjust over time to the exigencies of modernization
via a more marketable curriculum. Thus more for commercial than
for scholastic reasons, it broadened its educational base to accommodate the desires of clientele in the city, the state, and beyond.
The result is an academic community geared largely to undergraduate
preparation for service to business and industry, with sufficient attention to the liberal arts to justify its accreditation. While some departments did well in responding to the charge of their disciplines,
others have languished with limited success. Nevertheless, the atmosphere on campus remained entertainingly optimistic, for with
tongue in cheek the institution was heralded within as the Harvard of
the Midwest.

THE DEPARTMENT OF POLITICAL SCIENCE

Nestled strategically in the academic structure of YU is a department of political science, an integral and rather important component of the liberal arts college. Staffed by a faculty of eight, only
half of whom were full-time, the department was possessed of a relatively unique array of educators. Although all held earned doctorates, much unlike the status of colleagues in other departments of
the university, not all proved to be a measure of that level of intellectual achievement. The chairperson, an affable but unscholarly fellow,
had parlayed an affiliation with the headquarters of one of the national
political parties into the headship of the department of political science
as well as the leadership of the division of humanities. He had been
personally recruited and groomed by the then senior member in the
discipline, who, despite similarly weak academic and administrative
credentials, had utilized other skills in wresting the deanship of the
college. Thus two artisans of friendly persuasion had come to respect
a mutual interest, namely their complementary positions of authority,
and few with whom they dealt were unaware of that pact.

The productive work of the department rested in four full-time academicians. Senior among them was an Ivy League product, a seasoned scholar of limited renown beyond the campus, but one well known therein for excellence in teaching and considerable impatience with pseudointellectuals and administrative sycophants. Less aloof but occasionally as adamant toward the more glaring of academic abuses was the next senior in rank, a byproduct of the Big Eight, the principal published person in the group, a promoter of innovative programs, and otherwise among the better educators at YU. More than any of his peers, he maintained a cordial relationship with the chairman, but only a businesslike acquaintanceship with the dean, factors which might be borne in mind as this administrative case study unfolds.

Rounding out the full-time cast were two junior members of the department. One, a long-term servant of the institution, was highly respected as a lecturer, debonair with all entrusted with positions of authority, rather limited in his research and service obligations, and overly conscious of the excessive time taken in earning his highest degree from the Big Ten. The other junior member was the friendliest, most humane, and also the most insecure member of the faculty, an able teacher on his maiden voyage in academe by way of the Yankee Conference. His predicament had less to do with his competence and potential than with the fact that his efforts were subject to unwarranted reprehension.

Complicating, rather than complementing, the tasks of this staff was the presence of two part-time political scientists in the department. One was a handmaiden of the president of the institution, ostensibly an educator, but in fact an administrative trainee who taught a course per semester largely to justify his faculty fringe benefits. The other was a dedicated teacher in the older tradition, and a partisan political activist whose radical notions and ill bearing toward envious superiors won both their wrath and ostracism from the mainstream of the discipline.

Still the department of political science enjoyed a healthy enrollment of students. For despite its visible and latent shortcomings, this faculty was well respected on the campus, attracted a significant number of majors, and welcomed the task of staffing an introductory course in government which was required of all candidates for the baccalaureate. Beyond this accommodation, however, the interests of the students, faculty, and administration did not always coincide. For example, majors were known to be distraught by a departmental curricula which was clearly disproportionate with the number of students enrolled in each of the subdisciplines. Master's degree candidates were more embarrassed than vocal about an advanced study program in which all learning was accomplished in undergraduate courses, coupled with the requirement of an additional paper at the end of the term. And graduates at both levels were appropriately dismayed by a department which, administratively, was unresponsive to their placement needs. Meanwhile, their tutors evidenced the root nature of that consternation. By intent or circumstance, each professor was drawn into the power struggle within and beyond the department; more or less, one either favored all things sponsored by the chairman and the dean, or one was opposed. Communication, aside from the faculty grapevine and the student paper, was extremely limited. And the price of constructive criticism was at best a calculated risk, often taking its toll in salary adjustments and occasionally in questions of tenure and promotion. Indicative of the pervasiveness of this cancer at YU was the disposition of the higher administration. Aside from matters of campuswide consequence, which might affect the image and numerical strength of the institution, the president had no desire for addressing internal affairs, and his sycophants did not compensate for that executive narrowness. Yet, when faced with criticism on issues ranging from increased tuition to allowing credits for collecting garbage in a Model City, the superior will was vindicated with a vengeance, and, as this case study is about to reveal, it did not exclude recourse to the use of retribution.

A CHAIRMAN WANTS OUT

Such is the background of conditions and the cast of characters that set the stage for the evolution of a series of administrative problems. Aware of the inner turmoil of the department, and the detrimental effect of external management on the affairs of political scientists, the chairman rather courageously undertook a plan to vacate his office. Indeed it was a full year in advance of the proposed changeover that the head, Patrick Waldon, approached Joe Arthur, the second ranking member of the full-time teaching staff, and advised: "Joe, I feel that I have done all that I can for the department, and come the next academic year I would like to see you take it over. Are you interested?" Arthur did not hesitate in his reply, for he had cherished the thought of correcting some known deficiencies and instituting some standards that would enhance the professional integrity of the department: "Pat, if that is the way that you feel, I will look forward to giving the job all that I can offer." And so the procedure for succession began.

Following consultations on this matter, first between the chairman and the dean, and later between the dean and the proposed candidate, it was understood that the designee could anticipate his new duties the following fall, pending of course the affirmation of colleagues in the department and the approval of the higher administration.

Casually, over the course of the next month, each member of the affected faculty was informed of this development by current chairman Waldon and asked to react to the prospective Arthur appointment. The verdict, somewhat surprising in view of the spectrum of personalities and professional dispositions, was unanimous: it would be desirable for all concerned that this transition occur as planned. The dean thereupon was notified of that decision, and he in turn informed Donald Bayard, vice president for academic affairs, and Prentiss Seward, the president, of the recommendation.

A few weeks later, a pertinent but seemingly irrelevant episode was to take place. For the first time in the history of the university a new policy governing tenure was to be invoked, and, at the urging of the dean of the college of liberal arts, it was to have its initial application in the department of political science. Specifically, an evaluation was to be conducted of faculty members who aspire to long-term service at YU, with an eye toward developing a tentative appraisal of that likelihood. Moreover, this tenure policy was to affect those persons at roughly the midpoint of their probationary period. As circumstances would have it, only one instructor on campus was singled out for this potentially worthwhile review, namely James Laughlin, the younger and more insecure member of the department. Unfortunately, it took two lengthy sessions behind closed doors to realize what really underlay the proceedings: the assistant to the president was displeased with advantages given this junior colleague regarding academic courses and schedules which they evidently cherished in common; the dean let it be known that he was planning an early return to full-time teaching in the department and that he too favored the subdiscipline treated by the younger associate; and besides, it was alleged, the Laughlin appointment was not necessarily intended to become permanent. Of course, the candidate for tenure viewed the matter as self-serving to higher ups, essentially deceitful and unrelated to his performance, and a case of internal conspiracy.

After two months of subsequent piecemeal deliberation, during which virtually all other matters of importance to the department were held in abeyance, it was determined by the majority that Laughlin should prepare to seek greener pastures. A minority report, sponsored by chairman-designate Arthur, took exception to the finality of that verdict, pointed up the unprofessional character of the review, chided the tenure applicant for obvious deficiencies in his overall performance to date, and suggested another year of probation during which he might redress his shortcomings. This assessment was not appreciated by the assistant to the president or the dean, and the judgment proved to be a forerunner of things to come.

The really big controversy of that academic year was prompted by the university's attempt to respond effectively to an internal ground swell of sentiment in favor of making a contribution to resolving the so-called urban crisis. How might YU best serve in meeting the related problems in its immediate environment, and in what manner should it accommodate the altruistic desires of many of its faculty and students toward that end? These and other questions captured the attention of the higher administration and, upon consultation with interested civic and academic leaders, the president appointed and requested appropriate recommendations by a special task force of selected faculty, students, and administrators, to be headed by— you guessed it—political scientist Arthur. After meeting three times per week over a period of two months, the interdisciplinary group reached a number of unanimous conclusions, drafted its report, and submitted it directly to the president. Essentially, the recommendations called for the establishment of a Center for Urban Studies on campus, with an office and director to be designated as soon as reasonably possible. From this facility and with administrative guidance, it was envisioned that concerned faculty and students could render voluntary and meaningful research and service to the community. In addition, an innovative program was developed to take additional advantage of existing coursework, which, when supplemented by new offerings in urban studies and a civic internship, would facilitate the availability of a new academic major at the institution. These suggestions, incidentally, were to be implemented at a cost well within the financial capability of YU.

Another month passed. During this time only a law professor, a member of the special task force evidently closer to the higher administration, was informed of a follow-up development. He was selected to be a committee of one to recruit a director of the proposed urban center, and although he sought the advice of other members of the committee he could not explain the rationale for the procedure. Meanwhile the head of the special task force was not to hear an official word regarding the administration's reaction to any part of the committee's report. Nor was he given an inkling as to the disposition of the recommendation of his department relative to the chairmanship. As a result, pessimism and sarcasm began to characterize the remarks of faculty and students interested both in urban activities and political science. Finally, word of the obvious impasse reached the editor and staff of the campus newspaper, and student reporters swooped down upon the principals involved in a quest for clarification.

The result was an administrator's nightmare. In addition to charges of general mismanagement, the press carried headlines alleging wrongdoing by the higher administration ranging from undue secretiveness to downright corruption. When approached about the urban program proposals, Arthur was frank and to the point: "I have heard nothing from the president or from any of his aides regarding the status

of the committee report, and I am constantly being hassled by those
interested in answers." A less appropriate comment came from an
understandably unidentified source: "I don't know what they are up to,
but we faculty who were there know that an awful lot of booze money
is being spent to interview the candidates for the directorship." This
naturally riled the administration, and despite an element of truth in
the assertion, a spokesman for the president noted: "All the reports
that you have been reading are greatly exaggerated. We are making
progress on the proposals, and we will make an announcement when
the decisions are reached." Student activists were roundly displeased
with the brief pronouncement, and they continued to air their concerns
via pointed editorials.

Owing to his apparent disgust with these developments over the
past three months, Arthur decided that he no longer wished to bear
the burden of them. He resigned his headship of the seemingly defunct
task force on urban affairs, appending therewith an explanation of
events leading up to it; terse reaction resulted, expressing only regret for the decision. In the ensuing weeks the larger battle went on,
that being between selected students and a few administrators over
who had the ball and who may have dropped it. Finally the suspense
regarding Arthur's future at YU got the best of him and, in uncere-
monious fashion, he requested the long-awaited judgment of the administration regarding his colleagues' recommendation on the future
headship of their department. Surprise! With highly unusual efficiency
the question was answered. After all, the candidate for chairman had
not been cooperative in the tenure case; he had been outspoken on an
issue of campuswide concern; he had evidenced an air of independence
from the administration; his patience seemed to be limited; and he
could hardly be expected to join in the YU version of administrative
decision making.

In fact, Dean Enos Wyman extended an invitation to Arthur to
meet him at his office. The session was short and to the point as
Wyman indicated: "Joe, I am sorry to tell you that they—the
administration—would not go along with our recommendation." "I
expected as much," replied Arthur, "that is the way things are done
around here, and I am sorry to inform you that I can no longer work
for such people. You will have my letter of resignation before the
end of the day, to be effective at the end of this academic year."
"Now just a minute, Joe, this is not cause for rash action," advised
the dean. Said Joe in parting: "It is in my book."

So ended a phase in a succession of problems for the administration, both up and down the hierarchy and outside it. Those who decided
the political science matter were now confident that they had solved
a problem; in fact, they then unleashed a bevy of new issues heretofore latent. Was the decision on the chairmanship justifiable? What

is the effective role of the faculty in departmental affairs? Why were
affected students not consulted in this matter? Should the concerned
faculty be ignored in such cases? Where does the fault lie in this
series of interrelated incidents? It did not take long for another bar-
rage of editorials and front-page headlines to embarrass all concerned.
They led to the formation of a student committee to undertake an independent investigation of the facts surrounding the events of recent
months. Upon interviewing the affected faculty and administrators,
the result was a report to the president urging him to decline the
Arthur resignation, to apologize to him for the mishandling of his
case, and for the president to put an end to the pettiness and bickering
that characterized the stewardship of his administration. But the
chief executive would have none of that, and these pleas, along with
those independently offered by some members of the faculty, went unheeded. Again a problem had been solved, or so it seemed, for higher
authority had prevailed against the onslaught of those who would challenge its wisdom.

It is particularly instructive to recount the singular effort toward
reconciliation that followed. At the suggestion of the dean, a meeting
was arranged between the vice president for academic affairs and
Arthur. It proved to be short-lived and unproductive. But the ex-
changes between them may shed some light on a root cause of many
of these interrelated problems. The VP opened the discussion: "Who
do you think you are, Joe—God?" "No, I never suggested that,"
Arthur replied. "Well, then, Joe, I guess that you know by now why
we turned down the recommendation. There is no vacancy in the chairmanship, thus no need to appoint a successor." To that rationalization
Arthur did not choose to muster a suitable reply. "Besides," the VP
added, "you have only one face!" "If that is a fault, I must admit to
it," came the retort. In closing Joe was admonished: "Nevertheless,
Joe, you have been cleared for tenure and if you want to stay here
you can. Perhaps next year we will take another look at the chairmanship." "No thanks," Arthur countered.

In retrospect, the foregoing review of a disastrous experience
may serve to illustrate the coolness with which some manage the conduct of collegiate affairs. It may also depict the callousness of humans
under fire, or may be interpreted in terms of pervasive managerial
improprieties. All of these views, and undoubtedly more, hold some
degree of truth. Moreover, it is apparent that from the top of the
hierarchy on down, few in this case study exhibited an awareness of
the consequences of their action beyond the immediacy of the moment.
Whether good or bad, the president of the institution was too busy
with external affairs to get involved in these controversies; besides,
it was his style of administration to delegate internal responsibilities
to an appropriate vice president. However, the VP for academic affairs

was in process of gaining his initial experience in higher administration, and neither his preparation nor guidance was sufficient for the task. Parenthetically, both executives moved on to similar positions at other universities within the next year, suggesting that neither really had the will, if indeed they knew the way, to develop a positive solution to these problems.

Meanwhile, power politics was allowed to flourish at YU and particularly within the college of liberal arts. There the dean had elected to use his position of authority to further selected individual interests as opposed to academic objectives, and his protege at the helm of the political science department acquiesced in those decisions in the knowledge that his status might otherwise be put in jeopardy. As for the chairman-designate and the junior candidate for tenure, they proved to be pawns in the contest.

It is perhaps comforting to some that time marches on and that institutions tend to outlive their periodic adversities. Thus few affected by such dilemmas will stop and take the time to recount the courses of their action and to recognize their frequently unintended consequences. In this instance, it is doubtful that any of the parties concerned had willfully premeditated the adding of insult to injury, for even the dean evidenced some afterthought. Yet it is reasonably clear that all lacked a perspective, albeit in varying degree, of the long-range impact of their judgments. Surely none wished to subvert two productive academic programs, to inconvenience many students who later felt obliged to change the focus of their study, to encourage a further exodus of teachers from the institution, to incur the wrath of faculty, or to damage the credibility of the administration. Still all these things and more did occur, with the result that none were vindicated while an entire academic community was to suffer. That the board of trustees sat idly by throughout these episodes does not speak well for the calibre of decision making at that level.

THE HIGHER PRIORITIES

Fundamental in this analysis is the introspection required of those who seek to benefit by the experience of others. Accordingly, it is not difficult to single out faults, but it is preferable to learn from them in the hope of avoiding similar consequences. As applicable herein, it is less meaningful to ascertain the culprits than it is to deliberate about the premises of their judgment. Of necessity, such thought will lead one to consider his or her philosophy of administration and of academic responsibility, the limits of institutional loyalty and of professional obligation, the real meaning and extent

of decentralized decision making and of concentrated authority, the
requirements of leadership and of effective communication, and the
legitimacy of rule by men rather than by policy. These kinds of basic
inquiries, among others, are at the root of developments in this case
study.

To summarize, Arthur had been informally offered a chairmanship and, owing to peripheral considerations, the unanimously favorable departmental recommendation was disapproved. The incumbent
head, upon learning of the factors influencing that judgment, chose
to join his superiors rather than to risk questioning their motives.
The dean, assured of the resumption of the status quo, thereupon proceeded to defend a decision which he had been chiefly instrumental in
fashioning. Meanwhile, a heretofore vacillating higher administration,
at least with regard to the issues at hand, had reached conclusions
based more upon threats to its integrity than upon the heart of the
problems. Thus the leadership of one college in the university effectively used the higher administration to achieve a strategic end,
knowing that the judgment of an inexperienced vice president could be
directed and, further, that the well-known obsession on the part of
the president against being criticized would serve to reinforce the cor-
rectness of his aide's recommendation.

Although it may be entertaining to conjecture just when and
where each of the principals might have gone away, it is far more
fruitful to consider why. Arthur, after all, was the department's
choice for the position in question. His superior acknowledged that
and all of his colleagues concurred. But from the viewpoint of middle
and superordinate management, neither scholarship nor relevant experience were sufficient in meeting the qualifications for the post.
Indeed the higher priorities were compatibility with the dean and with
the vice president for academic affairs, not to mention acquiescence
in the administrative style of the president. Thus Arthur met the professional expectations of his peers, but he surely did not measure up
to the added requirements for managerial responsibility at YU.

LESSONS IN PERSPECTIVE

In addition to the lessons suggested and implied in the preceding
study, it seems appropriate in conclusion to also note some concerns
of overriding import. Although we may take for granted the imperfection of all humans and their institutions, it is difficult to accept
that the conditions of the foregoing case befit any college or university today. Yet they are based upon experience and the ramifications
of that fact alone should be cause for concern among those in and beyond the profession.

One is compelled to wonder how often comparable blunders are committed annually on campuses across the country. Are issues in academe frequently blown out of proportion by similarly insecure scholars? Are administrators increasingly prone to focusing attention in some directions at the expense of others? Are deans and chairpersons abandoning their hybrid character in favor of a role as functionaries for higher authority? Are faculty becoming apathetic in response to more forceful control of their earlier discretions? And what might the answers to these questions suggest in terms of the direction and quality of our institutions of higher learning? Hopefully there is little substantive ground for the foregoing intimations. If not, the state of the higher educational system is in great need of reevaluation and some fundamental overhaul.

Indicative of the potentially useful line of inquiry here suggested, some may wish to ponder the pervasiveness of administrative problem making as well as its problem solving. Though few would assert that all colleges and universities are beset with crisis management, it is equally implausible that any campus is without shortcomings in its decision-making process. Is it possible that the root cause of mismanagement, where found, rests less in intent than in administrative ineptness? Perhaps the record should speak for itself. How many presidents and vice presidents in academe have been professionally trained for their responsibilities? How many fewer deans and chairpersons can attest to well-rounded preparation appropriate to their tasks? Suffice it to submit that herein lies a basic problem in higher education, one generally ignored and not likely to be remedied soon, for the incumbents will tend to resent allegations of their relative imperfection. Thus on-the-job training, and the concomitant learning by trial and error, will continue to characterize much of the management of collegiate affairs, with the likelihood that sophistication in the arts of administration will remain largely academic.

11

PROBLEMS FACED
IN REDUCING THE
NUMBER OF FACULTY
John B. Duff

St. Robert's University, founded towards the end of the nineteenth century as a small liberal arts college and religious seminary, had changed fundamentally in the years following World War II. Although located in a metropolitan area, it possessed ample acreage for expansion; and the university had responded to the demands of returning veterans for opportunities to finish their education. The trustees approved an ambitious building program; and by the mid-sixties, full-time enrollment had exceeded 5,000 with an additional 5,000 students enrolled on a part-time basis. By 1965, the full-time faculty had grown to almost 300, supplemented by an equal number of part-time instructors. The college had achieved university status in 1965 and was comprised of five professional schools in addition to the College of Arts and Sciences. It had established programs leading to the doctorate in seven fields and enjoyed an increasing reputation for academic excellence.

But growth had brought problems. All too often, the university, entering the seller's market for professors in the early sixties, had been forced to act quickly without sufficiently checking references of new faculty members for the expanding departments. Complaints from department chairmen and deans as well as stringent criticism in a published student evaluation had convinced the President of St. Robert's, the Reverend James Kincaid, that more than a dozen faculty members had become serious burdens to the university. The situation had been aggravated by two major decisions taken by the Board of Trustees in the same year (1965) that university status had been achieved. First, acting upon the recommendation of the Faculty Assembly and the president, the board had approved a universitywide

John B. Duff, Provost, Seton Hall University.

reduction in the number of courses required in modern languages, history, English, philosophy, theology, and mathematics. Second, the board had reversed a seventy-year-old policy by now admitting women on a full-time basis in the undergraduate colleges. Enrollment had plummeted in several departments while increasing dramatically in sociology, psychology, communications, and fine arts. Some of the declining departments became seriously overstaffed. Their numbers would have to be reduced in order to enable the popular departments to expand.

To deal with these problems, President Kincaid brought in a new vice president for academic affairs. He charged the new officer, Dr. William Henderson, with the specific tasks of developing an intelligent policy on tenure and retirement, of reducing faculty in overstaffed areas, and of removing incompetent people in all areas.

Henderson began by instituting some obvious measures. He reviewed the staff of each department in the individual colleges with the appropriate chairman and dean. In those departments which had suffered enrollment declines, about six younger professors without tenure, with less than three years' service, and without any exceptional promise for the future were given nonrenewal notices in accordance with the guidelines established by the American Association of University Professors (AAUP).

After these steps had been taken, however, it was apparent that if he was going to be able to proceed any further Henderson would have to gain the cooperation of the faculty. He recognized the need to inform the faculty of the consequences of the rather easy policy in regard to tenure and retirement that had prevailed at St. Robert's. The year before he arrived at St. Robert's, sixteen individuals had applied for tenure and all had been approved. Over 80 percent of the faculty currently held tenure and the percentage gave every indication of increasing.

In addition, Henderson had perceived almost at once that the retirement practices of St. Robert's bore a direct relationship to the overstaffing and tenure questions. In theory, the retirement age at St. Robert's was sixty-five, but the faculty guide provided for the possibility of extension beyond that age through annual application to the president and upon recommendations by the retirement committees of the individual colleges and the dean concerned. When first announced a decade earlier, it had clearly been the intent of the policy that extensions would be granted only in exceptional cases and only for the soundest academic reasons. In practice, nearly every teacher who desired to continue teaching after sixty-five received an annual renewal of his contract. About twenty-five individuals past the mandatory age continued on the faculty; six professors who had passed the biblical milestone of three score and ten still carried full teaching loads.

Henderson decided to devote his remarks at the annual faculty convention to the two questions of tenure and retirement. He told the faculty that his analysis of the history of the rank and tenure committees of the various colleges revealed a tendency to treat tenure too lightly. He urged the faculty to remember that each recommendation for tenure constituted a lifetime appointment which committed over half a million dollars of the university's funds. Observing the record, the committee showed it to be much easier to get tenure than to get promoted. Henderson declared that tenure should be granted only to fully qualified teachers who were a definite asset to the university. He emphasized that the decision not to grant a lifetime contract to a professor occurred every year in hundreds of cases in American universities, with no dishonor being attached to a person denied tenure. Henderson hoped that the same type of attitude toward tenure appointments would come to prevail at St. Robert's University. Finally, he stated his belief that the university had reached the point where it would have to make some kind of a decision about tenure quotas.

On the retirement issue, Henderson noted that the retention on full-time contracts, with complete faculty rights, of thirty people past the mandatory retirement age contributed to the tenure problem. In several departments the university had not been able to bring in younger people of promise, since failure to follow the retirement policy had closed opportunities.

Henderson assured the faculty that he intended to work closely with the Faculty Assembly in seeking answers to the questions he had posed.

Within a week, committees to study tenure and retirement had been created. Within six months, Henderson was able to receive faculty approval for changes in the retirement procedures and for a long-range plan to reduce tenure. The new retirement procedures, while permitting extension of employment at a full teaching load and at the contract salary earned in the last year of regular academic employment, stipulated that Henderson would not normally recommend to the president an extension of a contract for more than one-half the normal teaching load, at one-half the salary. All employment would end at age seventy. The university agreed to establish a fund to assist retired professors who had taught at St. Robert's for a minimum of fifteen years and who had been unable to build a satisfactory retirement income.

On tenure, it was agreed that four years after the announcement of the new policy, no college or department would have more than 65 percent of its faculty on tenure. However, to secure faculty assent on this quota, Henderson agreed to a "grandfather" clause, stating that no faculty member currently tenured or who became tenured within the next two academic years would be counted towards a departmental quota. After four years, any department over the quota would not be allowed to make new faculty appointments except through term contracts of one, two, or three years with renewal possible up to a total of five years. If an opportunity to obtain a truly exceptional professor arose in a department already at its quota, it would be possible for the department, with the approval of its college's rank and tenure committee, its dean, and Henderson, to appeal to the university budget committee for an additional tenured position.

After less than a year, Henderson believed that he had taken substantial steps to fulfill President Kincaid's mandate. Yet, he also realized that his most difficult task remained unsolved. He must now deal with a number of tenured faculty members who either could no longer fulfill their professional responsibilities or who had been left without students due to curriculum revisions and changing student career objectives.

In the latter category were several elderly professors who had not reached the mandatory retirement age. Henderson decided to encourage early retirement in these cases by making favorable financial arrangements for the professors concerned. They were offered a year's sabbatical at full pay plus a substantial payment by the university into their pension plan, thus increasing their retirement benefits substantially. In addition, the university agreed to make up the amount of social security benefits the professors would lose by retiring at age sixty-two. Although these arrangements made a commitment of the university's money, they proved less expensive than continuing two salaries for an additional three or four years, especially since none of the professors came close to having the number of students in class needed to even approximate their annual salaries. Thus, in one case, Professor Donald Edwards, with a salary of $18,000, had enrolled a total of 60 students in two semesters; these students paid a combined tuition of $9,000 for these courses.

In another case, Henderson, to a limited extent, engaged in job retraining. A fifty-year-old professor of classics (another department in which enrollments had plummeted) attended a six-month course in student personnel services and was able to make the transition into the university placement office where he found satisfying work and proved to be an effective counselor. Henderson now turned his attention to two difficult cases which he knew would require special and delicate handling. First there was the case of Dr. John Martinson, a professor of geology who a year previously had been sent a letter of nonrenewal by the dean of the College of Arts and Sciences. The letter had informed Martinson that his services would not be needed during the academic year 1968-69 due to an anticipated decline in classes.

Initially after receiving his letter of nonrenewal, Martinson did not raise with the chairman of the department or other university officials the question of his nonrenewal. Then, he suddenly announced that he had de facto tenure under guidelines promulgated by the AAUP. Henderson made a careful investigation of the case and came to the conclusion that if St. Robert's counted every possible semester that Martinson had taught at the university and at St. Edelbert's College in North Dakota, which he had left some years previously, the university could possibly be guilty of a five-month-late notice in the case of Martinson. Henderson consulted with the representative of the regional office of the AAUP, who believed that if the matter were pushed by Martinson, the university would probably end up with a reprimand for the late notice. The AAUP official suggested a compromise might be proposed to the aggrieved professor, and Henderson decided this was probably the best course. He offered Martinson an extension of his contract for one more academic year together with a paid terminal sabbatical of one semester in the following year if Martinson would agree to resign from the university. After a preliminary meeting with Henderson, Martinson returned with an attorney and signed a letter which stated:

> I hereby resign from the faculty of St. Robert's University. This resignation is being tendered on the condition that I be granted a two-year contract; the first year at full salary and normal teaching load and for the subsequent academic year a sabbatical leave for one year at half-salary or one semester at full salary.

Henderson insisted that Martinson also sign a contract specifying the terms described in the letter, and with an added stipulation: "The acceptance of this contract by Professor John Martinson resolves the question of Professor Martinson's status at St. Robert's University and constitutes a full settlement by St. Robert's University for any claims that Dr. Martinson may have against the University arising out of the termination of affiliation with the University."

A year later, Martinson attempted to withdraw his resignation, claiming that he had signed his resignation under duress; the AAUP, to which Martinson had appealed, refused to support him on this matter. Although Martinson later threatened legal action against the university, nothing came of this threat.

Another case demanded even more delicate handling by Henderson. Professor Howard Jones had come to St. Robert's University in 1961 as an assistant professor in the School of Engineering. Previously he had taught three years at Johnson University. Therefore, under AAUP guidelines, he had achieved de facto tenure. He did not have de jure tenure under the regulations promulgated in the faculty guide of St. Robert's, since tenure could be achieved only by those

individuals holding the rank of professor or associate professor.
After three years, the calibre of Jones's classroom performance had
declined from being mediocre to downright abysmal. A student evaluation had given him the lowest possible rating; even more significantly,
it had become almost impossible to get more than a handful of students
to sign up for his class. In one recent semester, Henderson ascer-
tained, a total of twenty-six students had registered for the four
courses offered by Jones.

Dr. Frank Lewis, Dean of the College of Engineering, had held
several conferences with Jones over a two-year period. When the
dean expressed concern over the declining class registrations, Jones
replied that he had expected a decline; indeed, he had welcomed it.
He had been determined to set a higher standard than had previously
existed in the college. Certainly he had fewer students, but they were
better ones. Never would he become, Jones informed Lewis, a mere
crowd pleaser. Others would sacrifice quality for quantity; he would
not. To specific complaints about his failure to return examination
papers as required by departmental regulations, or about his tardi-
ness, Jones replied that these charges amounted to nothing more than
the empty soundings of malcontents. When asked about his failure to
meet eight sessions of one class in the previous semester, Jones
replied that he had not understood the academic world to be one which
required a professor to punch a time clock.

After three fruitless meetings and faced with the continuing
deterioration in Jones's performance, Lewis decided to submit the
Jones case to the rank and tenure committee of the college. The
committee at first agreed to review the case; but when they asked
Jones to submit a statement on his qualifications for tenure, Jones
refused, contending that he was already tenured. The committee,
therefore, asked Henderson to clarify the university's position on
Jones's claim to tenure.

Henderson faced a dilemma; Jones did not have legal tenure
under the university statutes, but there existed a strong probability
that the AAUP would hold him to be tenured, since he had received
seven successive faculty contracts, four of them from St. Robert's.

Henderson met with Lewis, and together they decided to ask for
Jones's resignation. They would state to Jones that while he might be
able to press his claim for de facto tenure, the university was prepared to remove him from the faculty for what it considered adequate
cause; the faculty guide reserved to the university the right to dismiss
a faculty member for adequate cause and specified incompetence,
grave misconduct, and neglect of duty among the causes which might
justify dismissal. Petitions from the students, Lewis's evaluations,
and Jones's proven record of absences, in the opinion of Lewis and
Henderson, justified removal of Jones on the grounds of incompetence
and neglect of duty.

Henderson realized, of course, that a removal for adequate cause could engender bad publicity for the university. Moreover, since, under the provisions of the guide, a faculty member had the right to request a hearing by a faculty committee, there existed a strong possibility that such a committee might stop short of recommending Jones's severance from the university. Accordingly, in his meeting with Jones, Henderson offered a carrot as well as a stick. If Jones agreed to resign, the university would grant him another full semester of employment beyond the end of the current academic year and give him an additional sabbatical year at full pay. If Jones declined to resign, he would be given a letter of dismissal showing adequate cause; and Henderson carefully explained Jones's rights of appeal in this instance.

When presented with the proposal, Jones asked for time to consider his response. After two weeks, he returned with an attorney and a counterproposal. After admitting he now realized that he must improve his teaching, he proposed that a final decision on his status be delayed for a year. He would resign and accept the proposal of the university for an addititonal semester of employment plus a full year's sabbatical only with the proviso that this resignation would be null and void if the rank and tenure committee and Lewis, after evaluating his performance during the coming year, recommended his retention. Henderson realized that this proviso would probably lead to a hearing at the end of the next academic year; still, he saw that at the very least, the university position on separating Jones would be improved. The burden of proof concerning classroom performance would rest with Jones in the following year, rather than with the university, as was the present case; and he agreed to the condition.

Jones submitted the required letter of resignation in March, and the matter rested until the following February when the rank and tenure committee of the college met once more. The rank and tenure committee voted three to two this time to retain Jones. This was a shock to Lewis, but he was convinced that a reluctance to act against a colleague had been decisive in the faculty's decision; and he believed more than ever that Jones was a detriment to the college. Lewis, therefore, wrote to Henderson that he did not agree with the rank and tenure committee, and that Jones's letter of resignation should, therefore, remain effective.

Henderson met with Jones and declared that since Jones had not received a recommendation from either the rank and tenure committee or Lewis, he (Jones) would, under the terms of the agreement, receive a terminal contract providing for the paid sabbatical. Jones strongly protested this action, claiming that, despite the agreement that he had signed, the favorable vote of the rank and tenure committee was sufficient for his retention by the College of Engineering.

He also, for the first time, alleged that there was bias in his case—a personal animus between he and Lewis. Lewis, Jones charged, had made several offensive personal allusions to Jones and had publicly disparaged Jones's classroom performance. Henderson replied to Jones by citing the faculty guide:

> When any faculty member feels he has been treated un-
> fairly he has a right and an obligation to bring his
> grievance to the proper authorities through administrative
> channels. A grievance should first be discussed with
> the faculty member's immediate superior officer. If
> the matter is not satisfactorily settled, the faculty
> member should request a conference with his immediate
> superior officer, the Dean concerned, and the Academic
> Vice President. If the faculty member is not satisfied
> with the settlement suggested by these officials, he
> may request a hearing by a Committee of the Faculty.
> A faculty member who desires a hearing by a Committee
> of the Faculty will file his request with the Academic
> Vice President. Arrangements will be made for a
> Committee to conduct a hearing where the complainant
> and the Dean concerned will present facts and viewpoints
> concerning the issues involved. The complainant may
> call witnesses and question them, present documents
> and read statements. The complainant may also question,
> within reasonable limits, any witnesses called by others.
> The complainant may, at his own expense, retain counsel
> of his choice to advise him at the hearing.
> The Dean may call witnesses, present documents and
> read statements. He may also question, within reasonable
> limits, witnesses called by the complainant. The Dean
> may have a counsel to advise him during the hearing.
> A stenographic or tape recording of the hearing will be
> made. After concluding the hearing, the Committee will
> study the recording and submit a report to the Academic
> Vice President, who will consult the President and then
> render a decision.

Henderson proposed that the University Rank and Tenure Committee serve as the faculty grievance committee to hear this case. This committee was composed of nine full professors representing the constituent colleges of the university. Jones accepted this arrange-ment and he duly presented his case to the committee. The committee then heard from Lewis and from Henderson. Henderson carefully explained the reasons why he had acted as he had; it was clear, he contended, that the university had acted properly. Henderson submitted the letter in which Jones had resigned from the university with the option to be retained only if approved by both Lewis and the College of Engineering's rank and tenure committee. Several faculty members on the grievance committee expressed their opinion that it was a mistake on the part of Jones to resign. As one of them put it, "If you don't intend to resign, don't resign." Others felt that the arrangement had been an equitable one and in any case, the severance of Jones would benefit the university.

Early in January, the committee reported its unanimous recommendation that the resignation of Jones had been duly accepted by the university; and it did not support Jones's claim for grievance. Jones made a final appeal to the president of the university, but the president sustained the decision of the committee.

Three considerations determined the methods employed by Henderson at St. Roberts's University. First of all and most importantly, he recognized the necessity of involving the faculty in setting new policies on tenure and retirement. The university faced severe problems in both areas; and under the circumstances, some administrators might have been sorely tempted to act unilaterally. Such a course would probably have divided the university.

Then, Henderson realized that the problems he had to deal with had developed over a period of years, and he could not expect to achieve an instant solution. The willingness of the university to take four years to implement a new tenure system and to tolerate inefficient faculty for an additional year or so contributed to an amicable resolution in several instances.

Finally, the new retirement policy, the early retirement of several individuals, and the granting of terminal sabbaticals in the most difficult cases cost the university a considerable sum of money. Without this willingness to invest a certain part of its resources in return for long-run savings and an improvement in faculty competence, St. Robert's would not have been able to achieve the results it desired.

12

THE RIGHT
TO KNOW
John D. Williams

One of America's great universities had as its bicentennial theme "Man's Right to Knowledge and the Free Use Thereof." Man's right to know is a fundamental principle of freedom implied in the Bill of Rights and other articles of the U.S. Constitution, as well as in the Mississippi Constitution. More specifically, the principle holds that a university faculty has the freedom to teach and students have the right to learn whatever there is to know.

A VARIETY OF CHOICES

Who is wise enough to perceive what students need to know today, the next five years, and beyond? Surely students themselves must have primary responsibility for these important decisions that are vital not only to their own future but that of the nation as well. Students are offered through their classes, seminars, laboratories, and libraries a vast array of information, theories, philosophies, and points of view that men have developed, accepted, or rejected over the centuries. In addition, students are provided estimates of the future and participate in the evaluation of the bases for such estimates. No student accepts all and no student rejects all. Each student accepts that which he believes to be worthwhile and of interest to him.

The faculty at the University of Mississippi, as all faculties at first-rate universities, is dedicated to the task of providing each

_____

John D. Williams, Chancellor Emeritus, University of Mississippi.

student with the knowledge that has been accumulated over the centuries. The student selects from courses, laboratories, and libraries what he wants to learn, for he knows that he has neither the time nor the capacity to learn everything.

CONTINUING CONCERN

As chancellor Emeritus of the University of Mississippi, I have been asked what I consider to be the most difficult task that I am called upon to perform. The answer is easy because it was uppermost in my mind continuously during the more than twenty-one years I served as chief executive officer. It is to keep the University of Mississippi "free and growing."

The struggle to develop a pervasive climate of learning on the campus and a spirit of creative inquiry in every member of the university community was always of topmost importance. The University of Mississippi "was not to be the university of zealous minorities, not the university of political powers, not even the university of the State itself, but quite simply and unalterably the university of the people," noted James Gray, in The University of Minnesota, 1851-1951 (University of Minnesota Press, 1951).

Following are but a few illustrations that will give point to the question and problem of maintaining a climate of freedom to learn on a campus.

The Communist Scare

During the days of Senator Joseph McCarthy it was politically popular in some quarters to find persons on university faculties who were Communists, were accused of being Communists, associated with Communists, or had ideas that could be labeled communistic. On one occasion a member of the Mississippi House of Representatives, on the floor of that body, accused three members of the faculty of the University of Mississippi of having communistic leanings. The press carried this accusation throughout the state just as the chancellor was leaving for a meeting of the National Association of State Universities.

While attending that meeting, the chancellor discussed the problem with the president of the University of Michigan and was told how that person had handled a somewhat similar situation. At a meeting of his Board of Regents, the president was asked if he knew he had a card-carrying Communist on his faculty. He said that he did. He said further that it had cost the university $2,000 to bring a chimpanzee from Africa so that some of the departments could study its behavior but that the "Communist hadn't cost a damn cent." It was a good story, but it seemed to have little bearing on the problem in Mississippi. Much effort on the part of many people, however, helped the university over this hurdle.

Publishing Problems

That a good faculty is a publishing faculty is a bromide of academe. The University of Mississippi has always encouraged its faculty to publish. What they publish is not always popular, however, as shown by the following incident.

One of the professors of philosophy at the university had written a scholarly book on comparative religions that was widely used in universities throughout the nation. One evening while the Mississippi legislature was in session (it seems that many of the problems involving freedom to learn coincide with meetings of the legislature when appropriations are under consideration), the university's chancellor received a call from the governor of Mississippi inviting him to breakfast the next morning. After a 180-mile drive to Jackson and a short night's sleep, the chancellor still could not figure out the purpose of the meeting. As he was walking from his hotel room to the governor's mansion, a car stopped and four legislators invited him to join them, as they also were on their way to the mansion for breakfast.

What a breakfast it was—everything one could want and well prepared. As the meal and the light talk came to a close, the purpose of the meeting became clear. The governor said something to the effect that he understood that there was a professor on the Ole Miss faculty that had written a book on religion. This fact was affirmed, and the good character, religious convictions, and scholarly qualifications of the professor were related. Then the governor told the chancellor that there was widespread disagreement with some of the contents of the book and opposition to having the author on the campus "teaching our children" such theories and opinions. He said, moreover, that the legislators had advised him that some action by the legislature was to be expected.

The chancellor suggested that before any action was taken Bible scholars of unquestioned reputation should be invited to appear before the appropriate legislative committee; otherwise there was the distinct possibility that the governor, the legislature, the university, and the people of Mississippi would be embarrassed. The subject was immediately dropped, and the legislators left. As the governor took the chancellor back to the hotel, he smiled and said that he did not think the chancellor would hear any more about the matter. And he didn't.

In another case, a continuing source of irritation to many citizens, alumni, and state officials was a member of the history department. He was one of the more prolific writers on controversial subjects. He wrote effectively, expressing his point of view clearly while stating the facts that led him to his conclusions. He was, throughout the conflict over the integration of Ole Miss, a vocal and staunch supporter of removing the racial barriers; and he had the ear of many students and others. In a sense, he was a great asset to the chancellor and the university. He was so controversial that he drew public attention away from other persons who were of like mind and who were also active.

The climax of this struggle came when he published a widely read book, Mississippi: The Closed Society (New York: Harcourt Brace Jovanovich, 1966). The university made every effort to defend his right to publish the book and to protect him from retribution that in any way could be considered punishment. The clamor and hostility from off the campus and throughout the state, however, led him to decide to take a position at a strong and well-known midwestern university.

A Speaker Crisis

Speakers who are invited to the campus and espouse unpopular points of view sometimes are the target of organizations, politicians, and private individuals who think otherwise. In the late fifties, for example, the student organization that encouraged religious activity on the campus invited an Episcopal minister from the Midwest to speak on "Jazz, the Theater, and Religion." The same speech had been given by the minister at other colleges and universities and had proven popular with many students.

Early in the fall, soon after the university had opened, a Jackson newspaper reported that the minister was to speak at Ole Miss in February of the following year; in an adjacent column the paper reported that the scheduled speaker had won $32,000 in a television contest and that he was giving a substantial part of his winnings to the National Association for the Advancement of Colored People. Immediately, demands for cancellation of his appearance came from all over the state. There were only a few state newspapers that did not concur in denying him the right to speak and denying students the right to hear what he had to say.

The chancellor went to the governor-elect and received from him assurances that the University of Mississippi had his full support and that most certainly a university should be open to all sides of a controversial issue. Convinced that the church pulpit should be free, the chancellor decided to secure also the support of the three bishops of Mississippi—Catholic, Episcopal, and Methodist. He called on his own bishop first and carefully explained the problem and its implications for the church. After some moments, the bishop put his hand on the chancellor's knee and said sympathetically, "Chancellor, you do have a problem." There seemed to be no need to seek help from the other two bishops.

Shortly thereafter a university representative phoned the minister in question and discussed with him his forthcoming appearance. Since the title of the minister's speech (mentioned above) did not include the word "integration," some persons thought he would not inject his views on the subject. This was not to be. In fact, the minister had strong feelings that the circumstances demanded of him the presentation of his personal views.

With this information in hand, the chancellor called on the new governor to thank him for his previous assurances of support for a free campus and to advise him that this was the time to speak out, since the press and the legislature were whipping the issue into a real problem that could have disastrous results not only for the University of Mississippi but for all of the institutions under the Board of Trustees of Institutions of Higher Learning. The governor was surprised at the turn of events and, with utmost sympathy and understanding, announced that he would be powerless to support the appearance of the minister because to do so would seriously jeopardize the pending legislative program.

Facing defeat, and with a heavy heart, the chancellor returned to the campus and called some twenty-five senior members of the faculty to meet that evening at his home. Finally, at 2:00 a.m., all individuals present but one agreed that the chancellor should call the minister and advise him that his appearance, while it had not been cancelled, had been postponed until a later and more propitious time. The heat was off, but few faculty or students were proud of the outcome. The minister never was invited again. Events were moving too fast, and he soon became lost in the rapidly developing crisis and confrontation over the issue of integration.

The Integration Issue

Regarding the integration issue, the political maneuvering and infighting that preceded the admission of James Meredith to the

university was classic. The chancellor many times urged the faculty
and students to take full advantage of this real drama of democracy
in action to observe, to feel, to appreciate, and to understand such
subjects as social psychology, government and political science, the
judicial system, and history. Some did. At Ole Miss was where the
action was; other faculties and students would have to study it from
the somewhat sterile press, radio, and TV. Never has a university
had a better laboratory for the study of human behavior and its relation to government. The chancellor cherishes the hope that those
students and faculty who were strong enough and courageous enough
to stay with the university through that year have benefited from the
experience and are better Americans for it.

The climax of the issue was a clash between the governor and
the attorney general of the United States. The governor later was invited to speak at the university and to give his side of the story. There
was little, if any, opposition. The chancellor was to be tested, however, when an invitation went to the attorney general to speak on
campus.

While some state officials and organizations brought pressure
to cancel the invitation, much of the press supported the university.
There was some fear for the safety of the attorney general, but there
had been careful planning. On the day of the event, the attorney
general and his wife enjoyed a private lunch with the chancellor, his
wife, and a restricted guest list. Later, the large coliseum on
campus was over half filled with students, faculty, and many citizens
from over the state. The attorney general's address was well received, and the ovation given him by the university community has
seldom, if ever, been equaled. However, when the plane carrying the
attorney general departed for the University of Alabama, the chancellor experienced a rare relief.

The School of Law

During the integration crisis, the School of Law at the university was a source of irritation to many persons because in its faculty
and student body were those who interpreted the U.S. Constitution as
the courts did. The popular sentiment in the state was to defy the
courts by using a questionable relic of state sovereignty referred to
as interposition. The lawyers then advising the chancellor were confident that the plea of interposition would be denied. (Three of those
lawyers are now federal judges.) It was.

Many state leaders thought that by changing the dean at the
School of Law the school would become a resource for the interposition forces. The dean at the time was being severely criticized because he was doing all he could to give the people the facts that

subsequent events have proved to be correct. The dean retired at the legal age and a new one was appointed. Soon it was discovered that changing deans did not change the law. By its nature a law school is a fruitful place for controversy, and the one at Ole Miss is no exception.

A Classroom Incident

On one occasion during the sixties, the chairman of the Department of Sociology invited some representatives of the Congress of Racial Equality (CORE) to bring their message to his classes and to make themselves available for questions. Their appearance was soon followed by calls to state officials and the press in Jackson. The diligent and alert chairman of the state's General Legislative Investigating Committee and four members of the Board of Trustees of Institutions of Higher Learning (as observers) soon were on the campus to find out who was responsible for the incident. After several hours of hearings, they took their records and returned to Jackson. And that seemed to be the end of that.

The Student Press

From time to time the student newspaper, the Daily Mississippian, publishes something that seems to endanger its freedom, a freedom that it has enjoyed for at least twenty-five years. These controversial articles always seem to appear while the legislature is in session. For example, soon after a newly elected governor had delivered his inauguration speech and his "state of the state" address before the legislature, the editor of the student publication felt called upon to express his own views. His editorial noted in closing, "Mississippi is fiftieth in almost everything and now it has the leadership to keep it there." Telephone calls began to come from Jackson and the press services even before the chancellor had had a chance to read the editorial. It is perhaps an understatement to say that it took time and a lot of doing to extricate the university from this incident.

CONCLUSION

Do not conclude from these illustrations that the chancellor had a bad time during the period of these incidents. The excitement and the opportunity to be joined by students and faculty in what some believe to be one of society's finest enterprises, the university, far overshadowed the failures, disappointments, and sorrows. The struggle continues, however, and the present chancellor no doubt could add incidents of a later time.

While the constitutional Board of Trustees of Institutions of Higher Learning, the American Association of University Professors, the Southern Association of Colleges and Schools, and the various accrediting agencies for the special areas and professional schools are powerful antidotes for the poison of fear that could pollute the climate of learning and the spirit of creative inquiry that are characteristic of every first-rate university, antidotes are not enough. What is needed is genuine support of the university in its continuing determination to safeguard man's right to knowledge and the free use thereof. Hopefully this study will enlist such support.

It is often presumptuous to assume that another wishes or needs the benefit of postmortem inquiries or observations. It is also fair to postulate that it is even more presumptuous to think that any other person has all of the right answers, much less the appropriate questions. In the hope that mutual humility will allow the consideration of the writer's afterthoughts, as well as those of the reader, let us now turn to some of the implications that may be deduced from the foregoing three studies.

Relative to the writer's case study on one's plight in the pursuit of a department chairmanship, are the cited circumstances atypical or indicative of such quests elsewhere in academe? To what extent are the processes and events common or unlike? Who appeared to be responsible for this clash between the administration and the affected faculty and students? How might the confrontation and result have been averted? Who among the principals should have taken the initiative toward that end? At what point in the unfolding of the events and in what manner? Would your judgment be affected by your role perception, that is, in the position of the president, vice president, dean, chairman, the candidate, or as a member of the concerned faculty or member of the student body? Would your action and decision in each of these capacities be consistent with the interests of all others involved in the controversy? In the final analysis, was this administrative matter treated in a professional manner? If so, why so; if not, why not?

In addressing the problem of reducing the number of faculty, the Duff study causes us to come face to face with a bevy of challenges in the academic community today, ranging from the transition to austerity through the consequences of zero population growth on many campuses. But, for the moment, let us wrestle with the problem area highlighted by Duff, for, as veteran administrators in large-scale organizations will readily advise, it will be traumatic and soon enough when one realizes that such discomforting experiences evolve a dozen at a time. So for the sake of enlightenment and some argument, what is right and wrong with imcompetent or surplus professors? Should the tool be equally applicable for use by the Faculty Senate to dispose of inept or bloated bureaucracies? Is the AAUP guideline for de facto tenure a rational policy statement or is it simply a byproduct of the emotional insecurity of its membership? On the other hand, once an institution commits itself to an individual,

whatever the probationary period, is it reasonable to expect that the
said person has earned a variety of rights, including dismissal only
for prescribed cause? And who really is the better judge of faculty
competence: peers within or beyond the college or university, administrative superiors, students, or a combination of such constructive
critics? Should that singular judgment, when applied to tenure, be
good for a lifetime? When one's services are no longer desired, is
severance the only solution? Might one be useful in other capacities
on campus and suitably retrained for such work? Or should we deduce
that more often than not the culprit is personally obnoxious rather
than professionally inadequate? In either case, what is good personnel
administration?

As the Williams study makes perfectly clear, there are many
and varying threats to campus freedom, conjured up and sponsored
by all manner and make of zealots. Still it remains remarkable to
recall the number of peers who have buckled under when tested by the
self-righteous causes of the political right and the political left. Conversely, it is no more commendable to note those who have used
these stresses and strains of our times to gain their fame and fortune.
To wallow in the field of intrigue is not our present purpose, but it is
undoubtedly profitable to consider it in microcosm. How applicable a
scapegoat is the "Commie scare" today for the disgruntled in our
society? If no longer in vogue, how else do critics manage to classify
their disdain for features of contemporary society which they may not
understand but clearly do not cherish? Are terms such as "socialistic
tendencies" or "un-American" still heard, or have they changed in
view of the counterattack under title of "fascist pigs" and "bourgeois
bastards?" Has anyone noticed lately the definitiveness of the substance of the complaints from such quarters, not to mention the
viability of the alternative that they offer? Interesting too is the deaf-
ening silence that tends to emanate from the ranks of the vast majority, caring not to get involved but nevertheless planning to be among
the leaders of tomorrow. To return to the scenarios of the Williams
study, what is your position on some of the nitty-gritty issues on
campus: the Communist lecturer, the anti-Christian researcher, the
advocate or adversary of racial integration? Would that position be
maintained in spite of popular or political opposition on and off campus? How could the related problems have been approached differently
from the author's approach? Do you favor or oppose academic freedom? Are your anticipated reactions and values consistent? Does it
matter? How much of our decision making is objective, and how much
is attributable to the peculiarities of one's life circumstances? Who
cares? Perhaps only those who are truly dedicated to the pursuit of
knowledge and the advancement of the human condition. We should not
expect less from our captains of erudition.

Perhaps the most striking characteristic of change is its inevitability. Although it is seldom viewed with certainty, it is a reality that should share equal billing with the assurances of both taxes and death. Unlike the latter guarantees, however, the phenomena of change seems generally to be unexpected, at least as evidenced by the behavior of too many members of large and small organizations. In academe as in government and industry, this is a matter of particular importance, for sheer bigness breeds not only bureaucracy but indifference and intolerance, and worse yet a tendency to wallow in the womb of the status quo.

As is well known among individuals receptive to change, resting on laurels is antipathetic to systematic evolution, whether of a personal or institutional order. Because change is constant, sometimes advancing and sometimes curtailing the goals of man and his institutions, it must be recognized and dealt with accordingly. That the course of change will not naturally follow the path of least resistance is well known in the sciences and to a lesser extent in the arts. Thus human direction is necessary for the proper fulfillment of objectives. The problem is that not all in command are truly aware of the nature of change, nor of its cause and effect with reference to their responsibilities. Herein lies the challenge: to discern its meaning, guide its course, and prepare for its consequences.

As applicable to the work of captains of erudition, this theme might be paraphrased as the management or facilitation of changing educational environments. To be sure, such words mean different things to different people and organizations, as will become apparent in the following studies. For Thomas F. Jones, whose study launches Part V, the efficacy of human learning and growth is again called into question, and he offers an answer in the form of a viable alternative. Of added interest therein is the role of higher authority in allowing and expediting a learning transformation, not to mention the utilization of subordinate leadership toward that end. Still it remains clear that superordinates can succumb to standards of educational efficiency that are not always tantamount to educational effectiveness. This is the major thrust of the case presented by Michael E. Browne, and many of his related observations are equally worthy of serious reflection by the most experienced of administrators.

Attitude and obligation in the face of change are subjects infrequently examined in the context of higher education. They are the focus of the subsequent study, by Mary Carman Rose, as she explores many of the moral and professional responsibilities of academic administrators. And how much change might the contemporary college or university accommodate? Samuel E. Kelly and Karen L. Morell offer a near-optimum example, replete with all of the difficulties and repercussions that one may expect. Perhaps few administrators have been so challenged, and few academic institutions have proven to be so universal.

CHAPTER

13

ON TURNING THE
INNOVATION CRANK
Thomas F. Jones

During my 28 years of experience in higher education, I have
given a major portion of my thoughts and efforts to changing student
attitudes toward learning and to increasing the motivation of students.
Throughout this time I have enjoyed a reasonably satisfying degree of
success. But my greatest fulfillment has come during the most recent
five years of a 12-year term as president of the University of South
Carolina, for during this time I have been able to participate in prov-
ing out a replicable experience which deals directly and effectively
with the affective behavior of students, including their attitude toward
the learning experience.

In Education and Identity (American Council on Education, 1970),
Arthur Chickering identifies seven areas in which those in the 18 to
22 age bracket should achieve significant personal growth: (1) competence; (2) autonomy; (3) purpose; (4) identity; (5) interpersonal relationships; (6) integrity; and (7) management of emotions. Although the
university traditionally has dedicated itself to the achievement of
competence in the cognitive domain, the university rarely has given
formal attention to the other six areas in this list. These, which lie
largely in the affective domain, generally have been relegated to

—————————————

Thomas F. Jones, former President, University of South Carolina.
This study would not be complete without giving special thanks to
the Ford Foundation, to Cy Mills of the National Training Laboratories,
to Robert Heckel, Manning Hiers, John Zuidema, and Barbara Fine-
gold of the Social Problems Research Institute, to John Kimmey who
masterfully headed our first-year teaching-learning seminars, and to
Jay Smith, education development officer, who helped in countless
ways.

extracurricular activities for the development of students as affectively skilled beings.

In recent years (since about 1965, it seems) this educational mode has proven increasingly inadequate for several reasons:

1. The influence of the home on the affective development of children and youths has been greatly reduced because of several changes in family life style. For example, communications within the family has been greatly reduced by television (the first TV generation arrived on campus in the 1960s), telephones, and automobiles. Constant and clear exposure to a system of attitudes and values has been correspondingly reduced or removed.

2. Communications regarding values, attitudes, and motivation seem to have been greatly diminished by the increasing speed of life, the increasing opportunities to be spectators, and the decreasing tendency to be participants.

3. The growth in size of our colleges and universities has tended to make extracurricular programs less effective in reaching the total student body.

4. The democratization of education has brought into conflict on the campus widely different value systems and protocols.

Out of these confusions has come large numbers of marginally motivated, undirected, confused, or alienated young people, many of whom use their energies condemning or pouting at the "system," which includes the university. In 1969 I first became aware of the possibility of a systematic and replicable way of dealing with these problems on the campus. Dr. Warren Buford, who had recently been honored as Outstanding Teacher of the Year in North Carolina, began educational experiments on our campus which gave startling results in the personal behavior and academic performance of his students.

Footnote from "Time To Take The Next Step" (1970-71): Thirty "flunkouts" who had been readmitted on probation were enrolled in the seminar for 3 credit hours. On the basis of previous experience 25 (85 percent) of these would have performed below standards and thereby flunked out again. In this case only 5 (17 percent) failed. The remaining 25 earned a semester GPR on a full load (12 to 18 hours) that averaged 0.7 points (out of 4.0) above their previous GPR average. All 25 qualified to remain in school. One student, whose previous GPR was 1.0, achieved a perfect 4.0.

A black student whose previous average GPR was 1.3 and who made 2.7 for the semester gave the following testimony to a meeting of deans and department heads:

If I had been invited to come before you last summer, I probably wouldn't have come, or if I had come I probably would have walked in, uttered an obscenity, and walked out. I come here today gladly and with very little fear.

Last summer I had only a few black friends, or perhaps I should say acquaintances since our relationships were superficial, really. But now I have both black and white friends, a number of them. And when we get together we talk about substantial things—not trivialities.

I used to suppress my thoughts because I expected people to laugh at me. I've learned that my thoughts are as valuable as my experience, that they do have serious meaning, and I'm not afraid to express them. I've been released from that hangup!

I never expected to graduate from this place. It seemed hopeless. I didn't believe in myself. I'm over all that bad thinking. I know what's expected of me and I know how to give it. I've had my first good semester, and it'll be easy from here on.

The seminar was a great experience.

Another student in the group had flunked out with a 1.46 GPR. A discussion with his father disclosed that he had had no motivation for school work since his high school freshman year during which he lost the sight of one eye in a freak accident. He was readmitted on condition he would enroll in the seminar. That semester his GPR was 4.0. He later graduated (overall GPR—2.75) and went to graduate school.

For some time it seemed as if Dr. Buford simply possessed strange therapeutic powers which might be prohibitively expensive to replicate (screening for appropriate personal characteristics and providing training which might possibly require several years of apprenticeship, for example). Out of protracted discussions among faculty and staff, including psychologists who had been deeply involved in our Upward Bound project, a concept emerged which lent itself to implementation. Our experience indicated that selected faculty could be developed into "facilitators" in 30 to 40 intensive hours of training, and that these could be effective in changing (for the better) the attitudes and motivation level of 80 to 90 percent of the students in seminar groups of 15 to 20 students each.

But how could such a radical educational effort be put into effect within a traditional university with all of its checks, balances, and other safeguards? Unusual tasks are difficult in any case, but are easier than money problems. Fortunately the University of South

Carolina, through my office, had been awarded a Ford Foundation
Venture Grant for the improvement of undergraduate education in the
summer of 1971, which was the point in time that our experiments
and thoughts began to jell. Subsequent events have contributed to an
air of considerable excitement on the campus, especially among the
younger faculty, though not all limited to that group, as we shall see.

Realizing that undergraduate education could be improved very
little by the standing processes of committee and legislative activity,
but would require significant changes in the attitudes and directed
efforts of people, we decided to concentrate our efforts on changing
the insights and outlook of the existing faculty members, as well as
looking for a limited number of new faculty with special attributes
needed to bring about changes seen as desirable.

Teaching-learning workshops open to all faculty were organized
for four evenings in the fall. Experts on such topics as good teaching,
educational technology, behavioral objectives, and psychology of the
student were brought in to give presentations and lead the discussions.
Average attendance was 60 to 80, or about 10 percent of the faculty.
The term ended with a weekend workshop using trainers from the
National Training Laboratories (NTL) and interested psychologists
from the faculty. Reactions were mixed. Engineers and some hard
scientists walked out of the first session. But a significant number
of the 50 participating were elated and gave the experience good exposure among faculty colleagues.

Subsequently, the administration announced the availability of
special funds for innovative teaching projects and a second, nondupli-
cative series of workshops were run in the spring with about the same
number of participants but with greater interest. At the end of the
semester another weekend workshop using NTL staff assistance was
planned, similar to the fall workshop but significantly different in
that the site would not be nearby but instead would be in a resort motel
on a beautiful South Carolina beach. Fifty-five members of the faculty
elected to participate, including several senior faculty and a vice
provost. The results of this workshop were electric: 50 of the 55
declared it to be a great experience that they would recommend to
their colleagues. (Two complained about the luxury of the accommodations.)

At this point, having built a reasonable base of faculty support
for experimental training, we chose a bold plan. Through the Faculty
Committee on Curricula and New Courses we proposed a freshman
seminar:

> UN 101—Elective seminar for freshmen: Introduction to the
> University, special resources, communication problems,
> the role of the student, subject area of professor—3 hours
> credit, pass/fail.

This was to be the first course in the university to carry the designation UN—university—instead of a disciplinary or collegial designation.

For the summer meeting of the Faculty Senate the committee reported on the proposal: recommended but without academic credit. Fortunately an ad hoc group of interested faculty had recruited power-center type faculty to speak out for credit and the new course was approved on a one-year experimental basis as originally proposed, on July 10, 1972.

Having crossed this bridge we now faced a significant staffing problem. Only a handful of faculty were qualified to teach the seminar. Thirty of those faculty who had reacted most positively to the weekend experimental workshops of the previous year were invited to my office, and I told them:

> Ladies and gentlemen, you have been especially selected and invited here to be offered an unusual opportunity to experiment with the new educational mode called University 101, a freshman seminar called Introduction to the University. Let me stress that your participation is entirely voluntary. No pressure will be exerted. But I am offering the following special proposition. If you will give 40 hours of your time during the month of August, my office will pay the costs of the special training that you will need. The training will be somewhat similar to that which you have experienced at the weekend teaching-learning retreat which you attended last fall or spring. After completion of training you will be asked to teach a section of UN 101 as an overload so that you may try out the new techniques you have learned. Your participation in this teaching project is voluntary. You are free to refuse without prejudice. For teaching UN 101 as an overload you will be given a stipend of $500 from Ford Foundation funds at the end of the term.

The floor was opened for discussion, which was lively, after which all 30 agreed they would like to accept the invitation. Some could not fit the training schedule, some found they were already too heavily committed for the fall, and, perhaps, some just wanted out. Eventually 22 did complete the training and 20 taught UN 101 in the fall.

The Social Problems Research Institute, which took responsibility for training and administration in the project, designed and administered evaluative instruments which were applied to faculty-in-training and, later, to students. These showed remarkably positive results.

Students were recruited for enrollment by the Division of Student Affairs during the summer orientation program, and most deans permitted entering freshmen to schedule UN 101 as an overload. The fall experience proved to be an exciting one for both students and faculty. Almost half of the faculty and staff involved insisted on the opportunity to teach another section in the spring, without extra compensation, but, instead, they were redeployed to other kinds of groups such as returning flunkouts and juniors in education. Thereby their experience was broadened, and UN 101 assignments were preserved for new trainees. In late fall another group accepted the project for the spring term. This group was full of surprises, including the volunteering of a dean of a professional school and the head of a science department.

The spring and summer of 1973 was a critical time. The UN 101 offering had been approved as a one-year experiment, and would, therefore, be terminated without further faculty action. At the last spring meeting in April, the Faculty Senate decided that no decision could be made before fall because the evaluation was incomplete. A motion was made and passed to continue the offering through the fall term, on an experimental basis.

Many, myself included, were surprised to find UN 101 on the agenda for the subsequent meeting of the faculty since the earlier decision was to defer action until the fall. This had happened because the evaluation study, made by the Social Problems Research Institute, was completed in June and a group of enthusiastic faculty had decided to wait no longer. My feeling of stress proved unwarranted. For UN 101 became a regular offering of the university by a nearly unanimous vote of the University Senate in July 1973.

The summer training groups for the fall term included additional department heads, a dean, and, believe it or not, a trustee who holds an adjunct professorship. And the fall enrollment was the largest ever. Some 45 sections enrolled over 800 students. In the spring additional faculty were trained and some 450 students were enrolled in 24 sections.

As I stepped up from the presidency to Distinguished Professor of the University, yet another group (of which I am an enthusiastic member) was in training, and an additional group of faculty was being trained in August 1974 to teach in the fall term.

What has been accomplished beyond adding another course to the offerings of the university? In my opinion we have made our first really significant effort on the affective stem of learning. The seminar is a sort of survey course in which the things surveyed are addressed to the specific needs of the individual students of the class. Everyone seems to profit considerably by the taking of individual, independent testimony, and the process indicates that each profits in a very unique way.

For example, students have noted the following. "I've always been very lonely, now I have twenty good friends." "I know Professor [X] better than any other official of the university. I can go to him about anything, anytime." "I was told the university was a large and completely impersonal place, but it's simply not true." "For the first time in my life I began to really listen to others, and then I began to read . . . and read, and read!" "I never believed I could finish university, but that will be no problem now that I have my confidence." "I never dreamed the administration had so many responsibilities, and that they were really willing to discuss them." And from a quiet, retiring young woman who normally had very little to say, "Before taking UN 101 I was a very shy person!" We have found UN 101 to be even more valuable for the older woman who either comes as a freshman or returns after an absence of many years. Getting closely acquainted with twenty or so other students closes the generation and time gap and makes it possible for them to completely embrace the university experience without feeling like a freak.

From the faculty one hears these remarks. "At last I feel like I am a member of a community of scholars." "My friendship with students reaches to every member of my seminar and does not feel forced in any way. They call me by my first name, but the respect is there." "I always learn more than my students." "I am adapting the facilitator technique to my graduate seminar with excellent results." "In these days I know fourteen people I've never seen before better than I know any faculty member in my department."

But the purpose of this study is not to explain or justify UN 101, but to expose the process by which a rather unusual new activity was taken on by a university which saw itself as rather traditional and flexible. I believe it is safe to say that it could not have been done without strong backing from all levels of the administration, especially the top ranks, and that it would have been very difficult without a modest amount of otherwise uncommitted funds—about $50,000 per year out of an institutional budget of $70 million.

AT WHAT PRICE
THE COST PER
CREDIT HOUR?
Michael E. Browne

The two decades following World War II were halcyon for American universities. The synergistic effect of returning veterans, a burgeoning population and unprecedented demand for goods and services resulted in growth and prestige never before experienced in higher education. The advent of Sputnik in 1956 provided an added impetus in the sciences. As a nation of competitors we rose to the challenge of the Soviet Union, and in the best Super Bowl tradition we gave it all we had. New mathematics, new physics, new biology, and new chemistry in the schools were among the fruits of this effort. In physics the glamor of nuclear energy and the laser helped to keep the ball rolling. Students clamored to enter graduate school, and departments expanded to accommodate them. In the resulting competition it is not unreasonable to assume that the best departments fared better than their contemporaries, and the growth of the programs at such prestigious institutions as Berkeley, Harvard, and M.I.T. attests to this. Consequently, in keeping with our indigenous free enterprise philosophy, it was natural for university administrators to associate growth with quality. They are not alone in this view, of course, and it seems certain that legislators also find this reasoning compelling.

During the 1960s the crunch of inflation began to be felt. As college enrollments leveled off, efforts were made to improve the management process in higher education. The much publicized successes of then Defense Secretary Robert McNamara at the Pentagon were viewed as a paradigm for similar approaches in other fields. The efforts then of President Hitch at the University of California perhaps best exemplify the push for better cost effectiveness in a

---

Michael E. Browne, Chairman, University of Idaho.

massive university system. However, even in the hinterlands the
gospel was heard, and the University of Idaho has been among those
trying to make the best possible use of the taxpayer's dollar. In all
cases the intent has been laudable. Few could argue that one should
not attempt to use objective criteria in evaluating educational programs. Physics, which has sometimes been referred to as the
science of measurement, would certainly be philosophically committed
to an effort to quantify the process of allocation of resources. Unfortunately, in actual practice efforts to improve the operation of the
higher education machine have too often resulted only in pressures to
increase enrollments and reduce costs. The number of credit hours
generated per dollar has become the prime factor in evaluating the
worth and performance of many academic departments. The experience of the physics department at the University of Idaho is a case in
point.

The University of Idaho is the state land-grant institution. Its
enrollment of about 7,000 full-time students has been fairly stable in
the 1970s. During this period job opportunities for people with higher
degrees worsened, and physicists were especially hard hit. The
federal government curtailed much of its expenditure for research
and phased out student fellowships and traineeships. Nationally the
number of students majoring in physics decreased steadily. Such has
not been the case at Idaho, however, with the number of majors holding steady; but the graduate enrollment has dipped sharply, with a
concomittant reduction in research productivity.

The bulk of credit hours generated in physics results from required service courses and from courses taken as electives to satisfy
science requirements. With only 50 undergraduate students majoring
in physics at Idaho, the number of credits taken by them in the physics
curriculum is not large. Consequently, it is primarily by attracting
students from other areas that the productivity of physics can be increased.

That there are strong pressures to reduce the cost per credit
hour is unmistakable. Comparison of such data for various academic
departments is published regularly by the university administration
and is a factor in subsequent budget discussions. The situation in
physics has been aggravated by the fact that the faculty is relatively
young. With almost no turnover and with numerous promotions, salary
costs have skyrocketed. This, coupled with inflationary effects on
expenditures for lab supplies and equipment, has resulted in cost
figures which make physics look relatively more and more unattractive
to the university administration. The expected, and implied, reaction
by the university is to reduce expenditures in physics by cutting back
on funds for research and for supplies for teaching, and by increasing
teaching loads. The department is unanimous in the belief that such

acts would have serious and deleterious effects on the quality of education at Idaho. As might be expected, the faculty has tried to cope with the exigency in order to continue to carry on what they believe to be a worthwhile endeavor.

It is perhaps worth digressing momentarily to comment on why a physicist thinks a strong physics program should be an integral part of a university. Although a wide spectrum of views is to be found in the profession, there is a consensus on certain points. Few see physics primarily as vocational training. If physics teaches anything, it is how to think and how to solve problems. Mathematics is the language of thinking, and physics puts this language to work as a means of communication between man and ideas. The simplicity of unifying concepts and laws is the very quintessence of physics, and hopefully the discipline gives the student a taste of the unfathomed order of the universe. The evolution of science and technology has had tremendous impact on the development of human civilization. Physics has become a vital part of our culture, and no person is truly educated without an appreciation of the role it plays. Like history and the language arts, physics will not be a source of livelihood to many students, but this need not lessen its impact. Although the number of professional physicists society is willing to support is limited, it remains crucial that some talented individuals enter the field if our understanding of the physical world is to advance. To this end a strong program for students majoring in physics is needed, even though enrollments are small.

The aims stated above are difficult to measure in simple quantitative terms. The payoff from studying physics is so vague, and often so delayed in time, that its assessment as a basis for making immediate operational decisions is of little value. Subjective judgments are required if the value of physics to the university is to be determined, and such judgments are not only difficult to make, but they open the involved administrator to criticism from many sources. It is much easier to fall back on simple-minded numbers, and here cost per credit hour rules supreme. When this becomes of paramount importance in conducting an academic program, the road ahead tends to be downhill all the way as far as academic quality is concerned. Two striking experiences in the Idaho Physics Department illustrate what can happen.

Faced with the problem of trying to reduce the cost per credit hour ratio, the department had two options: reduce costs or increase enrollments (or both). The department was determined not to dilute the quality of the program if this could possibly be avoided. Since the bulk of the departmental budget is consumed by salaries, costs could not be appreciably reduced without a reduction in faculty. This was considered undesirable from a number of standpoints. Not only would increased teaching loads result in poorer teaching, we felt, but a decrease in faculty would undoubtedly mean the demise of our graduate program. With a faculty of ten we are just barely above the critical mass needed to maintain a viable program. Hence it was decided that only through increased enrollments could the physics position be strengthened in the eyes of the university administration. The faculty felt that in order to achieve its true goals it was necessary to go along with the rather superficial aims of the administration in this respect.

One undertaking aimed partially at increasing physics enrollments was the introduction of a new course entitled Physics and Society. This was a project which many of the faculty could support with enthusiasm. Most feel there is a real need to expose a broad segment of society to the role of physics in our body politic. It is perhaps but a legacy of the atom bomb, but most physicists are blessed (or burdened) with a sensitive social conscience. Problems such as pollution, energy utilization, and weapons policy-making fit nicely into the above mentioned course and similar courses at most other universities. The first waves of students who enrolled in the course were caught up in the fervor of the ecology-now movement and the protests against the Viet Nam war. With the winding down of the war the peace movement in the United States became moribund. The gasoline shortage supplanted the drive to save the environment. The original idealistic Physics and Society students were replaced largely by warm bodies looking for an easy three credits to fulfill a science requirement. The competition for such students is fierce, and physics had to try to make a good showing against such courses as Man and the Environment (Biology 100), Chemistry and the Citizen (Chemistry 102), Politics and Pollution (Political Science 152), and Man in a Nuclear Age (Interdisciplinary 101). The clientele for these classes is not attracted by a rigorous course. They are not looking for "hard" science, and they do look for subjects where they can get a good grade with minimum work. An average class grade of B for Physics and Society is not unusual, and the work required is minimal. We could, of course, in a moment of mad idealism, raise our standards, grade as we do in a "real" physics course, and expect a full three credits' worth of work for three credits received. To do so would be to drop the enrollment to approximately zero. This would eventually lead to reductions in our budget, which in turn would harm the truly significant parts of our program. When data on costs per credit hour is compiled it doesn't matter where the credits come from. A Mickey Mouse course is as good as any other in the big ledger book.

It is not just in peripheral elective courses that the pressure to make enrollments grow is felt. The core of the lower division physics curriculum is a sequence of courses usually called Engineering Physics and required of all engineering and science students. At Idaho (and at other schools) these courses have been the focal point of significant conflict between the physicists and the College of Engineering. At Idaho the problem found its genesis when the engineers decided they must do something about their precipitously plummeting enrollments. (They, too, must compute cost per credit hour ratios.) Typically engineering students found it necessary to take an extra one or two semesters beyond four years to complete a bachelor's degree, since at Idaho they were required to complete some 138 credits (as compared to 128 credits for most other students). This was remedied in part by eliminating from the curriculum one of the three introductory physics courses taken by engineers. It was agreed to substitute a comparable engineering course as the prerequisite for the last two engineering physics courses. To further enhance the attractiveness of their program, the engineers decided to require their students to take a one-year orientation course designed to survey all engineering and increase career motivation. Some, perhaps unkindly, suggested the aim of the course was brainwashing. It was anticipated that this would alleviate the significant attrition experienced in engineering enrollments beyond the freshman year. It is perhaps no coincidence that the bulk of the students in these classes receive A's and B's. What better encouragement could they be given?

It is worth noting that the curriculum changes instituted by the College of Engineering were motivated in large part by the same numbers game that pervades so many facets of university life. This particular sequence of events culminated in a decision by the College of Engineering to dispense with the prerequisites for the second engineering physics course (having already discarded Engineering Physics 1). It was evident to the physics faculty that such a step could greatly water down the quality of our core courses, and this is indeed what has happened. No instructor is disposed to give bad grades to a large portion of a class, no matter how bad their preparation. The university utilizes a system of mandatory evaluation of instructional staff by students, and it is generally believed that there is a strong correlation between low grading and poor evaluations. Further, physics was faced with the publicly voiced threat of the dean of engineering to "teach our own physics." Confronted with the possible loss of large numbers of students in a major service course, we found that in academia as in the Congress, Sam Rayburn's admonition applies: "To get along you have to go along." Hopefully the weakening of our courses will not some day result in an engineer's bridge falling down, but one never knows. What is known, however, is that these curricular changes were brought about not on pedagogical grounds, but through expediency. The academic quality of a program, once it is above some pitiably low threshold, is never questioned. What does come under scrutiny is total credit hours generated. The incidents described here relating to physics at Idaho are symptomatic of a malaise that is widespread in institutions of higher learning. We have come to believe that a growing program is a good one. In a sense the university is a microcosm of the world around it. The economic well-being of the nation is based on the precept that the gross national product can increase in monotonic fashion forever. Since our natural resources are limited, the fallacy of such a view is obvious. Nonetheless, no one in the western world has yet come up with a solution that faces up to this verity and yet will enable us to maintain our present quality of life. Our socioeconomic system seems to doom us to an unending series of booms followed by recessions. Much the same pattern is followed in education. Just as the world's population will eventually be limited in one way or another, perhaps by natural factors if not consciously by man himself, so it is certainly evident that colleges and universities will have to learn to live with stable or decreasing enrollments. A crucial problem is how to do this and still remain dynamic and productive.

Too often efficiency has been confused with effectiveness in judging the merit of an academic program. To some degree this occurs because the latter is so elusive and difficult to measure. The threats to academic quality and integrity reflected in the examples cited here result not from undue stress on competition, but rather from competition in the wrong areas and for the wrong reason. There is little doubt that competition can be a strong motivating factor in any human endeavor, and teaching and research are no exceptions. However, when the competition is primarily for numbers of students the results can be catastrophic.

As is so often the case, the position of a department chairman in this problem area is ambiguous. He is close enough to the subject matter to be sensitive to compromising academic standards, but he is also sufficiently involved in the budgeting process to be aware of the importance of such real-life considerations as credit hour production. Perhaps no completely satisfactory resolution of the difficulty exists. Truly outstanding programs do tend to grow larger. Administrators have been known to block innovation and experimentation under the guise of maintaining academic quality. There is merit in basing decision on objective data when possible.

To an establishment enamored of computers and cost accounting the best remedy is probably anathema: simply to find university administrators imbued with that quality which once, long ago, used to be called wisdom.

THE MAINTAINING OF THE
LIBERAL ARTS ATTITUDE:
THE CHAIRPERSON'S ROLE

Mary Carman Rose

In this study I wish to discuss some of the problems, the obligations, the opportunities, and the importance of the role of the chairperson of an academic department in the maintaining of what I will call the "liberal arts attitude." I write out of 17 years of experience as chairperson of the Department of Philosophy in a college of about 1,000 students which is dedicated to providing liberal education, maintaining high academic standards, and preparing the student for postgraduate life in the world.

As is to be expected in these years as chairperson, I have met with some frustrations and restrictions along with a great deal of opportunity, success, and personal fulfillment. Certainly I have cause for gratitude for having received much understanding, support, and help from colleagues among the administration, faculty, and students. If in what follows I stress the problems I have come upon as chairperson it is because within the prescribed limits of this study I cannot also include the cooperation and support which have outweighed the problems.

From the perspective in which I view the liberal arts here, the liberal arts attitude is fundamental and, hence, determinate of the rationale, contents, and goals of liberal education. The liberal arts attitude has three dimensions which I will explain by way of illumining the role of the chairperson in the maintaining of this attitude.

First, the liberal arts attitude is a love of learning—that is, a love of the questions with which inquiry in any one area is concerned, of the processes of inquiry, of the conclusions of inquiry which are accepted as truth, and of the wise, dedicated appropriation of truth in

---

Mary Carman Rose, Chairperson, Goucher College.

action in the world. Thus, the liberal arts attitude includes an interest in the predominantly philosophical topics of the epistemological structure of inquiry in various areas (for example, in the natural sciences, in economics, or history) and the limitations as well as the potentialities of these modes of inquiry.

Second, the liberal arts attitude includes commitment to values—for example, to ideals for assessing decisions, commitments, aspirations, and hopes, and to criteria for determining fruitful uses of knowledge. And third, the liberal arts attitude includes aesthetic delight in many things—for example, in the products of the humanities, but also in nature, mathematics, the logic of scientific inquiry, scientific insights into nature, and the functional products of technology.

One reason for making the liberal arts attitude, rather than a specific set of subjects, fundamental is that there is virtually no subject that cannot be pursued with this attitude. And there is virtually no subject that cannot cease to be part of a liberal arts education if it is pursued without the requisite attitude. A course in techniques of elementary education can be pursued without the liberal arts attitude if it is taken only as entree to a particular job. But the same course can also be pursued with desire to know how in this particular social science we are in the process of seeking insight and clarity. And a course in poetry (or any other aspect of the humanities) can fail to be part of a liberal arts education if it is taken under duress—for example, to fulfill an academic requirement or as a prescribed part of vocational training.

A liberal arts education fosters, clarifies, develops, and frees the liberal arts attitude in the individual student. It provides courses in which, in accordance with his gifts, preparation, present interests, and aims, the student can study the various disciplines. And, ideally, it provides courses which will enable the student to think clearly and constructively about the fundamentally important topics of the nature of knowledge, values, and the aesthetic dimensions of human experience.

Also, as important as any aspect of the foregoing is the fact that all the key terms I have used are to be interpreted as variables. That is, the meaning of knowledge; the areas in which and the means by which knowledge may legitimately be sought; the meaning of values and which values it is wise to appropriate; the meaning of beauty and the loci and roles of beauty in the life of the individual and in the community—all these are matters of controversy.

These were not the same things to Plato, Aristotle, the medieval Jewish and Christian Platonists who dominated the first ten centuries of Western thought; or the Jewish and Christian Aristotelians who dominated much Western thought about education since the eleventh century. And in modern times they have not been the same things to

Spinoza, Rousseau, Kant, Hegel, Marx, Whitehead, Dewey—to mention only a few of the creative thinkers who have added to our store of insights on these topics.

Thus liberal education properly will foster an awareness and appreciation of the significance of the fact that there is now and has always been controversy concerning the very content and goals of liberal education. A corollary is that properly liberal education does not foster dogmatism, exclusiveness, or dislike in respect to what does not fall within one's own tastes or talents.

It is true that often in the past liberal education has fostered such dislike, dogmatism, and exclusiveness. But I suggest that we are ready for a development in our comprehension of liberal education and that the incompatibility between these negative and destructive attitudes ought now to be apparent to all. The defense of this lies beyond the scope of this study. Such a defense, however, would prove valuable to present-day understanding of the liberal arts attitude and would illumine the importance of fostering that attitude among our college students.

Also, the liberal arts colleges differ in respect to the ways in which they are able to foster the liberal arts attitude and in the ways in which they are able to come to terms with the negative attitude toward some aspects of liberal arts. The school which is committed to a particular interpretation of reality, man, and values (for example, a Roman Catholic, a fundamentalist Protestant, or a Jewish college) will teach a particular interpretation of some aspects of knowledge, values, and the aesthetic. But I suggest that such a school does not fulfill its own educational commitment at the present time unless it fosters in all aspects of its academic community an interest in other points of view and a willingness to attempt to comprehend them and the value they possess for those who accept them.

On the other hand, the secular school may, perhaps, be defined as an academic community dedicated to no one interpretation of reality, man, and values. Ideally it will foster openness and acceptance toward whatever points of view are held by its faculty and endeavor to clarify and comprehend—if not to foster—the various interests and commitments of its students. Perhaps, ideally, such a school is a microcosm of present-day views on these fundamentally important topics.

Finally, liberal education is not training for detached love of learning, nor a passive appreciation of the commitment of others. Liberal education includes training for action, for taking part in one's community, for courageous self-giving according to one's gifts and perspective on reality and on the needs of one's community.

To maintain the liberal arts attitude in a college community, then, is to provide a situation in which the student will be able to acquire the love of learning if he does not already have it and will be encouraged to develop it if he does have it. He will be encouraged to respect and never to treat reductively or destructively what he does not spontaneously appreciate and to be active in his community according to his opportunities and preparation.

All aspects of the liberal arts college have the opportunity as well as the obligation to further these ideals. Students ought to demand liberal education and attention to the liberal arts dimension of all courses. Administration ought to provide clarity concerning the goals of liberal education, support for those who wish to clarify and develop liberal arts ideals, and correction for those who do not. And faculty ought to maintain the liberal arts attitude in their own intellectual lives, ought to call attention to the liberal arts dimension of what they teach, and ought to prod the students who are not dedicated to liberal arts ideals.

There is, however, one group within the academic community which stands in a particular relation to the maintaining of the liberal arts attitude. These are the chairpersons of the academic departments. Their special opportunities, obligations, problems, challenges, and expertise stem from their experience in this role. Within the department the chairperson ideally is an intellectual watchman, coordinator, and leader. He mediates between administration and department. He carries to the administration the wishes and needs of the department and carries to the department those of the administration. According to his own lights he will protect the members of his department. But also he will speak out or act on behalf of the administration if he judges such action to be required to save or to develop the liberal arts attitude in his community. It has been my experience that sometimes the right is on the side of the department; sometimes it is on the side of the administration; and sometimes, albeit not clearly, it is shared by both.

Why must the chairperson continually act to maintain the liberal arts attitude? How are the liberal arts ideals threatened? Whence come these threats? Perhaps these questions are best answered by drawing attention to four types of attitude toward education which are not compatible with the liberal arts attitude and which as chairperson I have tried to correct: the lack of a love of learning; the love of a particular area but the ignoring of all others; the love of one area and dislike of others; and the love of one and the acceptance or even love of others accompanied, however, by the desire to dominate them.

Where there is no love of learning all effort to become educated arises from ulterior purposes—for example, the desire for financial security or for vocational status. As chairperson I have met with this attitude on the part of faculty and administration who pressed for a practical or vocational emphasis in the classroom and for a totally vocationally oriented course selection on the part of students.

I have known an example of a faculty member who, paradoxically, interpreted philosophy as the history of ideas and yet rejected the fundamentally important history of science as of no value or at most of only historical value. This same instructor also was given to the explicit rejection of all language-philosophy as of no significance.
And I have known an example of the dislike of a particular aspect of liberal arts in a talented, enthusiastic teacher of aesthetics who explicitly deprecated mathematics and the mathematical sciences in his classes. Apparently for him there was no beauty in mathematics or in the sciences.

My own field of philosophy has provided a superb example of the acceptance along with the dominance of a particular fundamental aspect of liberal arts. I have in mind the proponents of language-philosophy who have taught that all use of language in poetry, theology, and metaphysics has an emotive or noncognitive meaning. A generation of students brought by in that view were hardly being encouraged to interpret these traditionally important areas according to their own lights. That is, they were not receiving a liberal education.

These are attitudes which, as chairperson interested in maintaining the liberal arts attitude in my own academic community and in my department, I have tried to correct or to prevent. These attitudes have many sources in our society. And no one can be sure he has discerned all the sources. Yet I have found that some understanding of these sources has been a help in my efforts to curtail if not eradicate the attitudes. I suggest that the following are some of the more important ones, and I will illustrate each one from my own experience.

First, like many—I am tempted to say most—adults in our culture the persons who teach in liberal arts colleges have themselves been victimized by the very education which ostensibly was to prepare them for their roles as educators. For example, I have a deep love for mathematics. I love it for its extensive usefulness in the study of nature and in the creativity of technology. I also love pure mathematics for its own sake. But I have been entirely on my own in maintaining this love and in becoming clear as to what it is that I love in mathematics. There have been two reasons for this state of affairs.

One is the incredibly bad teaching of the basic concepts of arithmetic and mathematics I encountered in the elementary school. This, of course, is an all too familiar story. In this school I acquired a deep-seated conviction that I could not learn these topics. Obviously this conviction was utterly false, for later I graduated from a large midwestern university with a Phi Beta Kappa key and honors, having majored in astronomy, physics, and mathematics. And certainly nothing that went on in the classroom gave me any idea at all of the importance of the basic concepts involved and of their enormous importance for the way we think about time, space, motion, and so on. I developed a dual attitude toward these great subjects. On the one hand, there was the miserable, totally unrewarding classroom experience. And on the other, was my secret delight in numbers and the miracle of their usefulness in virtually all aspects of our encounter with nature. Fortunately the second attitude triumphed and only this attitude remains now as I speak out whenever I have a chance in an endeavor to prevent great subjects from being ruined through inadequate presentation in the classroom.

Alas, however, my love for mathematics and for the mathematical sciences met another profound challenge at the university. I spent my undergraduate years in the College of Science, Literature, and the Arts—that is, in the liberal arts college of the university. The Department of Mathematics and the Department of Physics were shared by students from the School of Engineering, and their vocational needs determined entirely how the courses were taught. All courses were courses in problem-solving. This benefited the engineering students who were also given training in the practical use of these techniques. We liberal arts students, however, learned only how to solve theoretical problems without having either the supplementary practical training or the liberal arts foundation which alone could have illumined the concepts and the theory of the various aspects of mathematics. And it has been my experience that this vocational stress in ostensibly liberal arts courses remains.

This second point, of course, is related to the vocationalism which properly is seen not as opposing liberal education but rather as underlying and fulfilling it. This point follows as a corollary of the view that liberal education is preparation for participation in one's community. In my own academic community there has been an increase in the students' vocational emphases. And this is all to the good. Even in the 1960s I frequently had occasion to regret that many of our students—some of our most talented students—enjoyed their liberal arts courses and only on the eve of graduation asked what they would do next. That attitude has virtually disappeared from our campus. But at the same time our clarity concerning the liberal arts dimensions of all courses has not kept pace with this interest in vocational preparation for postcollege life.

This vocationalism which is not leavened by emphasis on the liberal arts dimension of college courses is a second source of threat to the liberal arts attitude. I suggest, however, that ideally this vocationalism can become a valuable challenge leading to the rethinking of the character and value of the liberal arts dimension of courses taught in college, and of the role of liberal education in our society. The liberal arts attitude has never been free from the threat of serious misunderstanding or rejection. Always it has had to adjust to

172 CRISES IN CAMPUS MANAGEMENT

current practical interests and always it has done so by having its roots firmly in the practical realities of the society which has fostered it. The liberal arts attitude is not a frill in our culture. It is a necessity in the maintaining and development of that culture.

In the third place, however, many a liberal arts college currently is itself a source of threat to the maintaining of the liberal arts attitude. This is so when the college fails to achieve clarity as to what it means at the present time to be a liberal arts college. Students are invited to attend such a college but are offered no clarity as to what kind of education they will get or what is the value of the education they are offered or how that education will differ from professional or vocational education. In part this means that the exclusiveness, the narrowness, and the dogmatism of the students often go unchallenged and even undetected. Certainly in this situation we cannot be sure that the students will discern a love of learning in their instructors and will be encouraged to develop their own love of learning. They are not offered the liberal education for which, ostensibly, they came to college and for which they have paid. They cannot be expected to achieve that intellectual leadership for which liberal education is a prerequisite.

Fourth, quite apart from the destructive effects of inadequate teaching in the preparatory years and the lack of clarity concerning liberal education, there is in some—perhaps many—academic persons an unregenerate view which is as powerful a threat as any to the liberal arts attitude. This is the view that what one does not value is without value and that where one does not find value there is no value. I myself fell into this perspective in respect to a number of areas of inquiry. And for this state of affairs I do not think that I can justly blame anyone else but myself. Having at first only an exclusive love of mathematics and the mathematical sciences, I had no interest in any of the other great areas of intellectual activity. Paradoxically some aspects of the philosophical creativity in aesthetics and metaphysics which are now of central importance in my teaching and in my personal intellectual life were then closed doors to me. It was only after some difficult years of intellectual development in which I learned to pay attention not only to the small areas of my competence but also to the vast areas of my ignorance that I grew out of this narrowness and began to acquire the liberal arts attitude. Hence, as chairperson I have seen as part of my role the pointing of the way out of intellectual narrowness.

Through the years I have come increasingly to believe that in order to counteract the threat to the liberal arts attitude I as chairperson have an obligation to remain alert to the diversity of student needs, preparation, aims, and aspirations and to see to it that as far as possible our department comes to terms with these. And I have found that this work is complex. It has involved trying to protect the student from the undesirable professional bias of faculty and from undesirable effects of campus politics. And, of course, of first importance is the obligation to provide education in all aspects of the complex field of philosophy.

An example of professional bias on the part of the instructor which interferes with the liberal education of the student is the instructor's dogmatism and intellectual narrowness. Thus, there is the instructor who believes that his interpretation of any one of the philosophical classics is the only legitimate interpretation. To be sure, he must believe this to carry on his own reflection and creativity. On the other hand, however, his failure to remind the students that there have been many interpretations not only of the value but of the very content of, say, the Platonic archetypes or Kant's aesthetics and that the value and the meaning of all creative works in philosophy have been a matter of controversy does not foster the liberal arts attitude in the student.

So far as my own field is concerned, closely related to the foregoing as a threat to the student's liberal education is the instructor's dogmatic interpretation of what constitutes philosophical inquiry and philosophical conclusions. The truth is that in every intellectual generation and in every culture, both Eastern and Western, philosophy has been interpreted in many ways. In this century, for example, philosophy has been interpreted as language analysis; phenomenological-existentialist inquiry into the human condition; the history of ideas properly informed by the view that all truth is relative to the culture and the generation; and the optimistic search for objective truth concerning man and reality, as in the work of Whitehead, Teilhard de Chardin, and Aurobindo. And there has been a great interest in the creative comparing, contrasting, and synthesizing of Western philosophical insights and concepts with those of China and India.

Properly the person who possesses a doctorate in philosophy is committed to one of these interpretations of the work of his discipline. And in the classroom and in informal discussion with students he will teach philosophy according to his own lights. Yet his own understanding of his philosophical teaching and creativity (if he undertakes any of the latter) requires understanding of the interpretations of philosophy which he rejects. And certainly he has an obligation to make it clear to his students that, while he has chosen one interpretation of philosophy, there are others. And he has not finished explaining to his students what any one type of philosophical activity is unless he has also made it clear how the several interpretations of philosophy differ among themselves. If, because of his bias, he is unwilling or unable to teach any one of them, then to that extent he is incapable of serving the liberal arts ideal. And in my opinion the chairperson has

work to do in protecting the students from that bias. Sometimes I have
chosen to make it clear to the students that the very bias of a particular faculty member is offset by his strong dedication to and skill in
carrying out one type of philosophical work. And in fact, I should
think that a great many—if not all—chairpersons of departments of
philosophy would be kept very busy coming to terms with this problem. For in this country the graduate schools of philosophy have most
often fostered a professional narrowness and dogmatism in their students.

Also I have found that closely related to the foregoing is the role
campus politics and the lack of proper professional ethics on the campus can play in fostering the narrowness and dogmatism which many
a faculty member brings with him to the campus. Ideally, the vital
liberal arts attitude pervading a campus, or at least a particular department, can do much to enable the young Ph. D. to overcome the
limitations engendered in him in graduate school. By fostering the
liberal arts attitude the academic community can do a great deal to
offset the effects of graduate school. The truth is, however, that it
is very easy for the community to miss this opportunity and to make
it difficult for the chairperson to develop this attitude in his department.

As one example of the foregoing I have seen the destructive effects of the social-political clique. Even our relatively friendly campus has provided me with some experience of the destructive effects
of such a clique. The clique can be powerful. I have known it to dominate important faculty committees; politick successfully in faculty
legislation; influence students in their course selection; and now and
then have the ear of the administration.

On joining the faculty young persons have been looked over for
membership in a clique. I do not mean to imply that there is anything
formal about this procedure; nonetheless this does describe what has
sometimes occurred. Since those willing to be part of—or on the
fringes of—a clique are virtually never those possessed of a liberal
arts attitude, membership in a clique is one of the worst things that
can befall the professional and intellectual development of the young
faculty member. Having made it socially, the faculty member may
come to the non sequitur that his current intellectual development is
already all he can desire. And if he is dogmatic, if he has a narrow
professional interest which he imparts to his students, if he has no
appreciation of professional stances different from his own, he sees
no reasons for change.

As a result the task of the chairperson in relation to his young
colleague may become very difficult. He has responsibility for the
intellectual development of the colleague. And he gets no help in this
project from some of the leaders of the academic community. Further,

there is sometimes the conviction that those who are outside the clique are of little value on the campus. This means that the opinions, criticisms, direction, and example of the chairperson may have little effect upon the instructor who is part of the clique.

Such attitudes on the part of department members may make difficult or even vitiate the chairperson's efforts to maintain the openness and absence of dogmatism which are essential to the liberal arts attitude. As a teacher of philosophy I have tried to make it clear what my interpretation of philosophical inquiry is and what it is not. And I have encouraged students to make their own choices among the many significant interpretations of philosophy. The best students are aware of and grateful for the freedom of choice given them and also for the clarity with which the choices are offered. Such achievement in the inculcation of the liberal arts attitude is lost, however, when elsewhere on campus or, perhaps, on another campus nearby the view of philosophy which informs my teaching is psychologized away or rejected or transformed into another view from which, in fact, it is entirely different.

These conditions can also make difficult the chairperson's task of keeping departmental offerings in touch with potential areas of professional concern. This is particularly true in philosophy where there is a tremendous lag between the interests of the professional philosophical community and the de facto concerns of the American public. Ecology is a case in point. Ecology has many philosophical aspects, and it is a disservice to the students to leave these out of philosophical instruction. When members of the Department of Philosophy do not spontaneously develop an interest in them, the chairperson has an obligation to provide leadership in this area. This can be difficult in many ways. For it means urging one's colleagues to go against the mainstream of professional interests. And, thus, it also means urging them to be a bit creative themselves.

One last point pertaining to the chairperson's relations to students and to his colleagues in his department: It is his obligation to give support, appreciation, and honest counsel. And above all, while being true to his own conception of his discipline, he must also be an example of openness toward other interpretations of that discipline and toward other disciplines. But it has been my experience that given the level of intellectual and spiritual development of the present-day academic community, he cannot count on receiving support, appreciation, and honest counsel in return. If, indeed, he does receive them from students and colleagues, he will count this a blessing. But he cannot expect these as a perquisite of his role in the department and on campus. And he must be ready at all times to function without them.

This leads to the important topic of the role of the chairperson in respect to the administration. And here a reciprocal relation is a necessity for successful leadership on the part of the chairperson. On the one hand, the chairperson has an obligation to deal honestly with the administration. If he supports administrative policy, he ought to say so, and his actions ought to be true to what he says. If he does not support administrative policies he ought to say that too. The truth is, however, that these direct, honest dealings between administration and chairperson do not always obtain. But, on the one hand, the chairperson who is an administrative lackey or who uses behind-the-scenes political techniques to achieve his ends or who creates anti-administration feeling while perhaps remaining aloof from campus problems himself does a disservice to the academic community. These actions fail to give examples of the courage, clarity, and integrity which properly are the marks of members of that community. And, on the other hand, one necessary (but not sufficient) condition for successful leadership of a department is administrative support or administrative disagreement which is free from politicking. Keeping lines of communication open between departments and administration, honest discussion of differences of perspective and opinion, direct dealing which eschews behind-the-scenes manipulation by some persons, and the acceptance of accountability must be worked at by both chairperson and administration. Both have necessary roles in the development of this relationship.

Finally a word about the means whereby the chairperson can fulfill his roles: In my experience there are three things which he can do. And he must use his own judgment as to which one or combination of them will be effective in any one case.

First, he can speak and act directly. He can be forthright and clear in faculty meetings; in consultation with administration; in departmental meetings; and, above all, in informal conversations with colleagues. Sometimes, of course, he will choose to remain silent, judging—perhaps rightly, perhaps wrongly—that the time for direct speech and action is not now. If he is angry and unable to hide his anger or if another is too angry for fruitful conversations, silence may be indicated. If he finds a little behind-the-scenes-politicking which involves his department, he learns that it is not always wise to point it out immediately and directly.

Fortunately, however, it is not only by direct speech and action that the chairperson can have an effect and carry out his work. Sometimes what in the way of dedication to the liberal arts attitude, to high ideals of professional ethics, or to the importance of a basic humaneness in the academic community students have learned in his classes they can impart to other students and even to faculty members and administration. And thus indirectly the chairperson has an effect on the campus. Also, he has an indirect effect in what he writes and publishes for the general readership and that which is read on his campus.

Third, and most important of all, the chairperson has an effect by his example. He tries to put into his words and his actions all that he believes and wishes to introduce into his academic community pertaining to the dedication to liberal arts. Of course, the chairperson himself is heir to the temptations, the uncertainties as to which course to take, and the errors that plague the academic personality—and, in fact, any personality. And he is very apt to be misunderstood when he is acting in terms of his own convictions. But his own eschewing of dogmatism constantly reminds him that he himself may see only in part and that what he believes he does comprehend may be partly or wholly in error. And, on the other hand, his remaining charitable when he is misunderstood and his remaining true to himself when only a few of his colleagues—or, perhaps none at all—agree with him is not the least of his tasks and obligations.

CHAPTER

16

**ADMINISTRATORS OF CHANGE:
THE DEVELOPMENT AND
ADMINISTRATION OF CAMPUS
CENTERS FOR OFFENDERS**
Samuel E. Kelly
Karen L. Morell

Since the 1960s, some educational institutions have made
attempts to serve groups who were outsiders to the educational process. Staff and faculty committed themselves in varying degrees to
forthcoming innovations, usually being most concerned and willing to
change for those groups more closely associated with dominant
American cultural norms. Divergent groups fell into projects which
came to be called high-risk programs. In higher education this meant
admitting students who traditionally would not have been found on
college campuses.

Programs were labeled high-risk because of the unpredictable
performance of the group involved. In continuing education classes
for middle-class white adults, a faculty or staff member could feel
assured to a great degree of the group's behavioral patterns and
academic background. Thus, they were not considered to be high-risk.
Students from the ghetto, barrio, or reservation, however, performed
in more erratic ways, at least in the eyes of their white teachers.
Most campuses made some commitment to serve the nontraditional
student, whom they frequently called disadvantaged. The programs
designed for them, however, are not only high-risk to the institutions
who inaugurated them. They are high-risk to the students because
there frequently is no commitment of dollars—hard money—and understanding to the student. The disadvantaged were often destined to fail
because they as individuals could not academically survive without
additional institutional effort or because the programs created for
them disappeared from the institution's budget. Other programs

Samuel E. Kelly, Vice President, and Karen L. Morell, Assistant Vice President, University of Washington.

vanished because the head administrator could not obtain access to anyone able to make decisions to advance the course of the program.

Most high-risk programs have similar beginnings and encounter many of the same obstacles in the struggle for survival and success. The administrator of any such program can expect to confront administrative problems which are magnified beyond those of other tasks because of the fear and skepticism of both the campus community and the public. What follows here is an account of the development and administration of a campus-based center for men and women who are either on early release from penal institutions or diverted from prison by a prosecutor or judge. Being perhaps the optimum of the high-risk projects, the situations confronted here epitomize the problem areas faced by the administrator of many high-risk programs.

LAUNCHING OF RESIDENT RELEASE PROJECT

The Resident Release Project began in January 1972, within the University of Washington's Minority Affairs Office, as an early-release educational program for offenders. It developed from the immediate needs of offenders on training release who were attending the University of Washington. (To be on work/training release means that an individual has been incarcerated and is now judged by corrections officials as ready for an early release date. The person released under these circumstances is still considered to be in the custody of the level of government having jurisdiction over the case. If the individual makes satisfactory progress while on work/training release, he or she will be accorded parole status.) The state Probation and Parole Office housed these offender-students at a local halfway house designed primarily for men on work release. The distance from campus, the physical environment, and the workingman's atmosphere did little to encourage the student's academic success.

During the fall quarter of 1971, Cons Unlimited (the ex-offender student organization on campus which included men and women on parole and postparole status) discussed their concerns with the university's vice president for minority affairs. This initial meeting was followed by a series of discussions with the university president (Dr. Charles Odegaard) and other members of his cabinet. Additionally, a series of impromptu meetings were held with interested faculty, legislative representatives, and professionals in the criminal justice system. These conferences were extremely beneficial and finally culminated in a contract with Probation and Parole. As time was of the essence, the university president and the vice president for miniority affairs jointly wrote the request for approval of the contract which was presented 48 hours later to the Board of Regents. This act alone was practically unprecedented and immediately suggested the interest and commitment of the university administration towards penal reform. Despite the precedent set by the controlling bodies on other state campuses that had denied permission for similar early release centers, the Resident Release Project was unanimously approved by the Board of Regents, after considerable discussion by the board, in January 1972.

From January 1972 through fall quarter, 1973, a total of 57 men and women entered the Resident Release Project. The following data indicates the number of students participating in the project; a breakdown by ethnicity, sex, and age; and results of the project.

1972 Participants		1973 Participants	
Winter	4	Winter	
		New	5
		Continuing	9
Spring		Spring	
New	3	New	7
Continuing	1	Continuing	7
Summer		Summer	
New	3	New	11
Continuing	2	Continuing	9
Fall		Fall	
New	13	New	11
Continuing	0	Continuing	8

Ethnicity of Participants		Sex		Age Range	
Asian	1	Men	49	High	59
Black	18	Women	8	Low	18
Chicano	3				
Native American	5				
White	30				

Status of Participants

Continuing from fall into winter	9
Transferred to another work/release facility	4
Arrested before returning to prison	6
Returned after a revocation hearing—no arrest	4
Paroled	34
Total	57

IMPORTANCE OF HIGH-LEVEL DIRECTION

The importance of high-level administrative direction and sustained support cannot be overemphasized with respect to the development of a release program. Without this degree of institutional commitment the release program more than likely will deteriorate and ultimately fail because it is unlikely to withstand the daily pressure from state, local, and campus officials, notwithstanding the pressure generated after an unfavorable incident occurs. The problems and successes of the program need to be heard directly by the president of the institution. In order to have access to the president and the proper leverage within the key decision-making bodies, the person who should have the ultimate responsibility for the program must be at the vice presidential or equivalent administrative level. Moreover, it is extremely helpful that the administrator have faculty rank as well in order to legitimize the recommendations and decisions from an administrative and faculty base.

At the University of Washington, the Office of Minority Affairs was the logical office to sponsor the release center because supportive services, financial aid, a reading/study skills center, and academic advising were already operational, and the existing staff was willing to commit itself to the program by working overtime to promote and assist the disproportionate number of minority people who are incarcerated.

Certainly not all those who aspire to develop a resident release program will find it expedient or possible to have a vice president who will have ultimate authority to administer the program; this is an optimal condition. In those instances where this cannot be achieved, the commitment and direction of an influential faculty member whose voice may be heard and respected at the highest levels of the university is of paramount importance in insuring the project's survival. In this situation the support and involvement of the student constituency, professionals in the criminal justice system, and empathetic civic leaders is extremely vital.

In addition to enlisting the support of the vice president for minority affairs in our program, Cons Unlimited gained the assistance of several faculty involved in the criminal justice system. If the initial proponents of a release center have not done this, we urge it upon the head administrator of the newly established program. Contacting several faculty assured us of the dissemination of information about the project to other professionals and the receipt of valuable advice in establishing the program. Faculty are a source of information about new research and local contacts, besides being the foundation for training programs needed by the many offenders wishing to reenter the criminal justice system as professional staff. An ad hoc committee of faculty was created by the vice president for minority affairs during the first year of the program in order to advise him and discuss the future involvement of the university in the criminal justice system.

Although our Minority Affairs and Resident Release Project staff succeeded in establishing a good rapport with most components of the criminal justice system during the first year of operation, the campus police were an exception. Much of the suspicion with which each office viewed the other could have been avoided if our staff had initially contacted and briefed the campus police. They should be informed before anyone is brought into the university in order to deter suspicion about supervision and establish areas of responsibility and procedures amongst probation and parole, police, and project staff. In our situation the police were not even in close contact with probation and parole staff. While the law in some areas may not require that a list of releasees be submitted to the campus police force, project and probation and parole staff improve their image by issuing such a list. The police are important to the success of the project not only because they must be called to make arrests and searches, when warranted, but because of their conduct towards project members. To a great degree the police determine the extent to which a resident feels he or she has the opportunity to start a new life. Police surveillance of the project can undermine its foundation: the residents' development of a life style which keeps them within the law.

Several events at the close of 1972 led to a series of meetings between the heads of Minority Affairs and the police; the police chief was concerned about frequent changes in probation and parole officers and Resident Release Project staff and was suspicious, rightly so, of the involvement of one member in a few local burglaries. Since then the relationship between the three agencies has improved considerably. In return for providing basic information to the police, it is now possible for administrators in Minority Affairs to obtain satisfaction from them when any of the staff are overly anxious to supervise or harass project members.

Another group which should be contacted at the beginning of the program are the concerned, progressive business and civic leaders. This is another area in which our Minority Affairs and project staff could have improved. So much time was required during 1972 and early 1973 to establish the program on campus that staff were unable to venture outside and inaugurate new relationships. We can only hope that the experience of our project and similar programs will curtail the settling down period of other programs to permit them to begin their community involvement at an earlier stage. Empathetic members of the larger community, if adequately informed, can begin informally to provide the information which other citizens need to alleviate their fears of release centers and can create a forum to reduce misinformation about community-based corrections. When proposed local or state legislation affects releasees, this group can lend its name to encourage or hinder the proposal. Of most immediate consequence to project members, many individuals in the community group can be relied upon to provide jobs or a site for training or field work. If project members are to be reintegrated into the community, the program cannot maintain the university's traditionally isolated posture towards the larger population.

CONSULTANTS HIRED

In the initial stages of program development the Minority Affairs Office hired consultants with traditional academic credentials to assist in the review of the pertinent literature, exploration of funding possibilities, grant writing, and the development of contacts at the local, state, and national level. While ex-offenders were important for contact development, there were none available who had the skills acquired through years of exposure to academic discipline and professional social contact. While a truism, it is worth reiterating that the expertise and sensitivity of the academician and the ex-offender are quite different. The Minority Affairs Office, however, has found the two not only compatible but vital to the success of a release center. In planning for the Resident Release Project we requested that Cons Unlimited articulate the needs of offender-students to the conventionally trained staff who then wrote the first proposal for funding. This does not imply that the ex-offenders could not write or argue their own case. The fact that they could is evidenced by the Minority Affairs Office and other university and government personnel becoming interested in the first place. However, one must possess specialized skills and be conversant with the operation of universities and governments to assemble and process grants and contracts. This point had to be argued and occasionally insisted upon with some ex-offenders.

During the first year of operation (with the exception of a temporary part-time worker) the first-line staff were ex-offenders affiliated with Cons Unlimited. The first project director and members of Cons Unlimited began their work with the project believing in the erroneous notion that they knew how to provide for the offender-students and thus needed little direction or training. If the Minority Affairs Office could provide financial aid and academic advising, Cons Unlimited members believed they could do the rest. Unfortunately, their good faith and expertise were not sufficient. Their efforts were thwarted by their lack of administrative experience. The amount of record keeping and program administration required to operate a release center precludes the exclusive use of dedicated but untrained individuals. There is no doubt that ex-offenders should be a major component of the staff and that every effort must be made in recruiting

qualified ex-offenders for the various positions, but one should not
consign a program to failure because of the fallacious principle that
it takes one to assist one.

The administrative and supervisory difficulties which resulted
from the utilization of untrained staff contributed to or caused a high
staff turnover during the first year and a half. The first director of
the Resident Release Project left in August 1972 (after being employed
in that capacity for only five months); an acting director replaced him
until December. Subsequently, a new director remained two months,
was removed and replaced temporarily by the supervisor of the Asian
and Poverty Division within Minority Affairs, the most senior division
supervisor and a man of proven administrative ability. He was the
first key staff member who was not an ex-offender. While assigned to
the project he developed operational procedures affecting all phases
of the program from recruiting and screening to academic counseling
and rules for project members. After four months as acting director,
he codified these procedures in an Operations Manual and turned over
the directorship to an ex-offender who had proven his leadership abilities while inside prison and who had some administrative experience.
During the last half of 1973 this director developed stability and a
sense of purpose amongst project members and staff.

In concise terms, the director of the Resident Release Project
reports to the assistant vice president for minority affairs, in supportive services, who in turn reports to the vice president for minority
affairs, who ultimately must bear the responsibility for the program.
The vice president for minority affairs is assisted by the special assistant and director of the Prisoner Education Program, who is responsible for the establishment of policy, community relations,
funding, faculty participation, and state and national contacts. The
evolution and final organization of the Resident Release Project staff
component was not accomplished without some degree of difficulty,
as was the case in the development of the entire Office of Minority
Affairs. Indeed, in the development of both many of the same variables
were present: occasionally irate, rhetorical, and disfunctional tactics
from student groups and indifference, recalcitrance, and suspicion at
varied faculty and administrative levels.

FUNDING

The options available for funding a release project will vary
considerably among different campuses. In all probability, many
different sources will need to be explored, and this will require a
considerable amount of staff time.

The Resident Release Project was first supported almost entirely by Office of Minority Affairs funds. These monies were carved out of the office's budget through a series of internal readjustments which did not completely cover the new program. The unanticipated addition of the Resident Release Project with concomitant increased staff requirements was of such impact that it necessitated a major biennial budget revision to obtain the additional funds needed.

The contract with the state Office of Probation and Parole provided limited assistance to the operational expenses from January 1, 1972, through June 30, 1973. The request to them came in the midst of the biennium and thus little else could be expected. Since more funds were necessary to operate the project, staff began exploring various funding options. A variety of plans were outlined, some with academic departments having major responsibility for the grant, others with Minority Affairs solely involved. What evolved was a small request by Minority Affairs to the National Institute of Mental Health (NIMH) which provided some staff costs, travel to the prisons, and office expenses between August 1, 1972, and December 31, 1972. This additional funding allowed one of the consultants referred to above to become director of the Prisoner Education Program and special assistant to the vice president for minority affairs. The Resident Release Project was and continues to be the major component of the Prisoner Education Program, but beginning August 1972, the Office of Minority Affairs became increasingly involved in other phases of the criminal justice system.

During the five months of NIMH funding, the director of the Prisoner Education Program and other staff wrote and lobbied for a major grant from the state Law and Justice Planning Office, the distributor of Law Enforcement Assistance Act (LEAA) funds. This grant was approved and became effective January 1, 1973. Not only did it permit the hiring of three full-time and three part-time staff, which were necessary if the project was to grow, but it also paid the room and board of the project members. The initial plan for 1973 had actually included a provision by the Division of Vocational Rehabilitation for payment of all student financial aid. The capricious allocation and release of federal dollars, however, forced that agency to withdraw from the total package we had hoped to present when requesting LEAA funds. Because of the consistently uncertain flow of dollars from the federal government for student financial aid and because of the unpredictability of some campus financial aid offices, we strongly recommend that any plans for a release center take into account the entire financial needs of the future residents. Even with a most cooperative financial aid office, Prisoner Education Program staff has to devote an inordinate amount of time each quarter to, first, determining the capability of the financial aid office (which constrains the number of residents admitted), second, assisting the prospective resident in filling out the complicated forms, and, third, working as liaison between the residents and the financial aid office to assure the satisfaction of both parties.

Many difficulties in securing a source of funding are grounded in a common posture of the potential funding agency or department. Campus and, primarily, government personnel invariably seem to sidestep the assumption of financial responsibility for a release program in their office by claiming that such programs are someone else's responsibility. City, county, and state governments persist in the argument that one of the other two has jurisdiction. Campuses may reject appeals for funding because of reaction to those citizens who want the campus out of the business of rehabilitation altogether. Some believe the offender is taking their child's rightful place in the classroom and thus perpetuate the syndrome of "You have to be a slant eye, a nigger, or a bank robber to go to college these days." A release program needs financial commitment from both the campus and a level of government. Some hard money from each must be present at the beginning of the program, both as an act of faith to each other and the offender and for the match required for most grants. Indeed, as previously suggested, the demise of many high-risk programs came from lack of hard dollar commitment.

ADMISSIONS, RECRUITING, AND SCREENING

The Minority Affairs program was founded on the principle of guaranteeing access to higher education at the University of Washington to those groups who have been historically denied admission by the standardized admissions process. For minority students the traditional criteria of admission were often not valid predictors of success. Because the University of Washington, along with many other major universities and campuses, has a ceiling on its enrollment, some factions of the university community have questioned the validity of selective admissions. The experience gained as a result of program development for the Office of Minority Affairs was extremely valuable in providing the philosophical base and support for the Resident Release Project's admission policy.

Selective admissions procedures had been applied at the University of Washington in the past in dealing with admissions for students in the athletic and fine arts areas. This concept was extended in 1968 to embrace the basic philosophical tenets of the program for special students which then ultimately grew into the Office of Minority Affairs. The promulgation of this philosophical tenet to include the Resident

Release Project was a decision made by the vice president for minority affairs and ultimately supported by the president and other key administrators and faculty. It assumes that many of society's outcasts who have suffered incarceration for a year or more and who attempt to establish themselves in the existing society suffer from a high degree of alienation, frustration, and complete rejection. We are prepared to argue that regardless of color this disjunction from society, frequently coupled with a history of low socioeconomic status, is a criteria for minority status.

Efforts to secure the cooperation of university units involved with admissions proceeded far more swiftly than our attempts to work with personnel in the correctional institutions who are responsible for assisting residents in obtaining work/training release status. Part of the difficulty with the correctional institutions was a consequence of our staff making initial contact with the counselors and case workers, instead of talks originating with key administrators. At the beginning of our second year, we arranged a meeting, with the key personnel of the institutions, which we should have done at the beginning of the first year. After this meeting and visits of our administrative staff to the institutions, corrections personnel identified specific staff as contacts for us at their institution. Perhaps most importantly, the staff and administrators at the prisons became less suspicious of the Resident Release Project after having the opportunity to hear about the operation of the project and to ask questions to clarify rumors about our policies and treatment of residents.

As a result of our experience we would recommend that the highest ranking campus administrator possible write to the correctional institutions or other agencies to outline the program and request an appointment to brief the warden or other key staff. During the meeting, campus representatives can discuss their general philosophy and procedures in addition to requesting a commitment to cooperate with the educational institution. Brochures and other information about entry into the project can be left with the warden, head counselor, and educational director for distribution to other staff. Specific arrangements should be made with the institution staff to distribute literature and disseminate information to the residents.

The campus project director and staff need to firmly establish, and then monitor, a rapport with all of the institutions' counselors; without their cooperation and interest, the project cannot receive a reliable recommendation about an applicant. During our first year we discovered that a disinterested counselor may recommend an applicant who is disruptive, thereby removing him from the correctional institution.

In most states the process of gaining early release is troublesome and seen by the resident as fraught with irrational and arbitrary decisions. Many state officials have the power to block applications. Project staff need to identify the convoluted route on which an application is sent, who can stop it, and where appeals can be made. The head administrator should secure from the probation and parole office and the correctional institution the assurance that the campus office will receive word on whether an applicant is rejected and why. Obtaining this information makes officials accountable and prevents exclusion based only on the two words so frequently heard, "bad attitude."

Our experience shows that corrections staffs are especially prone to using these words to describe minority offenders. Doing so shuts the gate for many minorities who wish to participate in release programs. One reason why the Minority Affairs Office accepted responsibility for the Resident Release Project was to work towards the early release of highly visible ethnic minority offenders. Based on the general population, there is a disproportionately high number of ethnic minority people in prison. From the time of their arrest, if not before, minority people are often denied equal opportunity to participate in special projects and programs. Completion of education and training programs often means the difference between adhering to society's laws or returning to crime. Studies indicate that minorities are less likely to be diverted from the courts into a parole or probation system than middle- and upper-class whites. Projects involved in diversion need to be aware of this. We urge new projects to devote extra energy to assure that ethnic minority offenders are fairly considered at all stages of screening and processing.

For the project's own protection, the campus's contract with the state must give the educational institution the right to reject an applicant not only for educational but personal background. The resident would, of course, be informed of the rationale for rejection. Thus, along with the screening done by the state, the project must make its own assessment.

The Resident Release Project has one staff member responsible for liaison with the institutions to effect recruiting and screening. He provides information about the university and the project to staff and residents and interviews all applicants several times. The statements of ex-offender staff and present project members are added to those of the liaison officer to provide a dimension for screening not often found in the state's selection process. Project members usually know an applicant's reputation inside the prison walls, or they can find out about it rather easily. Release centers frequently have members who were cleared for release not because they had the greatest potential for it but because they had mastered the art of deception. Former residents have the best knowledge of who is sincere and who is "running a game" on the counselors. In fact, they may have knowledge on a resident's involvement in contraband inside the walls of which the staff of the institution is apparently unaware. Applicants seeking diversion to the project in lieu of prosecution or incarceration should be subjected to the standard interviews and checks on personal history.

RULES

The Resident Release Project, through necessity, was hastily assembled; thus, except for custody regulations spelled out in the university's contract with the state, the staff devised rules and operational procedures as the need arose. These are far from optimum conditions for the development of a high-risk program. Perhaps because of the project having no more than five members at any one time during the first three quarters, the ex-offender staff acted on the belief that they knew what should be condoned in individual situations in order to give each project member the maximum opportunity for self-development.

We learned that this degree of flexibility can become self-indulgence for both staff and residents. The staff so empathized with the resident's desire to be free again that they either encouraged a permissive situation with which the resident was unable to cope at that time or they excused a violation of the rules which on occasion developed into a more gross infraction. Project staff now believe that because the residents have left a highly structured environment, both in terms of formal and informal codes of behavior, the residents have even more difficulty adjusting if they are suddenly confronted with a lax environment. In conceptual terms, probably the best case for early-release centers is that they provide the opportunity for a bridge between an autocratic, regimented existence and the relative freedom of society. The center must keep the offender from getting the bends upon reentry.

The present rules for the project were developed during meetings between project members and the staff of Probation and Parole, Minority Affairs, and the Resident Release Project. They reflect a belief in the necessity to give the individual every opportunity for responsible self-directed action after the person has passed through an initial adjustment period. Certainly some individuals are ready immediately upon release for the greatest autonomy allowed by the state, but, since many are not, group morale and stability require the same orientation period for all. Members must immediately recognize that the staff will provide similar opportunities as well as disciplinary action to all members. The favoritism found in many penal institutions cannot be allowed to enter a release center. During an orientation period of several weeks, when there are more restrictions, the members need to be given a clear understanding of what they must and can do, and what will happen if they do not.

Individual progress is considered by a review board which has power to effect the concept of graduated responsibility. This board consists of the director, parole officer, counselor, and two project members. A majority decision determines guilt or innocence and any disciplinary action. When the board agrees that an individual is prepared to accept more responsibility, it can allow the student to be ruled by another preestablished set of guidelines. All new rules, however, follow those regulations established by Probation and Parole for work/training release centers.

An infraction of the rules is reported by the staff member on duty to the project director and the parole officer. If the offense is severe but does not entail police action or if it is the latest in a series of lesser infractions, the director and/or parole officer will call the review board into session. If the offense is judged sufficiently serious, the board can recommend that the parole officer call a revocation hearing. (The hearing can also take place at the request of only the parole officer or project director.) We have found that participation of project members on the board allows for a review by peers, thus increasing the acceptance of the decision by other residents. Their involvement also encourages active participation in the group's operation and progress. As a result, members are more likely to feel that their concerns will be heard, thereby reducing the number of gripes heard by the administrator.

Administrators need to be seen as responsible advocates of the residents' rights. If the state has not developed a plan of civil rights for offenders, the staff at the center need to obtain a legal opinion to ensure that due process is written into any decision regarding the transfer or revocation of a resident's assignment to the center. Promoting these rights makes the center closer to society than prison and encourages an image of the administrators and staff as individuals concerned with the residents' welfare and hence not remote authority figures.

UTILIZING CAMPUS HOUSING

Members of the University of Washington's Resident Release Project have been housed in a coed dormitory. The ex-offenders who lent their expertise to creating the program all believed that such a living situation would be conducive to successful reentry. The advice seemed reasonable to all the planners who saw that the integration in daily student life would assist in removing the members' sense of being branded forever as convicts. After establishing the residents in the dormitory, however, several staff, including initial advocates of dormitory living, questioned this arrangement. It was proposed that a house be found off campus. Because of staff time required to locate such a facility and the additional headache of hiring staff for cooking and maintenance, administrators decided to wait until more experience had been acquired with the release center and then to reassess the situation.

At the close of fall quarter, 1973, staff, residents, and administrators discussed the advantages and disadvantages of dormitory living. There was a unanimous decision to remain in the present facilities. Previous objections by staff were based on assumptions of incompatibility of residents and other students and increased difficulty of supervision. During two years of operation both assumptions proved false. Present staff realize that if a resident wants to violate rules or even escape, he or she will be able to do it whether in a dormitory or a private house, or even a prison. A few exits more or less make very little difference. At the beginning of the project ex-offender staff feared that differences in experience and, occasionally, age would cause friction between residents and other dormitory students. The few occasions when this has developed have been offset by an equal number in which residents have been elected to office within the student board of the dormitory.

Offices for project staff are now adjacent to the residents' quarters in the dormitory. Formerly they were the equivalent of a block away in the student activities building. The present arrangement facilitates staff and resident communication to such a degree that we would urge it upon all projects. Initially, some residents protested what they called the big brother approach of staff moving into their territory. It did indeed increase staff knowledge of residents' activities. Within a month, however, residents were sharing information about themselves and other residents, which they had never done before, even to an all ex-offender staff. The convict code (not telling on another) was broken for the benefit of all residents. Now situations can be confronted before they become serious problems for one or more residents.

EVALUATION

It is not our intent to describe how a campus-based release center should be evaluated but rather to call attention to its importance and the necessity for keeping records required in evaluations. To do more would be presumptuous since many special commissions and committees presently exist throughout the country whose sole purpose is to recommend criteria for evaluating community-based corrections programs.

During our two years of operation, the entire Prisoner Education Program has been subjected to the review of an outside evaluator contracted by us and to a statewide evaluation of work/training release facilities. The former was designed to assess the degree to which we had achieved the 1973 goals of the Prisoner Education Program as financed through the LEAA grant. It necessitated interviews with residents, staff, administrators, and faculty, but no audit or statistical review. The state review team studied records of expenditure and supervisory operations but not the attainment of goals. No one has yet evaluated the program in terms of either the residents' rate of recidivism compared to that of other programs or its long-range contribution to society. As professionals in the criminal justice system are aware, not merely the latter but the former are very difficult to assess.

Most administrators of release centers will not be well enough versed in corrections to enter the controversy on how to accomplish evaluation. They can, however, oversee the maintenance of records. The director of the Prisoner Education Program devised a questionnaire for Resident Release Project members which makes basic background information on residents readily available. It includes questions on educational history, attitudes towards education, conviction history, and more personal history. In addition to this questionnaire, Probation and Parole staff provide periodic revision of the status of former project members. Staff gather the quarterly GPA and a biannual review of former project members from the files of the university registrar. Following the path of former residents is difficult but must be done. Applicants for federal and state grants are finding the government's requirements for follow-up and the agony of producing it all too true.

Administrators need to be aware of new federal or, perhaps, state and campus guidelines relating to safeguarding the testing of human subjects. Prisoners have been among those most abused by medical doctors and social scientists. Any questionnaire administered by the project and the documents collected by faculty or outsiders as they scrutinize members of the project should be reviewed by the campus's Human Subjects Review Board. If such a board does not exist, a state or federal board should consider the proposed test.

CONCLUSION

A release center cannot succeed without a high degree of mutual respect among the administrator, the staff, and the offender-students. These students are aware of the hostility towards the program, always present in some quarters, which spreads quickly whenever an incident occurs. We have experienced the repercussions of a few minor incidents which led to the arrest of a few present and former project members. Unfortunately this kind of event not only reaches the papers and stirs up the public, but it also unnerves some officials responsible for overseeing similar state or local programs and leads them to impose more oppressive regulations or prompts them to question the existence of those projects. The project members know the program is vulnerable. They must have confidence in the administrators' commitment to the program and willingness to become a personal advocate of it.

On one occasion administrators of the Resident Release Project were informed by a state official that a candidate for state office intended to create an issue by publicizing the one sensational, illegal act of a project member which led to his incarceration. The candidate apparently wanted to gain the public's attention by recalling the act and stating that such a man was now a member of a state-sponsored program and living as a student on the University of Washington campus. Fortunately pressure from members of the candidate's party succeeded almost completely in keeping the story out of the press. During the two days when this outcome was in doubt, administrators had to be on call twenty-four hours a day in order to meet with project members and speak with influential people in the candidate's party. It was clear at the first meeting with the project that most residents were withdrawing to ward off the apparently inevitable decision that would send them all back to prison. They had learned to expect nothing from administrators, even protection. The key administrator must meet with project personnel every few months if for no other reason than to reassure them of the high-level administrative commitment to the program.

Project members and staff, especially the ex-offenders, function better if they see a constant display of empathy, sensitivity, and courage from the administrators. The latter must be careful not to confuse these qualities with permissiveness. Frequent contact among administrators, staff, and residents allows one to gauge whether a staff member or resident needs more direction and support or whether the person is abusing privileges and responsibilities. Our experience has shown that some offenders or ex-offenders who are acting irresponsibly can change if stopped early enough, reminded of the consequences, and given well-directed tasks. This, of course, can be true for non-offenders as well but seems particularly true for offenders. Administrators of release centers need to devote extra time and provide additional opportunities for offenders and ex-offenders but need to be prepared occasionally for suffering the consequences of misplaced confidence.

It takes courage and perhaps a bit of bravado to decide to create and administer a release center. These qualities are often found on the athletic field but not the administrative quarter of a campus. If an administrator recognizes that the majority population and a smaller group have failed to adjust and benefit from each other in society, that administrator can make a contribution to the community by reassembling campus resources in order to bring the smaller group in. Both groups can benefit from this synthesis.

The prison system in this country has failed to change for the better the lives of those sent to its facilities. Educational opportunity as an alternative to incarceration is an option whose merits should be more thoroughly explored. Our experience indicates that because of minority or low income status of many project members, education had not been seen as an option. Administrators can change this by creating release centers and monitoring the selection of individuals for the program. Education can provide the stimulation and the opportunity within society to raise the offender's sense of self-worth without having to resort to tactics which harm others. It has taken 200 years to see that penitentiaries do not create penitents. It has taken a life-span to understand that corrections have not corrected. It is time for affirmative and responsive action on the part of all sectors of society toward a cooperative effort to bring about sound changes in one of the most regressive areas of our civilization.

Change is inevitable and human organizations must adapt to survive. But why have some institutions responded to that challenge and others faltered? Are some organizations and individuals simply victims of circumstances beyond their control or do they contribute to the success or failure of their goals? What can or should be done to anticipate and monitor the direction and intensity of conditions that affect each academic community? Where such planning and analysis is ongoing, what usually is done with it? Do the better colleges and universities prove to be those which simply face up to the realities of the times? Suffice it to submit that the phenomenon of change is crucial to the survival and growth of human activity on the one hand, and it is fundamental in the decline or demise of others on the other hand. Thus it is a matter of serious consideration, especially among those members of organizations threatened by the advent of rapidly accelerating events.

As made applicable on campus in the study here by Jones, is learning also a function of changing conditions, educational as well as societal? If so, why is it that most efforts in teaching and research, not to mention administration, continue to be pursued in the traditional manner? Why, in the arena of scholars dedicated to the pursuit and dissemination of knowledge, is it so often necessary to secure governmental and eleemosynary support to rekindle the fire of learning? Could the innovative crank in this case have been turned without a grant, or indeed by someone other than the institutional chief executive? What do these circumstances suggest about the nature of academe? Have the students really changed, the faculties, or the times? And if all have changed, what accounts for the lack of similar innovation elsewhere?

Change agents, attractive though the characterization be at first blush, are not always positive expeditors of means towards organizational ends. Often their professional and personal aspirations intervene and effectively thwart the attainment of prescribed missions. For example, administrative preoccupation with comparative measurements may hinder rather than promote the cause of education, as suggested by the Brown study. Are such exercises in program justification usual or unique among colleges and universities today and, if so, who or what is chiefly responsible for the indulgence in rationalization? Is cost effectiveness really an appropriate standard of accomplishment in higher education, or might nonmonetary indices be more relevant?

Even if the former is preferred, why the primary reliance on cost per credit hour? Is supply and demand data all that should be considered in decisions affecting the learning process? What other variables may be equally as relevant? Are not some decisions on the campus basically academic and others fundamentally administrative, and should not the weight of the input be proportionate with the burden of responsibility? Or is wisdom solely a byproduct of relative standing in a hierarchy?

The maintenance of a professional attitude or liberal arts perspective towards the challenge of change is a special province of the academic chairperson, as defended in the Rose study. Is the inference valid that academicians have unique responsibilities, apart from those attendant to administrators? To what extent do line and staff managers operate accordingly? Is there such a clear dichotomy on most campuses? Are the dispositions of educators today generally compatible with the liberal arts attitude. Or has vocational study and the age of specialization preempted the love of learning? To what extent has the exigency of employment, for teacher and student alike, colored and narrowed the content of a well-rounded education? Does this suggest that perhaps the time has come to reclassify the forms of postsecondary learning, and frankly to distinguish academic from trade preparation? As a step in that direction, perhaps we need to reconsider the purposes of higher education.

Modern institutions of higher learning cannot escape their day in court; nor can they evade the embattled arena of public policymaking. Moreover, our colleges and universities cannot ignore increasing demands to remedy the problems of the larger society. To what extent can and should the academic community meet that obligation? The study by Kelly and Morell offers one rather courageous response, and at the same time prompts a bevy of pertinent questions. Is it the proper role of higher educational institutions to seek and facilitate solutions to all dilemmas in organized society? Or should academe be content in wrestling with the challenges directly affecting the halls of ivy? If not at the campus gate, the boundaries of a nearby ghetto, the police station or the prison wall, the unemployment line or the adjacent hospital, just where does one draw the line of the concern of higher education? Is there no limit to its purview, and is this then the essence of universality? Magnanimous though that be, what of the resources and competency of most academic centers in responding to such needs; if not adequate should they therefore be ignored? Is education a campus-bound concept or should it be offered without regard to site or condition of learners?

From all the foregoing it is evident that higher education is meeting many of the challenges of change. It can also be deduced that many academic institutions tend to falter under the strain. But that which is more intriguing is the circumstance of responsiveness and failure. Who or what is responsible for positive and negative action? Why do some institutions make meaningful strides under such conditions while others languish? What needs to be done internally and externally to improve the capacity and effort of every college and university? Why, indeed, must these questions be posed?

Periodically in the preceding pages we have had the occasion to allude to the external environment of the college and university system. The implication to be drawn was not unclear: institutions of higher learning, whereever their locale and whatever their kind, are interdependent with society and only as effective as they are serviceable to those in need. This is particularly true of their relations with immediate off-campus communities, from the town to nation-state. Thus the gown is by no means isolated in the confines of the campus and, with perhaps a few exceptions, all that it embodies tends to reach audiences and clientele far beyond its physical boundaries and formal enrollment. Thus it is appropriate that in this concluding segment of case studies we acknowledge the importance of town-gown relations and also illustrate the opportunities and tensions inherent therein.

First, and pointedly, Richard P. Bailey relates an experience which is not common among front offices on campuses across the country. In addition to pointing up a privilege and opportunity of higher administrators, Bailey reminds all that education is a process not limited to classrooms and students. An effort at expanding the horizon and context of education is next discussed by Margaret F. Heyse. From a planning and decision viewpoint, not to mention one of learning philosophy, it will be interesting to note the number and variety of complications arising out of this extension of an educational program.

Ralph C. John thereafter examines and relates a rather weighty issue between and among the academic community, the church, and the state. Suffice it to say that judicial notice of the fact that public policy greatly affects the campus is literally taken, and it is fitting that efforts are made to channel its development pursuant to institutional goals. Finally, Winthrop C. Libby addresses the subject of responsible judgment on campus and off. His concluding plea for understanding is timely, for the lessons and advice should not soon be forgotten.

17

**A PRESIDENTIAL
EDITORIAL COLUMN**
Richard P. Bailey

Administrators should be seen and heard.

I confess that I believe in high personal profile; I practice that belief unashamedly. If I had nothing to say, or were too bashful to give my opinion on assorted social phenomena, I would not be a college administrator, certainly not a college president.

One of the few advantages of "presidenting" is that one is assigned a soapbox and, standing on it, one can usually muster a "class" if often only of modest size and miniscule interest. I utilize the soapbox the position offers.

I write a presidential column, published irregularly on the editorial page of the Minneapolis Star. If the editorial column appears on a dull rainy evening its readership might surpass 100,000 in what is known as the largest daily newspaper in the upper Midwest. Men have been known to float over Niagara Falls before smaller groups and I am willing to risk ridicule and professional disrepute for the opportunity of speaking to a "class" of such magnitude.

For my efforts I receive $25 for each article published, and a thick file of flowers and brickbats. The intangible reward is spiritual satisfaction; I speak to thoughtful people, thousands of them, at "attitude adjustment hour," between Walter Cronkite and dinner.

Over one period of 20 months I wrote, and Star Editorial Page Editor Harold Chucker published, 25 articles. They averaged 750 words in length and can be classified as critical comment on education (6); miscellaneous humor with a slight educational twist (5); commentary on students (5); history of education back in my olden days (4);

Richard P. Bailey, President, Hamline University.

commentary on teachers (2); social-political controversy with a slight
education twist (2); and commentary on parents (1).

"(The articles) deal with human situations that are ever with us.
So much of the real stuff of life that surrounds us all each day goes
unnoticed because of the pots that are boiling over on the front of the
stove," wrote Mrs. Carl Ryberg of Jackson, Minnesota in the Star's
Letters to the Editor column. "Thanks to you, and to him." I don't
know Carl Ryberg, but I consider him a lucky guy!

Editor Chucker invited me to write the editorial column after he
had reprinted an article I wrote describing my seventh and eighth grade
teacher for the Hamline alumni magazine. She was "the woman who
entered my life" in 1936, Mrs. Kathryn Jennings. In that first article
I noted:

> Kate excelled in teaching word problems, sentence dia-
> gramming and the Palmer Method of penmanship. She
> seemed to me, in the year that "How to Win Friends and
> Influence People" was first published, about as relevant
> as a Thursday evening prayer meeting.
>
> It was not only the weekly sales of the (Saturday Eve-
> ning) Post that were important to me. I also sold a tabloid,
> Grit. I delivered the Dixon Evening Telegraph. I earned
> $1.20 a week delivering milk for Krug Dairy. And on Sat-
> urday I could scrounge 50 cents worth of scrap iron from
> back yards and vacant garages. Then in the spring I could
> earn 15 cents an hour cutting asparagus from 4 to 8 in the
> morning. In a good year I could plan on an income of $100.
> Relevancy was ambition, a charming smile, a 28-inch
> bicycle, a sharp knife, and a knowledge of back alley de-
> posits of scrap iron. Relevancy was not word problems,
> sentence diagramming, the Palmer Method and particularly
> not Kate Jennings. She sneered at Zane Grey and would
> not allow Horatio Alger's books on classroom library
> shelves. She had no apparent friends and she influenced
> us little people with a tyranny Dale Carnegie would have
> found totally unacceptable.
>
> Kate Jennings took sadistic delight, it seemed, in
> driving me to solve problems concisely, to write and
> speak with grammatical correctness and to discover that
> every accomplishment in life was not to be mine. Thiry-
> six years later when I slop through facts to an emotional
> answer, when I write or speak loosely and ineffectually
> and when I brag of personal accomplishments, I hear Kate
> saying: 'Richard, that will not do.'

Two of the columns raised up a paroxysm of disagreement. In one I reported: "Resign! You stupid jerk. You need psychiatric help. Don't you dare go to the polls, you Pinko."

In the same column I pointed out that a credibility gap existed between the man-on-the-street and educators:

My friends in other professions do not get the assistance
I do. Who helps the clergyman at a Christening? Where
is a critic in surgery? Who corrects and revises a judicial
opinion? Who in his right mind "discusses" a speeding
ticket?

I compared the gap to that which existed in a presidential election year between voters and "two incredible presidential candidates." For whom, then, should I vote? Since everyone knows you can trust a doctor—"AMA, that is, not NEA"—I admitted that I would cast my vote for Dr. Spock.

In the other column, which generated even greater heat, I took a stand beside Associate Justice Harry Blackmun, a friend and former Hamline trustee, following his written majority Supreme Court opinion on abortion: "There are moments when I want to stand beside someone I admire for no better reason than that he's right." I added, "The association is good for me."

On that flaming issue the letters (to the editor) ran ten-to-one against me. The local Catholic bulletin denounced me in an editorial (in fairness, Editor Chucker reprinted it on the Star's editoral page) without ever naming me. I was the "ill-tempered . . . president of a Twin Cities area private college," a "much-quoted college president," a "modern educator" (the unkindest cut of all), an "outspoken defender of Justice Blackmun," and a "degree-laden pedagogue."

Without altering my opinion of either the 1972 presidential candidates or abortion as a personal decision, I confess that neither column was appropriate. The advice to steer clear of religion and politics is good if men's minds are to be reached from an unsteady soapbox. I do not rule out either subject as fair game for open discussion but I do now (too late) admit that I should not have introduced them in an educational column for general readership.

There is too much chance for misunderstanding; too much emotional fog; too little education possible. I was wrong, and that's about as humble as a "modern educator" can be.

Editor Chucker and I get together regularly for lunch. We talk over the columns published, readers' reactions, and a list each of us keeps of possible subjects for future editorial treatment. Those luncheons are an added bonus; how else would I have a chance to visit with the brilliant but busy editor of a powerful newspaper? In what other way could he justify the time he takes to discuss issues with one of 100 college and university presidents in his readership area?

One seasonal column has been so well received that it has been repeated. It is a "translation" of the paper's annual Christmas letter and I expect to continue that column as an annual event. I qualified myself as an interpreter because "I spend much of my time separating flakes of truth from blizzards of flim flam."

Here are a few of the excerpts from the Christmas letter and my interpretive skepticism:

> Our eldest, Archimedes, is a sophomore now at Wesleyan. Remember, Mom caught Dad on the campus of good old Wesleyan, ha, ha. . . . Do you know the price tag the eggheads have tied on a college education? They're out of their trees at "good old Wesleyan." And the saddest thing is that the kids are running away with the place. Coed dorms and no hours, for the love of Wesley! Why can't they climb up the fire escapes or sneak out the windows like we used to? Everything's too easy for kids nowadays.

> We're following all the good advice we read and hear on saving energy during this time of crisis. . . . Our smart aleck youngest, of the modern math generation, has figured out that at 41 degrees in the house and 17 m.p.h. on the road we'll surpass the 100 per cent barrier. We'd like to export our surplus heat to bring Arab tents up to 180 degrees, spreading discomfort to all at this season of giving.

> Little Matilda is grown up now and she and Algernon are planning a spring wedding. . . . You don't know Algernon and that's another blessing for you. She met the nut on campus while Dad wasn't watching. Mom sheds a tear and allows as how we aren't losing a daughter, we're gaining a son. Dad sobs openly and marks off another total loss in a down year.

> The kids can hardly wait for Christmas Eve when we open the presents we've given to each other. . . . The squeals of avarice and shouts of greed are as wholesomely charming as a TV laxative commercial.

> Well, Merry Christmas. We sure look forward to exchanging greetings with each and every one of you at this season of peace and brotherly love. . . . What? Nothing from the Krumshaws again this year? O.K., that's it. Cross the crummy Krumshaws off our list.

The columns take a considerable portion of my spare time which means poorly paid overtime on Saturday and Sunday morning. Each must represent my best effort if I am to clear the editor and presume to speak to thousands of his readers. I have had three rejections; three excruciatingly painful experiences which I diligently try to avoid.

Everyone who writes has a personal method of composition, but there is one almost universally common practice—revision. It is impossible to churn out sparkling prose in one creative burst of scribbling. I write a sloppy original in pencil, let it lie at least overnight, revise, and type up a working copy. Usually I ask someone to read it and make suggestions (my wife is best at this since she has a license to criticize me). I revise the typed copy and come up with a final draft, if lucky, or another working copy if it still isn't right. I have revised and rewritten as many as a half-dozen times, but before that is necessary the copy usually ends up in my waste basket.

Such painful toil is the penance I pay for publication in the daily press. I must believe that writing is easier for others. I have read of authors who can dictate their manuscripts. Not I. Routine answers to letters and even service club and high school commencement addresses, yes, but not editorials.

If Hamline University is to avoid the curse of invisibility I must do my share as its primary spokesman. Let others hold national offices in the associations and deliberate on regional committees and task forces. Other presidents are younger, more handsome, more eager for advancement, and even more brilliant than I. There are those who sparkle in the pulpit; those who excel on the cocktail and banquet circuit; those who relate with students; those who inspire the faculty with scholarly production; and those who assume avocational civic leadership. For me there is the tedious loneliness of creative composition. It is, as my 15-year-old daughter would say, my thing.

I happen to think that a great many college presidents could, and should, be writing editorial columns for maximum visibility for themselves and for the institutions they head. It is difficult for me to understand any literate president ignoring such a potential audience. But some of my presidential friends would fault my disinterest in committees and convention. And there are Hamline faculty members who sigh longingly for a scholarly president.

Those faculty sighs of discontent surfaced in an evaluation I asked for (foolishly) and received (sadly). I was viewed with "tolerant but unenthusiastic contentment" and "about as much enthusiasm for Trail Boss Bailey as for a branding iron at roundup time." The evaluation inspired two columns, one headlined "Want to be a college president? First, attain divinity," and the other, "Every critic has his class."

"I hate criticism," I wrote. "It has never changed my mind although it has changed my friends." I gave personalities to a number of my most persistent faultfinders. Here are five:

Foster A. Snob. Often he holds advanced degrees but seldom is he intelligent. He has a technique: having labelled

me as a stupid dolt he leisurely knifes me with sophisticated thrusts. He and his smart-talk associates gather
together with booze and/or pot to itemize with titillating
eagerness every misstep I make.

Peter Luther Wesley. Not always ordained by man,
he piously considers himself touched by God. It is for my
own good that P. L. criticizes. If only I would repent and
join; but no, I sinfully struggle on, disenchurched, with
mistaken zeal and wasted motion. Oh, the shame of it.
Oh, the depravity of me. Oh, the blessed assurance of
having God on one's side. Oh, the satisfaction of ducking
another one of them in the pools of Salem.

Phyllis B. Kappa. I first met Ms. Kappa when I was
a classroom teacher and she took my class as my substitute. She gave a test to see how the kids and I were doing
and reported the results to the principal. She proofreads
my writing, splices my infinitives, nails down my dang-
ling participles, and misses all my points. She catches
every faulty reference, every wrong date, and every unintended double-entendre. Never does she err.

Ophelia R. McGood. I read the same books, maga-
zines and newspapers that Ophelia reads but she selects
excerpts which support her position. She is a professional
liberal. She quit thinking years ago; her opinions are now
delivered to her in predigested form, from doctrinaire
columnists and commentators, and from her liberal friends.

G. Dewey Dwiddledaddle. The youngest of my critics
is also the most numerous, surrounding me at home and
on campus. He dislikes my age, my position, my rules
and regulations, and my establishment friends in business
and profession. Me he barely tolerates. He expresses his
contempt in easily understood X-rated words often no more
than four letters long. He finds me wholly irrelevant, which
is as far out of it as one can get and still be a fellow pas-
senger on spaceship earth.

Some articles are, of course, more fun to write than others.
Often the most enjoyable is the one in which I can reminisce. In "Con-
fessions of a brat who was saved by love" I enjoyed myself so much
that pious readers reminded me that sin was not primarily for enjoyment. I remembered, editorially, the shocking of folks with a model
T Ford coil which could also disrupt radio reception; the removing of
distributor caps from parked automobiles; and the spraying of dog urine
on the trouser legs of standing spectators at auctions, fairs, and political rallies to attract stray dogs:

The look on a man's face when he observed a nonchalant dog, leg outstretched, wetting his trousers remains fresh in my memory even today.

I concluded in this column that, as an adolescent brat, I broke many of the laws of society and owed everything to "wise and long-suffering adults who waited out my brat-hood and rewarded my crime and delinquency with love." I can pay that debt by loving today's brats, "not liking the disagreeable little stinkers . . . but loving them." There is, I admitted, no other way.

Mostly for fun was a column, "Guide to pedagogical prose," in which I defined some of the words used by those of us who teach and administer:

> Coed dorms—College residence halls for coeds (if
> I get by with that definition I can certainly fool the older
> alumni and the trustees for one more year).
> Private college—Exclusive collegiate institution;
> admission restricted to young men and women who fill
> out application forms, submit registration fees, and
> walk or are carried into Old Main.
> Public college—A non-exclusive collegiate institu-
> tion. See "private college."
> Innovation—That new idea which has, until now, been
> properly ignored or wisely rejected. Will not work. One
> is worth a foundation proposal; five assure an operating
> budget deficit; and ten bring on a presidential resignation.
> Administration—The practice of making decisions;
> self-assigned avocation of every arrogant young student
> and faculty member; the duty of every tired old president,
> vice president, dean, director, and coordinator who is
> cursed with both the assignment and the responsibility.
> Non-tenured.

In a more serious mood I wrote of "million-dollar parents" who give a lifetime of support to their youngsters, of the student enrollment decline on college campuses, of the one lesson I would teach if I had only time for one, of allowing students to make mistakes in a controlled collegiate environment, of heightened rivalry between public and private colleges, of increased pressure on high school graduates to enroll in college, and on the changed atmosphere among students on campus.

One column was a personal adventure story—canoeing the wild rivers of northern Wisconsin with my family. I learned from irate letters that canoeing enthusiasts have a low tolerance level for the novice who finds "exquisite pleasure" in laying down his paddle after six days and five nearly sleepless nights.

During the 20 months of editorial column production I became
50 years old and the event was worth a column:

As it must to all men (and somewhat later to many women),
age 50 came to me this month. According to Socrates it
begins the golden age of philosopher-king, but after a few
days now at 50 it seems to me to be mostly a pain in the
neck, little better than 49. So few people read Plato now-
adays.

I summarized what I had learned about education in a half century: that the best teaching takes place in elementary school; that the
finest students are college and university seniors; that the senior year
of high school is "a social binge and an educational disaster"; that the
best teachers are married women; that kids who wear pretty clothes
and wash their ears get better grades than those who don't; that if I
had one thing only to abolish in education it would have to be grades;
that the most serious educational problem continues to be the lack of
minority educational opportunity; and that "the finest educational system the world has ever known, with all its flaws, is in operation today,
the American public school system."

Malcolm Moos resigned as president of the University of Minnesota during the period of my reporting and I took the opportunity to say
something about university presidencies by nominating, tongue-in-
cheek, three candidates for the opening. I nominated the 70-year-old
chairman of Hamline's Board of Trustees because he is an "avowed
gourmand" and could tolerate all the "dripping globs of potatoes and
chunks of hacked-up chicken" one must eat in such a position. I nominated Hamline's student dean for his disregard of public opinion
although I admitted that he has flaws—"He is soft on youth, particularly
those who ride bicycles and carry knapsacks and he distrusted Agnew
(too early) before it became popular."

My third nomination was my wife who "knows something about
everything" and therefore possesses the omniscience so necessary in
heading a major university. "Only those of us who know her mother,"
I wrote, "can understand how Ms. Bailey came to know so much, so
positively."

I, too, was queried, I modestly stated, as to whether I would be
interested in the presidency. "No," I told my 14-year-old daughter.

In possibly the most honest and certainly the most introspective
of my editorials I described myself as one of the failures of society.
"The world," I wrote, "is populated largely by successes." Kids fail
somewhat regularly, but parents lean more toward success. And no-
where do successes outnumber failures more often than in education.
I feel lonely "as one of the few self-confessed failures in midwestern
(education)."

As a practice teacher during my undergraduate days in college
I was advised, I pointed out, to "consider going into business or something."

My personal heroes are Charlie Brown and Henry David Thoreau,
both of whom share my proclivity to fail (Editor Chucker headed the
column with two pictures, one of me and the other of Charlie):

> As I begin a new year with another deficit budget at Ham-
> line, read another series of anti-Bailey student editorials,
> and prepare for the next faculty meeting I envy the suc-
> cessful folks. Is there no relief for us failures?

I had begun my second series of 25 editorial columns (I hesitate
to say that I'll be writing them for the rest of my professional life)
and, after a lengthy (vacation) break in my submission of typed articles,
I experienced the exquisite joy of a call from Editor Chucker.

"Get some more in?" he said in the terse manner he uses with
those of us he seems to admire.

"Well," I stalled with pardonable pride, "Are you getting hundreds of requests?"

"More like tens," he said.

That did it. I'll speak to "tens" any time I have something to say.

I shall keep trying for that high profile I cherish both for Hamline
and for me by continuing to write editorial columns for the Star. This
administrator will be seen and heard—and only then, if it must be, ignored or forgotten.

18

EXTENDING THE LABORATORY
INTO THE COMMUNITY
Margaret F. Heyse

A sparsely populated rural state, a small city, a small university—this is our community. The state has done an excellent job in supporting its educational institutions at all levels. It devotes one of the higher amounts per capita in the country to support higher education. The University of North Dakota (U.N.D.) is among those beneficiaries.

U.N.D. started a nursing program at a very early stage, but had allowed it to become inactive since at that time most nursing was taught in hospital schools. In the immediate post-World War II period, when it was decided to revive the nursing program, the university had to look to its larger community for clinical experience because no university hospital existed. Arrangements were made with a local hospital for use of its facilities, as well as with a neighboring university where certain clinical training could be taken by students, and credits transferred back to U.N.D. for granting of the degree.

The latter arrangement posed a number of administrative problems. The nursing unit (then the Division of Nursing) taught some of the beginning courses but depended on the local hospital school for sharing of faculty and supervision of students in junior level work. The Division of Nursing planned with the neighboring university for the senior level courses, but was not able to secure the courses it wished, such as Public Health Nursing, and settled instead for experience that overlapped that available in the local community. Not the least of the drawbacks was the fact that students, thus getting much needed clinical experience in the large metropolitan hospital center, tended to enjoy the glamour of the bigger city, and decided to accept employment or met and married men from the metropolitan area.

Margaret F. Heyse, Dean, University of North Dakota.

Thus, the number of students who returned to North Dakota for employment was distressingly low. Because students lived in the dormitories of the local hospital school during the junior year and at the neighboring university during the senior year, it tended to give them a feeling of divided loyalties with a tendency for less firm allegiance and commitment to their own university. Problems arose also in financial arrangements as students paid fees at the parent university which in turn transmitted fees to the neighboring university.

In the late 1950s the University of North Dakota decided that some other overall type of arrangement was indicated. The unit was established as the autonomous College of Nursing. A thorough review and revision of the curriculum was undertaken with a view toward having the university assume complete responsibility for teaching of the students in nursing. A second objective was strengthening the program to the point where national accreditation would be possible. The available community facilities were thoroughly reviewed for the possibility of teaching the entire program in the local area. At that time, however, it was felt that experience in the care of children was rather limited, as was experience in the care of psychiatric patients. It was decided to appoint an instructor to teach students pediatrics in the Twin Cities area (Minneapolis-St. Paul) with the students having psychiatric nursing taught by College of Nursing faculty at the North Dakota State Hospital. The major job of recruiting faculty, so that the university could assume its full teaching load, was undertaken. Arrangements were made to teach Nursing of Children at one of the private hospitals in the metropolitan area. This agency had space to accommodate students in a dormitory and was now happy to make arrangements for students to use these rooms. A faculty member was secured who spent a semester on the main university campus getting oriented to the philosophy and ideas of the University of North Dakota's College of Nursing, before taking the first group of students for this revised type of teaching.

Perhaps one of the most troublesome areas in terms of arranging experience at this period of history was in the area of Public Health Nursing. Because of certain problems within the community, it was felt not enough experience was available locally, and thus arrangements were made for the Public Health faculty member to serve almost as a "circuit rider" with students having experience in several small community health departments. The faculty member went from one to another to provide supervision and teaching, almost on a one-to-one basis. This was very time-consuming and expensive teaching and led to reevaluation within a few years as to how teaching could be handled more efficiently. Although this arrangement had the advantage of extending our contacts into a number of communities, a change was needed in order that instructor and student time might be better used.

Plans were developed to have the teaching in the Grand Forks area, utilizing city and county health departments as well as some work occasionally in nearby communities, notably the one across the river in our next-door community. Thus, we were actually utilizing three health departments for securing clinical experience but it meant faculty and students could remain at home.

As time went on, although the experience remained excellent at the state hospital, there were problems in having students away from campus so much as well as problems of securing faculty for this more isolated location for teaching. In addition, with the development of facilities in the local hospital for a small psychiatric unit as well as the Regional Mental Health Center, it was decided to focus more on the broad community aspect of psychiatric nursing rather than the acute hospitalized patient; thus this experience was returned to the main campus.

All of these agencies were happy to work with us in providing experience for the students. It seemed all of us would be better protected if some type of agreement were signed. A form was developed in consultation with the agencies which would set forth the university's responsibilities, the agencies' responsibilities, and those which would be undertaken jointly. The university's responsibilities related to assignment of students, numbers, dates, and teaching arrangements. The agency's responsibilities related to provisions for office or classroom space, coatroom, library or other space needs, and provision for securing meals. Joint responsibilities related to meetings to discuss problems and to plan experiences. These agreements are renegotiated each year and signed by administrative officials of the university, the College of Nursing, and the administrator and director of nursing in each agency.

During the time the student body was small, much of the arranging for student experience and their assignments, arranging for contracts and other administrative details were relatively routine, uncomplicated, and not unduly time-consuming. As the school began to grow and expand rapidly, complications set in. It became essential to utilize every available agency in the local community and others nearby. About this time the College of Nursing decided to plan for students to have a period within the senior year in which to select a location in which they would like to function—their own option on clinical functioning, with the recognition that there might well be some special areas not available locally in which students were particularly interested. When the first student requests came in, they seemed highly unrealistic. Students asked for experience in what sounded at first like rather exotic locations. A year and a half later, we now find ourselves encouraging students to seek such locations, since we have found it is not greatly different to assist students in arranging for experience across the country than it is to make arrangements across the county.

Probably a bit more explanation of this course is needed here in order to point out the administrative aspects of this type of extention of the laboratory into the broad community of the nation. Half of one semester of the senior year is dedicated to this course, which was titled Nursing Options. Recognizing that one of the objectives for this experience was to help students see what functioning as a graduate nurse might be in a particular area, we wished to have a block of time as free from classes as possible. It was decided to concentrate classes in the first and last week of the time period, allowing approximately six weeks' time for students to function in the clinical area in the agency of their choice. Students are assigned approximately 32 hours per week so they can have the feel of continuity and responsibility of a graduate staff nurse, but also so that they have some time for reading, studying, and pondering new clinical learnings and problems. Students have selected a wide variety of special areas, such as the emergency room, intensive care units, coronary care units, the operating room, special clinical areas of all varieties, ranging from pediatrics to geriatrics, and specialties such as neurology, neurosurgery, and obstetrics. In some instances they have functioned within the general hospital, in others in specialized hospitals such as the Indian Service Hospital at Belcourt, North Dakota or the one at Cass Lake, Minnesota or the National Institutes of Health's Clinical Center in Bethesda, Maryland. Some students have worked in out-patient facilities; others have worked with physicians, serving essentially as nurse practitioners with physicians, some of whom have been general practitioners, some obstetricians, some pediatricians, and some in other special areas. Some have been located in Grand Forks, others have been in small communities with the physicians, or in small community hospitals. A number of them have sought additional fields for Public Health Nursing experience, including school nursing, a large city health department nursing service, and the Frontier Nursing Service in Kentucky. One student, interested in the area of psychiatric nursing and drug abuse, sought her assignment at one of the Synanon Centers in California. Others have been in the Twin Cities area in large metropolitan hospitals for maternity, operating, emergency, and intensive care units, either in private hospitals or large public hospitals. They seem to have covered a rather full gamut of work; yet undoubtedly each new group will uncover new experiences.

This type of arrangement differs from the previously described situation in Public Health Nursing in the earlier periods of the school in that, though we keep in close touch with the students, we make no pretense of direct supervision in this senior period. In the option situation, the agency agrees to provide the supervision of students, which also means that we need some type of evaluation from the agency so that we know how adequately the student was prepared for the experience and any other comments the agency has. From the standpoint of both student and agency, we are available at any point by phone. Fortunately, to date, there have been no profound emergencies. For the locations closer to home, we do make an effort to get out and visit the agencies and the students in order to ascertain how things are going. With those located across the country this is hardly practical, but the telephone serves as our medium for communication.

Contracts are written, again defining the university's responsibility and the agency's responsibility. In this Nursing Options experience, students are asked to make their own living arrangements, though we appreciate whatever help people in the agency can give. In some instances the agencies have housing available, while in other instances students have had to seek apartment or other temporary housing. Those who have their Nursing Options experience in the Grand Forks area continue with whatever type of housing they have had, including university dormitories or apartments.

As a means of helping its agencies to feel more a part of the university, the College of Nursing each year plans an Agency Conference to which representatives from all the participating agencies are invited. The invitation is extended to those even at a distance as a means of letting them know that if they could arrange to attend, we would be happy to have them do so. No effort is made to pay for transportation of people coming to the university, although they are our guests for the day of the conference. At this time, arrangements are made to help them understand what the university's special projects are, what new developments it is undertaking, and how it is proceeding. Probably one of the most valuable and helpful portions of the day is giving the agencies an opportunity to share with each other what their particular projects and problems are; the new developments going on in each agency. Not infrequently, agencies from within the same community are greatly surprised to discover what their neighbors are doing. During some part of the day, an outside speaker is planned for, generally from the university community but outside nursing, to help people know of developments in other, though usually somewhat related areas.

Planning for this wide variety of contracts and the assignment of students on such an individualized basis has taken a greatly increased amount of time. Every effort is made to provide students with their first choice of location, although this has not been possible in every instance. Students are asked to list first, second, and third choices. Occasionally, students have to decide between a choice in clinical experience or a time when the experience is arranged since in some instances this relates to planning around university or even family situations, especially in the case of married students.

With only one of the agencies has there been a financial arrangement. In the case of the prime agency where the largest number of students and faculty are located, rental for office and instructional space is paid by the university to the agency. It is also expected that when faculty secure supplies from the hospital supply areas or pharmacy for class use, these will be paid for by the university. No effort has been made to charge or to reimburse on a per student basis or on a credit hour basis or in any other type of arrangement of this sort. While it is true that students undoubtedly cause additional expense for the hospital in terms of use of linens, extra use of disposable equipment, etc., it is also true that though the staffing is planned theoretically without the students, the students contribute a profound amount in terms of nursing care rendered. It is also true that the presence of students and faculty has a stimulating effect on staff and personnel at all levels. It is quite probably also true that occasionally they must feel that there are so many around that they wish we would get out of their hair. Such feelings are not very often expressed, even if felt. The attitude of staff generally has been one of great cooperation in sharing, with everyone eager to give students the best learning experience possible. The faculty for their part have endeavored to make it possible for individuals to share in learnings, especially as new things have come along.

A part of this overall approach in the optional area has been to increase the amount of teaching for students in overall patient assessment. A representative from each agency was invited to participate during the summer session, when visiting faculty presented a two-week workshop for College of Nursing faculty on assessment. Since this content was material that people in the agencies are increasingly eager to get, they were most anxious to participate and felt that this was very helpful to them. It might be commented that this invitation was not extended to all of the broad scope of agencies where students are assigned for options, but merely to the major agencies nearby, such as those in the immediate environs of the universtiy community.

In spite of the administrative problems in terms of arranging for such a variety of experiences, the university feels that this is a valuable way to utilize the community. For one thing, students see a variety of different ways of providing care. They are not tied to just one institution as is sometimes the case when a large university medical center is utilized. They know from observation that there is no one way, but have the opportunity to see a variety of ways and to evaluate these. Students have the opportunity of functioning in a large metropolitan area as well as a small community. They function in general hospitals, in specialized hospitals, in varying types and qualities of nursing services; they work with a variety of nurses, noting levels of nursing care and varying philosophies of approaches to care.

They experience private hospitals and governmental hospitals. Thus, these young people should be better prepared to meet community demands, wherever they may function. The university for its part believes that by working with these various agencies it assists them in keeping their services up to date and attuned to latest developments. Faculty share the ideas that they bring from the variety of agencies and are able to keep their teaching in tune with a variety of different approaches as well.

Sometimes it seems as if life would be simpler if we were all comfortably located in a single institution with only a single set of policies and ideas to cope with. However, the faculty currently feel that they are better off in this type of setting than in that of a big medical center.

The university has dealt with some other problems as well as the administrative problems cited. For example, in the early years of experience, nothing was done about any form of insurance. As hospitals were added to our group of community facilities, the question was raised about responsibility if something went wrong as a student was giving care. Thus, the university began providing a basic type of liability insurance, perhaps not very large by some standards, but minimal insurance to cover potential emergencies. Fortunately, no call has ever been made on this insurance. It is greatly hoped that it need never be used.

During the time that Public Health was being taught in a number of the small agencies, a mobile library was provided. This is no longer necessary. Many of the agencies now have provided their own libraries, in no small part as a result of stimulation from the students. When students are in residence at the university, they of course have access to the student health facilities. It was agreed that those in the home community would continue to use the student health facilities, except in cases of those who might be taken sick while on a unit. When this does occur, students are then taken to the unit emergency room, seen there, and returned to the university for follow-up care at the student health service. The student is expected to pay whatever normal charges would be incurred or the university reimburses the agency through the normal student health service fees. During the time students are involved in Nursing of Children in the Twin Cities, if they become ill, they are seen in the emergency room there; the billing for this is then sent to the university so that the student has, in essence, the same kind of coverage that would be present if he were at home. The student health service is not set up or intended to cover a long period of hospitalization or major medical expense. Students are expected to carry hospitalization insurance toward this end.

Faculty members located in the Twin Cities commute to the campus for faculty meetings. Every effort is made, through frequent telephone conversation and other provisions, that is, inclusion in announcements, mailings, etc., to make them feel as much a part of the university faculty as possible. There probably are some difficulties in making them feel fully a part of the university since they are here so infrequently and for such short periods of time. Nonetheless, this has seemed to work out quite satisfactorily with minimal difficulties.

A good deal of additional travel money is needed for this type of commuting as well as the necessity to transport faculty and students to some of the special observation areas, such as some of the special units at the state hospital, which we continue to utilize, for example, the alcohol and drug unit or the adolescent center. Every effort is made to plan these trips as economically as possible, both from the standpoint of student and faculty time. A fairly good system has evolved at the present time with students spending about four days in observation areas.

Probably for many of the agencies, one real benefit accruing to them is an opportunity to recruit students for employment after graduation. Especially with the optional experience, students have not infrequently returned gloating "and they offered me a job when I graduate." Although it is not our effort to plan these experiences for job placement interviews, we are happy if the community sees our product as desirable and employable.

Within the past several years our horizons have broadened from seeing our community as the city of Grand Forks, or even the State of North Dakota. Just as our graduates have scattered over the whole country and, to a lesser extent, the globe, we now see our laboratory-community as just as broad. We have not yet resolved potential administrative problems for the time a student requests an option aboard Skylab, but that seems no more unrealistic than the present scope would have appeared a few years back. It is our hope that we can produce the quality of student that will enable succeeding generations to be welcomed wherever our community may be.

19

THE PRIVATE COLLEGE AND
THE CHURCH-STATE ISSUE
Ralph C. John

It has been observed that private colleges and universities with an historic denominational affiliation face ten years of testing on the church-state issue. Accordingly, suits have been entered in several states to disallow the distribution of public monies to this class of private institutions of higher education.

The three most celebrated cases to date are Tilton v. Richardson (Connecticut, 1971), Hunt v. McNair (South Carolina, 1973), and AUSCS v. Bubb (Kansas, 1974); all three have generally been settled in favor of the defendant colleges, the first in the U.S. Supreme Court and the next two in U.S. District Courts. There is a growing body of law in this field, some of it based on principles or precedents established in litigation relating most directly to parochial elementary and secondary education. The best survey is found in Charles H. Wilson's Tilton v. Richardson: The Search for Sectarianism in Education (Association of American Colleges, 1971).

THE CASE INVOLVING WESTERN MARYLAND COLLEGE

Western Maryland College is basically a four-year liberal arts institution with a fraternal and mutually voluntary relationship to the United Methodist Church. There are no references to the denomination in the college's charter, no ex officio trusteeships, no favoritism toward Methodists in admission or hiring practices, and no required religious observances or religion courses. The college is listed,

Ralph C. John, President, Western Maryland College.

however, as one of the institutions related to the denomination, and
has received modest annual support ($25,000-$50,000 toward a
$5,500,000 budget) from the Baltimore Conference of this church body.

In the past there was a formidable clerical presence on the
governing board, though only one clergyman has been elected by this
board, which has been entirely self-perpetuating.

In 1972 Western Maryland was named codefendant with four
Roman Catholic colleges in a suit to disallow state institutional grants
authorized by the Maryland General Assembly in a bill—Higher
Education-Aid to Private Colleges—passed in 1971. These grants are
capitulated on the basis of $500 for each degree, undergraduate or
graduate, awarded by an accredited private college or university in the
State of Maryland. Western Maryland's annual benefit under this program is approximately $145,000. Also codefendants in the 1972 case
were the Maryland governor, the Board of Public Works (which de
facto is the state bureau of the budget), the state comptroller, and the
Maryland Council for Higher Education, along with the colleges themselves.

The original plaintiffs were the Maryland branch of the American
Civil Liberties Union, AUSCS (Americans United for the Separation
of Church and State), John C. Roemer, and several other individual
Maryland taxpayers. The case was filed in the 4th U.S. District Court,
Baltimore, which disqualified the ACLU and AUSCS as having no standing because each is a tax-exempt organization which suffers no loss
or penalty consequent to the expenditure of public funds for the colleges
in question. The individual taxpayers, however, were recognized as
having standing, so that the case has come to be known as Roemer, et
al v. Board of Public Works.

The claim was that these institutions should be denied state institutional grants because, as church-related colleges in whatever
degree, they are sectarian and, therefore, are ineligible under the
First Amendment of the Constitution of the United States. The arguments turn on the establishment and free exercise clauses and, again,
on alleged sectarianism, which is defined to involve the propagation
or inculcation of a religious point of view or tradition as a substantial
part of the institutional purpose.

Preparation of the Case

The first question faced by the college in preparation for the
trial was choice of counsel. Two of the other codefendant institutions
expressed an interest in Western Maryland joining them in engaging
Williams, Connolly and Califano of Washington, D.C. Edward Bennett

Williams, senior partner in the firm and noted trial lawyer, had successfully represented the Connecticut colleges before the U.S. Supreme
Court in Tilton v. Richardson. Wilson, perhaps the outstanding legal
authority in this field, also is a member of that firm.

The decision was to engage separate counsel because of belief
in substantive differences vis-a-vis the legal situation of the other institutions. Western Maryland, in effect, opted for a free-standing
trial with its own counsel: Semmes, Bowen and Semmes of Baltimore.

As the legal processes began to function interrogatories and depositions were required. The attorney for the plaintiffs submitted 43
interrogatories which mandated answers with exhibits (over 2,000
documents) on details in many areas in the corporate life of the college,
particularly where evidences of preferential treatment on the basis of
denominational affiliation, religion requirements, or any form of institutional dependency upon the United Methodist Church might be indicated.

In the meantime the college's own counsel began developing its
case. This too placed heavy demands for the production of documents
and information on the operation and spirit of the institutional program,
to counter, of course, the claims of the plaintiffs.

It became obvious that one person should be made responsible
for the assembly, accuracy, and release of these materials. The designee was the college's dean of admissions who has a recognized competence in the field of institutional information and research. While
he typically reports to the vice president for academic affairs, he was
attached to the Office of the President for this special assignment.
The college's attorneys were authorized to deal directly with this liaison person, though copies of all material transmitted between them
(except exhibits which were too bulky) were sent to the president and
the chairman of the Board of Trustees to keep them informed.

The plaintiffs' counsel required depositions from the president,
vice president for business affairs, and chairman of the board. Here
the focus was on the possible commingling of state funds in support of
sectarian activities through the budget of the college (How can you
prove that none of these funds goes toward the support of the dean of
the chapel?), the possible application of denominational considerations
in the recruitment of students and faculty, and the concrete meaning
of the church relationship in terms of exhibits gathered through the
interrogatory procedure. And so it went through two hours or more
of intensive oral examination covering many aspects of the organization,
practices, and offerings of the college.

The interrogatories, which were legally certified, and the depositions, which were taken under oath, became official parts of the
court record. Typically their content is not duplicated in the cross-
examination of subsequent hearings, though they frequently are cited

in other stages of litigation. Preliminary briefs were prepared by the attorneys for both the plaintiffs and the defendants, and the dates for the presentation of evidence were fixed.

Presentation of Evidence

The presentation of the evidence was before one judge of the three-judge panel named to hear the case. The final hearing, several months after findings of fact by the judge and pleadings by the attorneys, was before the full court or all three judges.

It is impossible to fully detail the court procedure or the thrust of arguments. Enough has been said, however, to suggest the direction of probings and defense.

This case, as previously indicated, involved several public officials and five colleges. In a sense the General Assembly of Maryland, too, was a part of the situational milieu. Initially the plaintiffs argued the unconstitutionality of the Higher Education-Aid to Private Colleges law prima facie, because no provision had been made in the original bill for institutional accountability to the state relative to the actual use of the funds. This imperfection in the law itself, however, had been corrected by an amendment passed in a subsequent session of the legislature, so that the court ruled favorably on the prima facie validity of the law.

The public defendants (governor, board of public works, comptroller, and Maryland Council for Higher Education—the local "1202" agency) were defended by the Maryland attorney general. The major emphasis was upon the ability of the state to protect against a sectarian misuse of public funds under a careful system of accountability.

The four Roman Catholic colleges, in separate trials, argued their primary secular purpose and the academic freedom of faculty in the implementation of academic programs. All disclaimed a sectarian institutional character.

The plaintiffs found Western Maryland nonsectarian, and so indicated the fact in preliminary briefs, on the basis of information gathered through the deposition and interrogatory process. Hence its attorneys moved a summary judgment which, in effect, would have thrown this college out of the case. The one judge who was scheduled to hear the evidence, however, ruled that he was not in a position to act on this motion, since it would require the concurrence of the other two judges, who would not sit as a panel until the final hearing.

It is impossible here to treat in detail the long and complicated pattern of arguments on both sides. These have been suggested, in broad sweep, in what already has been stated. The administrative and legal strategies, however, do demand attention.

During the year of preparation, which also happened to be the first year for a new president at Western Maryland, Dr. Earl J. McGrath, one of the America's most outstanding scholars in higher education, had been intermittently on campus as consultant for a study of the governance, organization, and management systems of the college. He was engaged as an expert witness and testified that in his thoroughgoing study of the institution, just completed for other purposes, he found no evidence of church dependency or control.

The college has a Department of Philosophy and Religion which offers majors in these disciplines. As in the instance of many small colleges, particularly those with an historic church relationship, the department is a combined one, though separate majors are offered. Also religion courses are among the options which students have in fulfilling a humanities general education requirement. The attorney for the plaintiffs pressed hard to find witches in this heather.

Hence Dr. Samuel H. Magill, executive associate of the Association of American Colleges, whose specific portfolio is with the Commission on Liberal Learning, was brought in as a second expert witness. He defended religion as an academic discipline (as distinguished from a system of sectarian beliefs), pointed out that as such it has been incorporated into the curriculum of many state universities, and argued that a comprehensive approach to the liberal arts requires attention to this important aspect of the human experience—whether one is a believer or not.

The third such witness was Dr. Keith J. Edwards, associate research scientist at Johns Hopkins University, who had run a statistical analysis of admissions practices and performance at Western Maryland over a three-year period which demonstrated no evidence of discrimination against non-Methodists, or favoritism toward Methodists, in the acceptance of students for admission.

Those from within the college called upon to testify on the witness stand—by the plaintiffs, the college's attorney, or both—were the college's chairman of the board, president, dean of faculty, dean of admission, dean of the chapel, and head of the Department of Philosophy and Religion. Whereas the presentation of evidence on the other colleges had taken two or more days, this was accomplished in one short day in this instance.

Compacting extended, tedious procedures or arguments into necessary oversimplification, there were several bothersome factors, in the judge's subsequent finding of fact which otherwise seemed favorable to all the colleges. Those factors relating to Western Maryland were the following:

1. The college historically has accepted support on a regular
   basis from the Baltimore Conference of the United Methodist
   Church.
2. It is listed as an institution related to the church in the denomination's publications.
3. All four faculty members in the Department of Philosophy
   and Religion are ordained Methodist clergy, though they hold
   earned doctorates in the areas in which they teach. (This situation is partly vestigial, partly reflective of the heritage of
   the college.)
4. The college lists itself as church-related in its own catalog.

Internal Administrative Accommodations

An experience such as this one, if its values are appropriated,
results in a serious reappraisal of the nature and objectives of the
college and in a careful evaluation of its public representation of itself.
It is a memorable responsibility to defend under oath everything said
or published over a five-year period with the outcome having clear
implications for the continuing viability of the institution.

If Western Maryland loses this case it will be placed at a serious
competitive disadvantage among its collegiate peers in continuing as
a quality college, because of resultant ineligibility for substantial state
aid which others receive. On the other hand, there is a history and
heritage which cannot be discounted. Herein lies the dilemma.

The response of the college to the suit, at this writing, is as
follows:

1. No disclaimer has been entered on the fact of a fraternal and
mutually voluntary relationship to the United Methodist Church. In
this respect, and in these terms (which are honestly descriptive of
fact) the college holds to its heritage.

2. The Board of Trustees has requested that the college be removed from the budget of the Baltimore Conference of the United
Methodist Church for the modest annual appropriation which it receives
from that source. The fact of regular financial support appears to be
legally damaging and pragmatically, in this instance anyway, is not
worth the risk. This request, as expected, is interpreted by some as
defection, but is not intended to be under the terms indicated above.

3. All literature of the college (catalogs, brochures, president's
reports) have been carefully screened for honest, carefully descriptive
language where there is any reference or implication for church-
college liaisons. The problems of the suit have seemed to relate more

to extravagance of language in secondary (noncharter or bylaw) publications than to the formal corporate situation. (There is no reference to the United Methodist Church, or any other ecclesiastical body, in the charter and bylaws of the college.)

4. The Division of Higher Education of the United Methodist Church, the national church agency, has been advised of the problem, with the request that it give attention to its published definitions or descriptions of relationship too. There is the same problem of loose language there, when—again—in a period of legal testing there must be precise language.

Editor's Note. At the time of submission of the forgoing study, the case was in the hands of the courts, with a decision expected in some 60-90 days. That decision was rendered on schedule in November 1974, as follows:

> Washington (AP) . . . The U.S. Supreme Court has rejected a request to halt payment of $1.8 million in state funds to four church-related colleges in Maryland. By a 5-3 vote, the Court refused to block an order of a U.S. District Court that upheld a state law aiding the four colleges—Loyola and Notre Dame in Baltimore, Mount St. Mary's in Emmitsburg, and Western Maryland in Westminster—as well as 13 other financially troubled private institutions. The first three institutions are Roman Catholic, the fourth Methodist. The lower court had ruled that "the religious programs at each school are separable from the secular programs, and the latter are the only beneficiaries of state aid."

20

THE PUBLIC
BE DAMNED
Winthrop C. Libby

The chicken had been consumed. The president had talked for 15 minutes viewing with optimism and modest humor the academic and economic progress made by the university during the past 12 months. The alumni group was attentive and courteous. The question period arrived. The first question was from an alumna whose voice quivered with indignation. "Why", she asked, "does the university encourage promiscuity and immorality by establishing a fund from which money can be borrowed to finance legal abortions in New York State?" The question was followed by her personal views of the matter. Her position was eminently sane and quite traditional expressing as it did the common feeling of many whose Maine roots had been nourished by a morality standard which considered premarital sexual activity as the most serious of deviations from acceptable mores.

During the winter of 1971 this scene was repeated time after time. The alumni circuit covered much of eastern United States and almost invariably this question was raised in one form or another at every meeting. With practice the president became reasonably adroit at handling the issue and, while people understood, few accepted the validity of the abortion fund's existence.

THE GENESIS: AN APPEAL TO STUDENTS

For three years the Student Senate of the University of Maine had financed a visit to Orono by Bill Baird, an abortion crusader.

Winthrop C. Libby, President Emeritus, University of Maine at Orono.

Baird's honesty, frankness, and knowledge appealed to students. He
gave straight answers to their direct questions. They needed information; he provided it. Local evidence had accumulated that a number
of young women from homes of reasonable affluence had gone to New
York for legal and safe abortions within that state. Women from less
affluent backgrounds, caught in a trap of despair, turned to quacks.
Evidence from the student health center indicated that in some cases
this resulted in physical damage of a serious nature. Students, moved
by Baird's descriptions and their personal knowledge of the needs of
young women confronted by the emotional crises of unwanted pregnan-
cies and the physical hazards associated with illegal abortionists, decided to do something about it.

Without consulting university officials, the student senate created
the University of Maine Abortion Loan Fund. The motivating force
was humanism. Capitalized at $5,000 the source of the original finan-
cing was the student activity fee, collected by the university and under
student senate control.

THE ABORTION LOAN FUND PLAN

The fund was under the supervision and administrative control
of a committee of five students appointed by the senate. The chairperson was a well-known and highly respected student from a Maine
Catholic home. A maximum loan level of $400 was established with
applications made directly to the committee. These were handled
with a minimum of red tape and in complete confidence. There was
no advertising. The fund existed but knowledge of its existence was
entirely by word of mouth. The plan had been in operation for about
two months with loans having been made to three women and one man
when the fund's existence became a matter of common knowledge.

PUBLIC REACTION

The story was unearthed by a capable reporter of the local Ban-
gor Daily News. It was a low-key and factually accurate account carried on one of the inside pages of the paper. The wire services picked
up the story and featured it widely as a national first. The story was
carried not only in weeklies but in such daily newspapers as the Boston
Globe, Long Island Newsday, the Washington Post and numerous others.
University officials learned about the fund at the same time as the
general public. The reaction was swift and voluminous; the criticism

vehement and virulent. With two notable and most pleasant exceptions, the hundreds of letters and phone calls blamed the university for allowing this situation to happen.

As a public institution, the University of Maine is vulnerable to public reaction. The county attorney studied the possibility of prosecution. There was public condemnation by the governor and an implication by responsible legislative leaders that the university's budget recommendations would be affected negatively by the development.

Interestingly enough, many students, learning of the Abortion Loan Fund for the first time, were bitter about their dollars being used for this purpose. Student clamor became loud enough to require the student senate to issue assurances that a student's 73-cent involuntary contribution to the fund would be removed and diverted to other projects sponsored by the student senate. It later developed that, from a managerial viewpoint, such a transfer could not be made, but the assurances from the senate quieted the student critics.

UNIVERSITY ACTION

Given the extent of unsought presidential involvement in the issue, it became necessary to consult with the involved student leaders and to seek advice of university counsel. The students were crystal clear in their reactions. Their conclusion was a simple one: the public be damned! They argued that the senate action in creating the fund was entirely legal. The need, while limited, was very real and the interests of humanity were served well and without publicity for those involved. Since it was right, no other criterion mattered.

It was very easy to understand and to be sympathetic to this line of reasoning. The president felt that the matter was outside administrative jurisdiction since the university's board of trustees had earlier delegated full responsibility and authority to student governmental units for the expenditure of activity funds. These dollars were collected by the university at the rate of $6.00 per student per semester, with the collection being made at registration time. However, legal counsel came into the act. They advised that since the activity fee was a condition of enrollment the delegation of authority to spend the dollars so collected did not in any way alter the responsibility of the board for the manner in which the money was spent. This opinion made it necessary to take administrative action. At no time did the trustees ever involve themselves either as a group or as individuals in the matter, other than to refer to the president all letters of criticism received by board members.

After considerable stirring about, the resolution of the problem was simple. By administrative edict, the University of Maine Abortion Loan Fund was abolished. It went out of existence. It was recognized, however, that students like any other group of people have financial emergencies of all kinds. They have a very legitimate need for having dollars quickly available without the necessity for unwinding a lot of red tape. Consequently the Student Emergency Loan Fund was created to which students could make application for small amounts of emergency dollars. Students are sensible. They recognize that a rose is a rose is a rose.

THE LESSON LEARNED

On balance little was learned from this extended, frequently bitter, and essentially unimportant episode. At best it simply reaffirmed a number of basic facts or principles involved in the administration of public, higher education institutions.

Taxpayers, alumni, parents, and citizens at large feel that they have a vested interest in the way a public institution is operated and are willing to make their thinking known in no uncertain terms. Administrators cannot ignore these expressions. Principles must be upheld in a reasonable and factual manner while at the same time understanding the expressions of concern from those who choose to express themselves. The grass appears much greener, however, on the lawns of the private institutions. Administrators in private colleges can better afford the emotional outbursts from the general citizenry. Furthermore there is a broad, general sorting of students on an economic basis between private and public institutions. Public institutions by their very nature attract students from middle, lower middle and low income families. Private schools enroll a larger share of their populations from upper and middle income backgrounds. And there is a tendency for family income level to affect the degree of family sophistication in the area of personal behavior. Students in private, higher educational institutions are less apt to be first-generation college students, less concerned about college preparing them for jobs, more convinced of the value of general education, and hence more willing to let others do their thing, no matter what this may be. Parents of such students are less apt to expect the institution to protect and guard their offspring.

College students in the 1970s continue to be very idealistic and are moved to action by injustices of all kinds, real or fancied. The level of concern for others has never been higher. The Abortion Loan

Fund was created by students not to encourage premarital sex, as was
frequently suggested by the critics, but for purely humanitarian reasons. It came as a shock to the involved students to find that so many
people regarded the fund as providing license for increased sexual relations. Certainly in a rural state, such as Maine, there is considerable concern about the sexual behavior of young adults, and a quick
readiness to condemn behavior which does not fit into a traditional
view of what is right and proper.

To convince parents and citizens that the ethical standards of
young people are formed in the home, in the church, and in the public
schools during childhood and early adolescence is almost impossible.
The best the university can hope to accomplish is to refine and focus
the standards already a part of the young adult's being. People do
change as they mature and gain understanding. Yet their fundamental
nature remains unchanged. The 18-year-old man or woman is an adult
entitled to all the rights and responsibilities of adults. The university
must consider students as such until they prove otherwise.

As a final thought, some people even at 40 or 50 never rise
above adolescence. To such, condolences are in order.

On the basis of the preceding studies, and hopefully as evidenced in the experience of the reader, it is readily apparent that the environment of higher education is by no means limited to the classroom. Nor is the academic community to be understood as solely campus oriented. Gown meets town in more ways than the unacquainted might imagine, for the college and university are integral parts of the social, economic, and political fiber of society as a whole. Thus it behooves the administrator, more than faculty and students, to weigh carefully his or her role off campus, and to be especially mindful of the ramifications of one's acts and judgments as a major representative of the educational community. As most veterans will attest, this task is much easier said than accomplished.

As implied by Bailey, education is a process of communication that ought not exclude the participation of administrators, off campus or on campus. But is the role of columnist a common or unique expression of the interests of an academic administrator? If compatible with the talents of the individual, is this form of outreach more the province of a chief executive than any other campus personnel? Might that judgment be different if the focus of the editorial commentary is unrelated to the business of the institution or the professional qualifications of the writer? In any event, could it be persuasively argued that such public relations may serve to better educate the general public and to advance the goals of academe than is normally possible through efforts characteristically within the halls of ivy? At what point might the risks of such efforts outweigh their potential merit?

In reflecting upon the Heyse study, what are some of the basic issues raised by the concept of the extended university? Is it generally accepted that any professional work program belongs in the university, much less in its undergraduate schools? What are the arguments, pro and con? Given a general awareness of the professions given academic sanction to date, which are more and less entitled to collegiate accreditation? For what specific reasons? And which worldly professions, currently excluded, might be equally entitled to scholastic inquiry and degreed status? What is desirable and what is unfavorable about the concept of the extended university? To what extent does it complement educational efforts on the campus? To what extent does it detract from those goals?

Gown-town relations of the order encountered by John should be sufficient to excite any higher administrator. Aside from the question of institutional survival, it is not often that one has the opportunity to help shape the course of public policy toward similarly situated schools. Do you favor a strict construction of the constitution, or, as in this instance, a clear dichotomy between church and state? Would it make any difference if you worked for a denominational university versus a municipal college? Was the decision in this litigation sound; if not, what other decision and/or rationale might have been more appropriate? Are the grounds cited of a constitutional order or of a personal nature? Given the humanity of judges, churchmen, and politicians, not to ignore the balance of us mortals, is there really any difference between the legal and value bases of such decisions? In any event, what are some of the major ramifications for higher education that will grow out of this case?

The Libby study raises many questions that are equally troublesome. What are the rights or privileges of students on campus? Do they differ if the board of control is private or public? Are students entitled to pass judgment on all policies within the academic community? If not, which areas are excluded and on what grounds? Are the prerogatives of faculty in these excluded areas clearly more justifiable? How much of that defense can be attributable to vested interests on campus and off campus? Are faculty associations, public opinion, political alliances, or corporate donors sincere advocates of student welfare? Where then does the objective administrator turn for sound advice? How and where should he draw the line between paternalism and permissiveness, if and when the challenge is brought to the fore? Or are the extremes of liberty and order self-adjusting? If not, who else can seek to steady the ship in troubled waters; if not the chief administrator, who else will dare?

PART

VII

CONCLUSION

21

**FINDINGS AND
IMPLICATIONS**
George J. Mauer

As indicated in both the preface and introduction to this book, the purpose of this collaborative effort has been to fill a discernible gap in the literature on higher education administration. Specifically, it was emphasized that the profession lacks a record of case studies which, from the vantage point of those who experienced them, served to depict many of the trials and tribulations of academic administrators at each of the major hierarchical levels in the college and university system. By bringing together a reasonably representative group of presidents and chancellors, vice presidents and provosts, deans and heads of departments, each offering a different perspective on the troublesome nature of their offices, we believe that we have accomplished the objective for which we set out. The task has not been simple, nor do we surmise that the result is perfect, for the exploration of new territory is often fraught with some perilous prospects. Nevertheless a void has now been filled, and the authors join in the hope that a fuller awareness of the plight of academic administrators may also have been communicated.

THE FINDINGS

On the premise that hindsight can assist in the development of foresight, it remains our task to consider what we have learned throughout these readings and in what thought directions they lead us. The findings thus become a prelude to the drawing of relevant implications. In retrospect, it is pertinent at this point to try to fathom what in all of the preceding pages may have contributed to a better understanding of the administrative process in academe. Without reverting to the agony of redundancy, we believe that a wide array of instructive observations may be gleaned from the foregoing studies, some obvious but generally left unstated and others latent but seldom brought to light.

Contrary to occasional rumors "on the outside," campus management is in the hands of human beings, probably no more nor less gifted in the administrative arts than their counterparts in the public and private sectors of the so-called real world. The consequences are not to be unexpected: imperfect organizations managed by imperfect beings will tend to produce imperfect results. Educational institutions are no exception, for ineptness in the selection and use of their administrators, faculties, and students will have its toll in the success and productivity of all. Such problems, characteristic of large-scale organizations at least in western societies, are oftentimes influenced by externalities, but on balance they are frequently administrative dysfunctions or errors in judgment that can be corrected only with compensating decisions. This practice of trial and error, rather than of scientific investigation and prescription, is common to most institutions, and the college or university is structurally and socially a prime example of that application. So it is in this context that higher education seeks, through its officialdom, to cope with the multitudinous problems that confront the larger society, some quite serious and most not, some infrequent and most routine, and some near impossible to solve while most remain soluble.

Although the foregoing comments are mundane to the astute observers of organizational life both on campus and off, they do entail a list of fundamentals about the nature of man and administrative systems which can help others in perceiving more fully the sometimes seemingly peculiar if not impractical behavior of those in academic decision-making authority. Actions are not always what they seem, nor are they taken in isolation. Thus it becomes advisable to know the environment in which people function, as well as the context of the dilemma they face, before proceeding to analyze the alternative responses and to pass judgment. Constructive criticism without such facts and procedure is reduced to the level of irrational ridicule. The same holds true for those superiors who condescend in the face of legitimate inquiry from lesser levels, a practice not uncommon among pseudoacademic administrators. To such unfortunate beings, inadequately prepared for their tasks and appropriately insecure with them, the recourse to rank or rationalization rather than to remedy is SOP, and such incompetency in defense of ignorance is no excuse in academe.

Despite these assertions and innuendos, it is quite clear that most institutions of higher learning in America and abroad do manage to survive, whether by design or good fortune. Putting aside the more important questions of their effectiveness and efficiency, the positivist would admonish that the proof of fulfillment of any enterprise lies in its continued existence. To the extent that this hypothesis is valid, it follows also that most academic administrators must therefore be performing their duties at par or better. We wish to concede to that assessment for we too would hope that all colleagues are sincere and dedicated servants of the goals of higher learning. However, there is reality to contend with, and a public record to the contrary: some colleges and universities have failed as a result of administrative mismanagement, many academic and extracurricular programs are dead or dying owing to inept leadership, and regrettable though it be even corruption has been unveiled on some campuses. That the frequency of these events is not great is small room for comfort, and those who would rest on such laurels are a part of the problem itself. Suffice it to consider that we still know little of the true effectiveness and efficiency of higher educational programs and processes, and only a profession in atrophy could not care less.

Given this fundamental food for thought, it is timely to turn to some of the overriding features of the previous studies. As most analysts will acknowledge, it is an axiom of modern collegiate management that positive reactions to the challenges of change are crucial to the survival and development of our educational institutions. Such reactions do not come easily, whether premeditated or accidental, and more often than not they are the product of many years of preparation or experience coupled with sound judgment. In contrast, negative responses to academic management problems are common, for treatment of an effect is less burdensome than surgery into its cause.

But what a bore it would be if somehow our colleges and universities were to be without problems. Alas, it would be unnecessary for managers to minister unto the needs of teachers and students, and the latter would have only one another toward whom to vent their anxieties, academic and otherwise. Perhaps then we should rejoice in the plentifulness of bureaucracy and be on with the business of slow but sure progress. Administration at all levels needs all the help it can get, particularly when advisors are mindful of the fact that critics are a dime a dozen and constructive observers few and far between.

For better or worse, it is self-evident that the issues that commonly precipitate problems on the campus are most often the visible, and sometimes the latent, reflections of the turmoil that besets the society at large. Thus academe may properly be viewed as much of the real world in microcosm; the principal difference being that the former can anticipate as well as express the promises or fears of the latter. Where doubt may exist, witness the collegiate scene in the mid-1950s as contrasted with the mid-1960s, and ponder the social, economic, and political plight of the nation during those decades. Still, when all is said and done, it is disturbing to note that most of the same basic educational policies and problems remain on the campus, most often without a changing of the guard.

So the "steady state" is hardly novel in higher education, despite the good intent of those who may think the term to be fashionable or, better yet, that it depicts the contemporary condition of fiscal levelling off owing largely to declining enrollments. We've been there before in the history of this and other countries. That a temporary peak has been reached in clientele and in the financial support of higher learning, from which we have subsided, there is no argument; that this reality is either steady or different from earlier experience, there is much room for debate. Indeed, the business of typology is rather risky, especially when it seeks to explain institutional behavior. Therefore it may be more meaningful to acknowledge a pulsating state on the collegiate campus, one in which expansion and contraction of functions is the essence of viability. Suffice it to submit that those who cannot adjust to the exigencies of the times are no longer with us, for as another had long ago stated, only the fittest survive. Both academic institutions and their administrators can take that admonition to heart.

Whether pulsating, steady, or vegetating, it is widely accepted that despite their individuality most colleges and universities are beset with comparable concerns. Be they more or less financial, organizational, curricular or political in nature, institutions with similar educational goals are bound to have like problems, differing of course in scope and depth depending upon their occurrence and intensity. Administrators in turn will approach these problems somewhat differently, depending upon their strengths and weaknesses. Thus analogous conditions often get dissimilar treatment, which may or may not be appropriate in remedying academic ailments.

However laudatory or miserable the result of such attempts at problem resolution, it is most unfortunate that the decisional process seldom enlightens any beyond those directly involved. This brings us full course in asserting once again a serious shortcoming in the state of the art: little if anything has been done heretofore to capture the lessons of experience in the hope that peers and successors will not have to duplicate those predicaments in order to learn. Ideally, in the long run, the solution lies in appropriate academic and professional training for such aspirants, but in view of the number and kind of positions in question, the natural resistance of bureaucracies to change, and the current attraction in being elevated to one's level of incompetence as reward for nonadministrative excellence, it is unlikely that the optimum course of action will be fully realized for at least another generation. Besides, few universities or professors are now geared for the task, and, among those which currently pave that way, it is quite clear that their programs are very much in the formative stages.

Alternatively, for both the long run and short urn, we must settle for a substitute or surrogate system of academic administrative education. Perhaps better called the Academy of Hard Knocks, it is otherwise known by the marriage of the Management Conference with In-service Training. Whether of the weekend, week-long or half-a-summer variety, it should be clear that such piecemeal approaches to higher learning are woefully inconsistent with the level of knowledge required of incumbent administrators, and the resultant certification is downright hypocritical in light of the standards they thereafter impose upon persons seeking comparable professional credentials. That on-the-job training, in the name of the internship, may last as long as a year, is good; still it is insufficient grounds to justify unsophisticated preparation.

Academics may be promoted out, stumble upward, or simply learn to play the game for all that it is worth, and thereby accede to positions of administrative authority. Some have done so, and some have been a credit to their institution nevertheless. Many have simply found themselves employed as pseudoacademic administrators, to which a surprising number will admit, and their colleges and universities reflect that quality of management from the chairpersonship to the presidency. Few campuses can afford the resultant luxuries of ineffectiveness and inefficiency, but the status quo will persist in the absence of more rational planning and action in this field. Meanwhile, we can rest assured that the aforementioned semiformal and informal learning experiences will have to suffice in preparing or upgrading the managers of collegiate affairs.

Given this assessment of the status of the profession of academic administration, past, present, and in the foreseeable future, it will be interesting to see how much more rationalization, apathy, or fear will permit a further delay in the quest for ultimate truths and understanding in this profession. Lest the reader think that this challenge may be a bit overdone, it will be profitable for one to reconsider the relevant qualifications of the parties in question, the manner in which our wisdom has been brought to bear on their selection for administrative responsibility, and the quality of the pertinent curriculum at any institution of higher learning in America and abroad. Then one might consider the administrative achievements, rather than the housekeeping chores, at selected colleges and universities, and only then begin to evaluate what ought to be versus what is, at least in terms of effective management of academic resources. The prospects are that most professors are too busy or insufficiently interested to bother, or like so many of their colleagues in subordinate administrative posts, they dare not explore that which is not assigned to them. Administrators at all levels know this cardinal rule of bureaucratic behavior, and they therefore shall be the last to recognize their own failing. Of

course, there are exceptions to the rule, and they have come to be
well known for their creative thought and innovative action. Parenthetically, it may be instructive to mention that the truly great centers
of learning would accept nothing less at the helm.

SOME INFERENCES

Although a wide variety of issues and problems have been brought
to the fore in the preceding pages, it may be cause for bewilderment
that somehow we failed to account for many additional nitty-gritty aspects of contemporary higher education. Be not bewildered, for we
stand properly accused. But more importantly, why the absence of
case studies on other vital subjects, such as admission practices,
tuition rates, the grading system, degree requirements, faculty recruitment, teacher evaluation, collective bargaining, etcetera? It
is tempting to rationalize these exclusions on the grounds that no single
book can do all things for all persons. True though this be, it is also
apparent that still other conditions have influenced the restraints or
limitations of our work.

Novel ventures usually require imaginative thought as well as
esprit de corps, and it is noteworthy that this investigation has found
that it tends to correlate highly with perceptions toward one's position
or, for purposes of this inquiry, the relative standing of one in the
academic hierarchy. Put another way, project participation proved to
be a function of administrative rank, with greater involvement and
enthusiasm associated with ascending order of office in the education
bureaucracy. Presidents and vice presidents, often considered too
preoccupied or overly defensive, were more receptive to the opportunity to discuss their experiences than were subordinates. In contrast,
and despite a quadrupled effort at enlisting a representative number
of collaborators, the response among deans and especially chairpersons was generally apathetic, the present group excluded.

What inference might be drawn from this unexpected consequence?
Perhaps that the administrative arts are felt to be more the prerogative
and duty of staff-level as opposed to line-level management personnel.
It also may mean that higher authorities find it professionally advan-
tageous to make such a contribution, whereas the lesser authorities
find it a bothersome imposition. Or one may deduce that superiors
are less insecure about revelations of choice, while subordinates may
be uptight about extradisciplinary matters. Then again it is conceivable that those atop organizations know well the meaning of their work,
and those below, especially in positions of quasi-responsibility, are
simply much less committed to their extra assignment. Wherever the

truth of the matter, it appears that higher administrators are psychologically and emotionally attuned to the rigors of their adopted profession, and lesser administrators are more often than not enamored by the concerns of their chosen academic discipline. Therefore, the former seem to be more readily reached by communications of administrative consequence, while the latter tend to be turned off by a matter of marginal interest.

But why then would these extraordinary collaborators, at each level, elect so obviously to sidestep many of the other major issues and problems on the scene of higher education today? Again we can only speculate. Given the liberty to expound on a topic of one's choosing, it is not unexpected that one will prefer a subject of personal interest, one within one's sphere of competence and experience, and one which it is hoped will communicate something of value to another. Though the guidelines of the editor directed attention to a problem oriented case study, it is human nature not to latch onto the worst or most controversial illustration. Thus the modest studies, considering some possible alternatives, which on balance provide a proper and realistic reflection of the ongoing kinds of concerns of academic administrators.

Still, the absence of case studies of greater notoriety may require further explanation. What additional reasons can be offered in defense of the existing material? A few come to mind. Administrators are manipulators and as such they learn to utilize the arts of politics. One unwritten principle of that field of endeavor is not to cope with troublesome alternatives until compelled to do so. Incidentally, those who choose to cope at first blush are called statesmen (now, statespersons), a title normally conferred upon one's demise! Being appreciative of life and the art of getting things done, we did not choose to compel the authors to do anything more than to relate an administrative experience or commentary that would offer something of value to peers and students. Consequently, when allowed to determine the focus and development of one's observations for public consumption, the astute and responsible writer will tend to follow a course of moderation and challenge rather than the route of sensationalism and condescension. The result is earnest, forthright, and generally low-key, and, we submit, an appropriate characterization of the tasks and demeanor of modern academic administrators.

Moreover, in further defense of the nature of the cases and observations herein, it should not be overlooked that 20 studies on distinguishable levels of higher education administration is no small or narrow achievement under one cover. The dubious will become true believers once they attempt to find a comparable collection of observations. Besides, the issues that are raised in these pages already number in the hundreds, and in fact they are limited only by the

perception of the reader. Thus it may be argued that the failure to
isolate additional problem areas in systematic fashion is a figment of
the critic's imagination. Nevertheless it is clear that more about our
captains of erudition can be explored, and all that are party to this
effort join in encouraging others who are able and willing to do so.

Still the curious mind must ponder why more in positions of administrative authority are not evidently interested in such matters as
budgetary theory, organizational analysis, group dynamics, model
building, decision-making processes, and other similarly important
aspects of large-scale institutions. After all, are not such perceptions
an integral part of the nuts and bolts of maintaining and developing the
contemporary college and university? Academically speaking, there is
no doubt about this; administratively, there seems to be a different
point of view. Shallow though it appears, most centers of higher learning have little concern for analysis along the foregoing lines, particularly as they apply to their own institution. Even among our
research-oriented campuses one will find a far greater disposition
toward the study of others rather than self, and lesser entities are
commonly inclined to maintain an office of institutional research for
the collection and partial dissemination of mundane data. Again, the
overriding problem is not so much in few knowing what ought to be,
but rather that so few in positions of power are sufficiently aware of
such maladministration to redirect it.

But whether attributable to traditional lack of staff support for
good information gathering systems, fear of the consequences that
might be unveiled by such research, or simply not knowing the potential
value of factual analysis, it is most unfortunate that colleges and universities do not plan and administer their affairs at a level of sophistication equal to their standing as centers of advanced learning. Yet,
with all the rhetoric aside, the ship will go the course of the master,
and it now seems commonplace that the cargo will go along for the
ride! Perhaps it is for these reasons that most academic institutions
are caught unaware of the new trends in higher education, and then
almost in chorus their leaders cry loudly of the unforeseen developments that must now negatively affect the future of the educational
enterprise. It is doubly sad that so many other interested parties
stand by in the interim, from boards of control and public officials to
parents and faculty, leaving the task by and large to students who re-
volt at the sight of superficial management wherever it is found.

Underlying this dilemma on too many campuses is the harsh
reality that very few persons in higher education administration are
professionally trained in the arts of public or private management.
What is worse, it shows! From enrollment procedures to property
utilization, and virtually all points in between, it is seldom that a college or university can escape the charges of gross inefficiency and

general ineffectiveness as regards the "business" of the institution. And the collateral characteristics at such learning centers are not to be unexpected: politics takes precedence over principle, human relations gives way to the organization manual, purpose and process take a back seat to fiscal requirements, students are treated as products rather than as evolving personalities, faculty is regarded as labor rather than as creators and disseminators of knowledge, and both alumni and facilities come to mean more than campus-bound activities and educational programs. In its decadent state, this and more is rationalized under the title of exigencies for survival; and it is a pleasure to report that most often such practices do not salvage what little is left at such quasi-academic institutions.

That there are very many exceptions to this example we have no doubt. Yet we remain very much aware that many centers of advanced learning have prospered in spite of unsuitably prepared executives, as others might define or describe such personages. We mean only to submit that leadership qualities, coupled with preparation and experience in academe or professionally allied fields of management, can be sufficient criteria for success as a college or university administrator. Indeed, it is conceivable that wholly unqualified individuals, by any standard, may successfully manage a given activity. But here we address the subject of established competency, and we are concerned that too many academics, without an appropriate administrative record but very likely with widely respected technical credentials, have acceded to positions in management, all too often with relatively little subsequent achievement to show for it. Therein lies the nub of a problem not yet faced up to by academe, and it exists at all levels of the administrative hierarchy from the presidency on down to the department head.

If constructive criticism is in order, so must be creative suggestion. And if none of the latter has been evident, perhaps a few additional observations will be helpful. Higher education administrators ought to be better trained than heretofore, and despite the prevailing air of contentment among those who made it without, there is every logical reason to believe that their successors will be vastly better qualified, especially in the next generation. Meanwhile, there are still other methods whereby academic management can be improved. For example, positions can be reclassified, such as at the departmental or division levels, to diminish the exaggerated need of advanced and marginally relevant degrees to satisfy responsibilities which tend to be preponderantly housekeeping in nature. Most of these functions can almost always be better served by administrative aides or able secretaries, thereby leaving the costlier academician free to perform work for which he or she is more clearly qualified. Reorganization also may help by eliminating unessential administrative posts, or, alternatively, by reconstituting the organizational framework to allow productive managers to coordinate the efforts of the less successful. Likewise, duties might be redefined or persons relocated, such that the end result will be a superior form of administration. But, in the final analysis, both rational recruitment and proper placement will make the real difference between progress and failure of our academic institutions, and higher level personnel management on the campus leaves much to be desired as measured by most comparable professional standards.

CSHEA: IMPLICATIONS FOR THE FUTURE

The managers of collegiate affairs, especially in the academic tract of the administrative hierarchy, are no more or less fraught with the challenges of changing circumstances than are their peers in similar public and private service agencies. After all, change, as in nature and society, is fundamental in human and institutional development, and management to be of value ought to be able to assess and control its direction and momentum. Thus the capacity to clearly appraise all phenomena affecting a college or university, coupled with the ability to lead all concerned in the directions made evident, are basic among the prerequisites or qualities of higher education administrators today and tomorrow. Moreover, lest more be deduced than intended, it should be pointed out that higher education credentials, as appropriate to the administrative service but not necessarily in the form of advanced degrees, should continue to be among the criteria for appointment to positions of authority in academe.

It is also worth noting that philosophically and attitudinally there is much commonality in the perspective of those who elect to join and promote the objectives of the not-for-profit institution. In the world of education of every description, as in other human service pursuits in the private and public sectors, organization and program administrators are prone to a similar commitment to work for the betterment of others, to seek the advancement of humanity or insight as may be appropriate to their efforts, and to reap therefrom those satisfactions as well as whatever economic reward may be forthcoming. Conversely, these kinds of managers are expected to be alike, empathetic and dedicated to be sure, but also competent to grasp the full dimensions of institutional problems, able to weigh alternative solutions in terms of organizational goals and impact, and to evidence leadership sufficient to guide the chosen course of action toward its intended objective. And only the breadth or depth of decision-making should distinguish such administrators, for the sophistication of the art ought to be equally applicable without regard for hierarchical standing. Though this is admittedly not a fact of administrative life today, it assuredly will become so in the near future.

Unlike the past, when relative abundance justified spending, the current and foreseeable status of most colleges and universities admonishes administrators to give equal attention to saving. Indeed the readily available data on birth rates, school-age persons, and both real and potential collegiates suggest a keen eye for innovative or alternative educational opportunities while recognizing that asterity has become a precondition for survival. Needless to say, the resultant challenge for decision-makers has seldom been greater, for their judgment and skills will be tested to the fullest. And their preparation should be equal to the task.

On the fiscal front, the relatively sparse appropriations of state legislatures is well known to followers of higher education budgets, and especially to those professors who earn little more than their most recent proteges. Still, barring something of a cultural challenge in the seventies or eighties approximating that laid before the scientific community in the fifties and early sixties, it is unlikely that a new financial harvest will soon save or expand many public centers of advanced learning. Private academic institutions are already suffering the consequences of declining enrollments and external monetary support, to which the snowballing economic stagflation of the 1970s offers even less room for optimism. Moreover, as some higher education administrators are aware, slightly more than half of our high school graduates are going on to larger campuses these days, and half as many again are finally degreed. But these trends at the undergraduate level are declining and disfavoring most senior colleges and universities as well as a particular array of disciplines. The student and cost data at the graduate level is worse yet, with only six earning the master's degree and one the doctorate for every one hundred who matriculate, and at an expense increasingly greater by all accounts. Perhaps more than ever before, these and similar data bear meticulous examination and consistent replanning per that evaluation.

It is reasonable to conclude that analysis and action upon the foregoing kinds of information and events require individuals adept in academic management, receptive to the pursuit of relevant knowledge, and otherwise basically appreciative of the aspirations of most institutions of advanced learning. This demeanor does not develop by chance, nor is it secured without special preparation and dedication. What is more, if the arts in question are to be brought to a level of true sophistication, they necessitate far greater academic and applied study than has been brought to bear to date. Administration, generally, primarily in the private sphere and secondarily in the public, is a subject of inquiry of rather long standing. As applied to higher education,

it has been far less analyzed, both in abstract and pragmatic terms.
On the one hand the literature is testimony to our modicum of understanding in this field and, on the other hand, the collegiate curriculum
and the credentials of administrators from coast to coast will attest
to the unenviable state of the profession. The findings are neither
pleasant nor really warranted, for the campus is the repository of
knowledge for the development of management talent and yet it has not
garnered its share of applicable insight and service.

Although it is expected that this concern will be resolved in
piecemeal fashion at some distant time, it is more comforting to consider an early and more efficacious solution toward meeting these
pressing problems of most colleges and universities, not in a generation or in a decade when it will be too late for many, but within a year!
For lack of a foreseeable singular educational institution to bear the
burden of this proposal, and in the likely absence of a comprehensive
approach wherever it could be adopted, it is suggested that the time
has come for the establishment of an Academy for Higher Education
Administrators to meet the in-house research and service requirements of the collegiate community. Whether incorporated as an independent entity, as an offshoot of an established national association,
as a consortia of interested centers of higher learning, or even as a
byproduct of one or more governments, we envision the development
of an organization that can prudently and effectively meet the objectives
of producing highly competent higher education administrators, of exploring the wide-ranging academic and applied questions involving the
suitability of the work of presidents through chairpersons, and of
bringing such talent and learning to bear on the conduct of management
on every campus desirous of redirection.

Funding of the academy would be derived in part from the sponsor, a fee schedule for user academic institutions, tuition from its
postgraduate students, philanthropic contributions, and contract research. The areas of expenditure are self-evident. Organizationally,
the academy should be directed by a board of trustees experienced in
the education or application of the administrative arts and representative of their various levels at differing kinds of academic institutions.
The executive director could not be less than an esteemed member of
collegiate management and preferably a former university president.
His immediate staff and each of the educators and researchers would
be both versed and experienced at an appropriate level of academic
administration. The curriculum of the academy, offered at its site
and interrelating theory and practice as well as an interdisciplinary
view of the subject matter, should require a full year for completion.
Of course, entrants ought to be considered on the basis of their institutional recommendations and need, plus an independent evaluation of
requests in light of the capabilities and resources of the academy.

Credit would be extended to applicants who have earned or experienced
selected levels of understanding, either as established by coursework
or the combination of examinations and interviews. Graduates should
be formally certified for a given management position in academe,
thereby becoming eligible for the next higher position, and encouraged
to return for advanced work as soon as they or their sponsor sense
the need.

The academy, in conjunction with the academic institutions which
otherwise will continue to be operative in this field, could manage to
meet effectively the relevant needs of interested colleges and universities, from the community system to the multiversity complex. In
addition, it would pursue a continuing program of research in higher
education administration, both theoretical and applied. In the area of
theory, for example, the nature of organizations and leadership might
be among the first order of inquiry. To what extent is academic management predictive and descriptive, at which levels and under what
circumstances, and how applicable are the contemporary perspectives
or explanations under title of the structural, decisional, human relations, systems, and institutional schools of thought? Are models relevant to the interrelationships between and among the various actors
in academic administration? Is the hierarchical, collegial, democra-
tic, or some other framework more or less conducive to achieving
the multiple objectives of academe? And to what extent and at what
foreseeable cost can we expect evaluative research to bring us closer
to the answers we seek?

On the applied side of the research agenda, what precisely can
be done to advance the capability of managers, both novice and veteran,
to better plan, develop, and execute policies and programs within
their jurisdiction? Where should the line be drawn between staff and
line administrators, and on what grounds, and to what extent does the
distinction affect operations in higher education? Is policy development distinguishable from policy administration; if so, how so and
under what circumstances? For a change of emphasis, what new forms
of postsecondary education may be conceivable for cooptation by
higher educational institutions in the immediate and long-range future?
To what extend would those redirections be compatible with the presumed goals of advanced learning outlined in most catalogs? Even if
rationalized, could innovative efforts become viable without regard
for present notions of education affected by time, space, method, and
content? What consequences can be expected, from the allocation of
resources to the psychology of effecting change, and to whose overall
betterment?

These and thousands of other similarly intriguing questions cannot be answered by periodic and marginal academic inquiry which,
unfortunately, characterizes the depth of contemporary administrative

research in higher education. Thus sophisticated analysis of management in academe is no more advanced than is the level of training of administrators in the relevant arts. If this condition in the profession is to be different tomorrow, preparation must begin today. We submit that the most meaningful step in that direction will come with the establishment of an educational entity akin to an Academy for Higher Education Administrators. The sooner this task is completed the earlier we will be relieved of some of our ignorance and ineptness. The longer it takes, the greater the risk that we will continue to endure failures in higher education. In any event, to try and to fail is at least to learn, but to fail to try is to suffer the inestimable loss of what might have been.

HIGHER EDUCATION ADMINISTRATION

Aside from occasional references found in the literature on public management, it is seldom pointed out that the field of
administration—as an academic discipline as well as a profession in
the United States—is largely attributable to the late nineteenth century
literary efforts of one Woodrow Wilson. Reaction to his pleas for serious attention to the administrative arts and sciences was far from
immediate, either in the institutions of higher education that he served
or in the governmental services that he was later to lead. Indeed, it
was not until the turn of the twentieth century that Charles Thwing
authored the first book on the administration of the American college,
and only later did the study of public institutional management gain
legitimacy as a part of the curriculum on campus. And despite the
subsequent proliferation of universities, it is ironic that we continue
to witness a paucity of programs designed to analyze and improve academic administration, and in particular to study and upgrade the talents
required of those who courageously elect to serve the cause of higher
learning in such capacities.

Still there is comfort in the knowledge that research and writing
have compensated for the lag in teaching in this field, for available
today are tens of thousands of articles and books on higher education
administration. Although the critical student will question the relevancy of much that has passed for analyses of academic institutional
management, it is not the purpose here to make that delineation nor
to classify or evaluate the full spectrum of that productivity. Rather,
it is our intent to facilitate the access of concerned administrators
and scholars to a bibliography of substantive value. After an examination of over 20,000 pertinent citations, we have concluded that the
appended works, directly and indirectly related to the management of
collegiate affairs, are representative of the better products among
their kind.

These references will prove useful to the generalist as well as
the specialist in academic administration, at all levels of the hierarchy, for they include considerations that range from the ideal to the
mundane. Moreover, these writings can be helpful to the veteran as
well as the novice in the field. Many of the former, but by no means
all, will be acquainted with the titles; none of the latter are advised
to ignore their contents. Substantively, these works give sufficient
attention to most matters of concern to university managers. Hence
theory is compared with practice, humility with arrogance,

prognostication with fact, seriousness with satire, and success with failure, all being made possible by the sometimes complementary and sometimes contradictory insights of classicists and contemporaries. Thus, collectively, these authors have served us well by placing into meaningful perspective the dilemmas and opportunities which confront the leadership on campus, in any time period. It remains to be established whether we shall profit by their wisdom.

BIBLIOGRAPHY

American Council on Education Faculty-Administration Relationships. Washington, D.C.: The Council, 1958.

Andrews, K. R., ed. The Case Method of Teaching Human Relations and Administration. Cambridge: Harvard University Press, 1953.

Anello, M. The Future College Executive. Boston: Boston College Press, 1973.

Armour, R. Going Around in Academic Circles. New York: McGraw-Hill, 1965.

Barnard, C. I. The Functions of the Executive. Cambridge: Harvard University Press, 1938.

Barzun, J. The American University: How It Runs, Where It Is Going. New York: Harper and Row, 1968.

Bauer, R. C. Cases in College Administration. New York: Teachers College, Columbia University, 1955.

Benjamin, H., ed. Democracy in the Administration of Higher Education. New York: Harper, 1950.

Bennis, W. The Leaning Ivory Tower. San Francisco: Jossey-Bass, 1973.

Berdahl, R. O. et al. Statewide Coordination of Higher Education. Washington, D.C.: American Council on Education, 1971.

Blackwell, T. E. College and University Business Administration. Washington, D.C.: American Council on Education, vol. 1, 1952; vol. 2, 1955.

Blau, P. M. Bureaucracy in Modern Society. New York: Random House, 1971.

Bolman, F. D. How College Presidents Are Chosen. Washington, D. C.: American Council on Education, 1971.

Bowen, H. R. The Finance of Higher Education. Berkeley: Carnegie Commission on Higher Education, 1968.

Bowen, W. G. The Economics of the Major Private Universities. Berkeley: Carnegie Commission on Higher Education, 1972.

Brown, J. D. The Liberal University. New York: McGraw-Hill, 1969.

Brubacher, J. S. Bases for Policy in Higher Education. New York: McGraw-Hill, 1965.

Brumbaugh, A. J. Problems in College Administration. Nashville: Board of Education, Methodist Church, 1956.

Burns, G. P. Administrators in Higher Education. New York: Harper, 1962.

Burns, N., ed. The Administration of Higher Institutions Under Changing Conditions. Chicago: University of Chicago Press, 1947.

Capen, S. P. The Management of Universities. New York: Foster and Stewart, 1953.

Carnegie Commission on Higher Education. Governance of Higher Education—Six Priority Problems. Hightstown, N.J.: McGraw-Hill, 1973

Carr, R. K., and Van Eyck, D. K. Collective Bargaining Comes to the Campus. Washington, D.C.: American Council on Education, 1973.

Cattell, J. M. University Control. New York: The Science Press, 1913.

Committee for Economic Development. The Management and Financing of Colleges. Washington, D.C.: CED, 1973.

Corson, J. J. Governance of Colleges and Universities. New York:
    McGraw-Hill, 1960.

Curtis, M. H. Oxford and Cambridge in Transition. Oxford, England:
    Oxford University Press, 1959.

Deegan, W., McConnell, T., Mortimer, K., and Stull, H. Joint Par-
    ticipation in Decision Making. Berkeley: Center for Research
    and Development in Higher Education, 1969.

Deutsch, M. E. The College From Within. Berkeley: University of
    California Press, 1952.

Dewey, J. Democracy and Education. New York: Macmillan Co.,
    1916.

Dibdon, A. J., ed. The Academic Deanship in American Colleges and
    Universities. Carbondale: Southern Illinois University Press,
    1968.

Dill, D. D. Case Studies in University Governance. Washington, D.
    C.: National Association of State University and Land Grant
    Colleges, 1971.

Dimock, M. E. The Executive in Action. New York: Harper, 1945.

Dodds, H. W. The Academic President—Educator or Caretaker?
    New York: McGraw-Hill, 1962.

Doyle, E. A. The Status and Functions of the Departmental Chairman.
    Washington, D.C.: Catholic University Press, 1953.

Dressel, P. F., Johnson, F. C. and Marcus, P. M. The Confidence
    Crisis: An Analysis of University Departments. San Francisco:
    Jossey-Bass, 1973.

_____, and Pratt, S. B. The World of Higher Education—An
    Annotated Guide to the Major Literature. San Francisco: Jossey-
    Bass, 1971.

Dykes, A. Faculty Participation in Academic Decision Making. Wash-
    ington, D.C.: American Council on Education, 1968.

Dysinger, W. S., ed. The Functions of the Dean—His Duties and Re-
    lationships. Stillwater: Oklahoma A&M College, 1954.

Eells, W. B., and Hollis, E. V. Administration of Higher Education. Washington, D.C.: U.S. Government Printing Office, 1960.

Eliot, C. W. University Administration. Boston: Houghton Mifflin, 1908.

Eulau, H., and Quinley, H. State Officials and Higher Education: A Survey of the Opinions and Expectations of Policy Makers in Nine States. Berkeley: Carnegie Commission on Higher Education, 1970.

Eurich, A. C., ed. Campus 1980: The Shape of the Future in American Higher Education. New York: Delacorte Press, 1968.

Falvey, F. E. Student Participation in College Administration. New York: Teachers College, Columbia University, 1952.

Fashing, J. J. Academics in Retreat: The Politics of Educational Innovation. Albuquerque: University of New Mexico Press, 1971.

Foote, C., and Mayer, H. et al. The Culture of the University: Governance and Education. San Francisco: Jossey-Bass, 1968.

Frankel, C. Issues in University Education. New York: Harper, 1957.

Gibson, R. C. The Challenge of Leadership in Higher Education. Dubuque, Iowa: W. C. Brown Co., 1964.

Glenny, L. A. Autonomy of Public Colleges: The Challenges of Coordination. New York: McGraw-Hill, 1959.

_____ et al. Coordinating Higher Education for the '70's. Berkeley: Center for Research and Development in Higher Education, 1971.

Glenny, L. A., and Dalglish, T. K. The State: Its Government and University. Berkeley: Center for Research and Development in Education, 1973.

Goldwin, R. A., ed. Higher Education and Modern Democracy. Chicago: Rand McNally, 1967.

Gross, E., and Grambach, P. University Goals and Academic Power. Washington, D.C.: American Council on Education, 1968.

Hack, W. G., ed. Educational Administration. Boston: Allyn and
    Bacon, 1965.

Harris, S. E. A Statistical Portrait of Higher Education. New York:
    McGraw-Hill, 1972.

_____, ed. Higher Education in the United States: The Eco-
    nomic Problems. Cambridge: Harvard University Press, 1960.

Hartnett, R. T. College and University Trustees: Their Backgrounds,
    Roles and Educational Attitudes. Princeton, N.J.: Educational
    Testing Service, 1969.

Heckman, D. M., and Martin, B. M. Inventory of Current Research
    on Higher Education. New York: McGraw-Hill, 1968.

Hefferlin, J. B., and Phillips, E. L. Information Services for Aca-
    demic Administrators. San Francisco: Jossey-Bass, 1971.

Heilbron, L. H. The College and University Trustee. San Francisco:
    Jossey-Bass, 1973.

Helsabeck, R. E. Collegiate Decisionmaking and Effectiveness: A
    Conceptual Framework and Set of Propositions. Berkeley: Center
    for Research and Development in Higher Education, 1973.

_____. The Compound System: A Conceptual Framework for
    Effective Decisionmaking in Colleges. Berkeley: Center for
    Research and Development in Education, 1973.

Henderson, A. D. Policies and Practices in Higher Education. New
    York: Harper, 1960.

_____ et al. Training University Administrators: A Pro-
    gramme Guide. Paris: UNESCO, 1970.

Herron, O. R. The Role of the Trustee. Scranton, Pa.: International
    Textbook Co., 1969.

Hodgkinson, H. L. Institutions in Transition: A Profile of Change in
    Higher Education. New York: McGraw-Hill, 1971.

_____. Campus Governance—The Next Decade. Berkeley:
    Center for Research and Development in Higher Education, 1970.

_____. The President and Campus Governance. Berkeley: Center for Research and Development in Higher Education, 1969.

_____. Current Alternatives in Campus Governance. Berkeley: Center for Research and Development in Higher Education, 1968.

_____, and Meeth, L. R., eds. Power and Authority: Campus Governance in Transformation. San Francisco: Jossey-Bass, 1970.

Hodinko, B. A., and Whitley, S. D. Student Personnel Administration: A Critical Incident Approach. Washington, D.C.: College Guidance Associates, 1971.

Hughes, J. M. Human Relations in Educational Organization. New York: Harper, 1957.

Hutchins, R. M. The Higher Learning in America. New Haven: Yale University Press, 1936.

Hyneman, C. Bureaucracy in a Democracy. New York: Harper, 1950.

Jencks, C., and Reisman, D. The Academic Revolution. Doubleday, 1968.

Jenson, T. J., and Clark, D. L. Educational Administration. New York: Center for Applied Research in Education, 1964.

Kaplowitz, R. A. Selecting Academic Administrators: The Search Committee. Washington, D.C.: American Council on Education, 1973.

Keeton, M. Shared Authority on Campus. Washington, D.C.: American Association for Higher Education, 1971.

Kerr, C. New Challenges to the College and University. Berkeley: Carnegie Commission on Higher Education, 1969.

_____. The Uses of the University. Cambridge: Harvard University Press, 1963.

Knight, E. W. What College President Say. Chapel Hill: University of North Carolina Press, 1940.

Knorr, O. A., ed. Long-Range Planning in Higher Education. Boulder, Colo.: Western Interstate Commission for Higher Education, 1964.

Knox, W. B. Eye on the Hurricane: Observations on Creative Educational Administration. Corvallis: Oregon State University Press, 1973.

Ladd, D. R. Change in Educational Policy: Self Studies in Selected Colleges and Universities. Berkeley: Carnegie Commission on Higher Education, 1970.

Ladd, Jr., E. C., and Lipset, S. M. Professors, Unions, and American Higher Education. Washington, D.C.: American Enterprise Institute for Public Policy Research, 1973.

Lahti, R. E. Innovative College Management. San Francisco: Jossey-Bass, 1973.

Law, G. C. The Urgency of New Leadership in Higher Education. Philadelphia: Ivy-Curtis Press, 1962.

Layton, E. N. Higher Education Administration and Organization. Washington, D.C.: U.S. Government Printing Office, 1951.

Lazarsfeld, P., and Thielens, Jr., W. The Academic Mind. Glencoe, Ill.: The Free Press, 1958.

Lee, E. C., and Bowen, F. M. The Multicampus University: A Study of Academic Governance. Hightstown, N.J.: McGraw-Hill, 1971.

Lehrer, S. Leaders, Teachers and Learners in Academe: Partners in the Educational Process. New York: Appleton-Century-Crofts, 1970.

Lloyd-Jones, E., Barry, R., and Wolfe, B. Case Studies in College Student-Staff Relationships. New York: Teachers College, Columbia University, 1956.

Lowell, A. L. What a University President Has Learned. New York: Macmillan, 1938.

Lunn, Jr., H. H. The Students' Role in College Policy Making. Washington, D.C.: American Council on Education, 1957

Lunsford, T. F., ed. The Study of Academic Administration. Ann Arbor: University Microfilms, Inc., 1963.

March, J. G., and Cohen, M. D. Leadership and Ambiguity: The American College President. Hightstown, N.J.: McGraw-Hill Book Co., 1973.

Margolis, J. D., ed. The Campus in the Modern World. New York: Macmillan, 1969.

Mayhew, L. B. Arrogance on Campus. San Francisco: Jossey-Bass, 1970.

McGrath, E. J. Selected Issues in College Administration. New York: Columbia University Press, 1967.

McVey, F. L., and Hughes, R. M. Problems of College and University Administration. Ames, Iowa: Iowa State University Press, 1952.

Metzler, K. Confrontation: The Destruction of a College President. Los Angeles: Nash Publishing, 1973.

Millett, J. D. Decision Making and Administration in Higher Education. Kent, Ohio: Kent State University Press, 1968.

_____. The Academic Community: An Essay on Organization. New York: McGraw-Hill, 1962.

Minter, W. J. Campus and Capitol. Boulder, Colo.: Western Interstate Commission for Higher Education, 1966.

Mood, A. Papers on Efficiency in the Management of Higher Education. Berkeley: Carnegie Commission on Higher Education, 1972.

Mosher, W. E., and Kingsley, D. Public Personnel Administration. New York: Harper, 1941.

Ness, F. An Uncertain Glory. San Francisco: Jossey-Bass, 1971.

Nevins, A. The State Universities and Democracy. Urbana: University of Illinois Press, 1962.

Newsom, C. V. A University President Speaks Out: On Current Education. New York: Harper, 1961.

Nigro, F. A. Modern Public Administration. New York: Harper and
    Row, 1970.

_____. Public Personnel Administration. New York: Henry
    Holt and Co., 1959.

Palola, E. G. Changing Centers of Power in Education: A Challenge
    to Institutional Leadership. Berkeley: Center for Research and
    Development in Higher Education, 1968.

Palola, E. G., Lehmann, T., and Blischke, W. Higher Education By
    Design: The Sociology of Planning. Berkeley: Center for Research
    and Development in Higher Education, 1970.

Perkins, J. A. The University As An Organization. New York:
    McGraw-Hill, 1973.

_____. University in Transition, New Jersey: Princeton Uni-
    versity Press, 1966.

_____, ed. Higher Education: From Autonomy to Systems.
    New York: International Council for Educational Development,
    1972.

Perry, R. R., and Hull, W. F., eds. The Organized Organization:
    The American University and Its Administration. Toledo, Ohio:
    University of Toledo, 1971

Peter, L. J., and Hull, R. The Peter Principle. New York: Morrow,
    1969.

Pfiffner, J. M., and Presthus, R. V. Public Administration. New
    York: Ronald Press, 1967.

Pigors, P. J., and Pigors, F. Case Method in Human Relations. New
    York: McGraw-Hill, 1961.

Plank, E. H. Public Finance. Homewood, Ill.: R. D. Irwin Co., 1953.

Poore, W. Personnel Practices in College and University. Cham-
    paign, Ill.: College and University Personnel Association, 1958.

Reining, H. Jr. The Administration of Development and the Univer-
    sity's Role. Chicago: Comparative Administration Group,
    American Society for Public Administration, 1964.

_____. Cases in Public Personnel Administration. Dubuque,
    Iowa: W. C. Brown Co., 1949.

Retzlaff, B. R. Higher Education Administration: An Annotated Bibliography of Research Reports. Washington, D.C.: National Center for Educational Research and Development, 1971

Ridgeway, J. The Closed Corporation: American Universities in Crisis. New York: Random House, 1968.

Riesman, D., and Stadtman, W., eds. Academic Transformation: Seventeen Institutions Under Pressure. New York: McGraw-Hill, 1973.

Ritterbush, P. C., ed. Let the Entire Community Become Our University. New York: Acropolis Books, 1973.

Rivlin, A. M. The Role of the Federal Government in Financing Higher Education. Washington, D.C.: The Brookings Institution, 1961.

Rogers, R. D. et al. University Library Administration. New York: H. W. Wilson Co., 1971.

Rourke, F. E., and Brooks, G. E. The Managerial Revolution in Higher Education. Baltimore: Johns Hopkins University Press, 1966.

Ruml, B. Memo To A College Trustee. New York: McGraw-Hill, 1959.

Runnion, N. Up the Ladder. Garden City, N.Y.: Doubleday, 1969.

Russell, J. D. The Finance of Higher Education. Chicago: University of Chicago Press, 1954.

Sammartino, P., and Rudy, W., eds. The Private Urban University. Rutherford, N.J.: Farleigh Dickinson University Press, 1966.

Sargent, C. G. Educational Administration: Cases and Concepts. Boston: Houghton Mifflin, 1955.

Schoenfeld, C. A. The University and Its Publics. New York: Harper, 1954.

Simon, H. A. Administrative Behavior. New York: Macmillan, 1961.

Smith, G. K, ed. The Troubled Campus: Current Issues in Higher Education. San Francisco: Jossey-Bass, 1972.

_____. Agony and Promise. San Francisco: Jossey-Bass, 1970.

_____. In Search of Leaders. Chicago: National Conference on Higher Education, 1967.

Sofer, C. The Organization From Within. London: Tavistock Publications, 1961.

Sperle, D. H. The Case Method Technique in Professional Training. New York: Teachers College, Columbia University, 1933.

Stahl, O. G. Public Personnel Administration. Evanston, Ill.: Harper and Row, 1963

Stenzel, A. K. Learning by the Case Method. New York: Seabury Press, 1970.

Stoke, H. W. The American College Presidency. New York: Harper, 1957.

Tead, O. The Art of Administration. New York: Macmillan, 1958.

_____. Trustees, Teachers, Students: The Role in Higher Education. Salt Lake City: University of Utah Press, 1951.

Thackrey, R. I. The Future of the State University. Urbana: University of Illinois Press, 1971.

Thompson, V. Modern Organization. New York: Knopf, 1961.

Thwing, C. F. College Administration. New York: Century Co., 1900.

Towl, A. R. To Study Administration By Cases. Boston: Harvard University Graduate School of Business Administration, 1969.

Veblen, T. The Higher Learning in America. Clifton, N.J.: Kelley, 1918.

Waldo, D. The Study of Public Administration. Garden City, N.Y.: Doubleday, 1955

Walker, W. G. Theory and Practice in Educational Administration. Brisbane: University of Queensland Press, 1970.

Warnath, C. F. New Myths and Old Realities. San Francisco: Jossey-
    Bass, 1971.

White, L. D. Introduction to the Study of Public Administration. New
    York: Macmillan, 1958.

Whyte, W. H. The Organization Man. New York: Simon and Schuster,
    1956.

Williams, R. L. Legal Bases of Boards of Higher Education in the
    Fifty States. Chicago: Council of State Governments, 1971.

_____. The Administration of Academic Affairs in Higher Edu-
    cation. Ann Arbor: University of Michigan Press, 1965.

Willings, D. R. How to Use the Case Study in Training for Decision
    Making. London: Business Publications, 1968.

Wilson, L., ed. Emerging Patterns in Higher Education. Washington,
    D.C.: American Council on Education, 1965.

Wilson, R. E. Educational Administration. Columbus, Ohio: C. E.
    Merrill Books, 1966.

Woodburne, L. S. Principles of College and University Administration.
    Palo Alto: Stanford University Press, 1958.

Wriston, H. M. Academic Procession: Reflections of a College Presi-
    dent. New York: Columbia University Press, 1959.

Pertinent Periodicals

Administrative Management

Administrative Science Quarterly

Administrator's Notebook

AAUP Bulletin

AAUW Journal

Carnegie Corporation Quarterly
Change

College and University Bulletin

College and University Business

College and University Journal

College Management

College Public Relations Quarterly
Compact

Education Administration Abstracts

Education Administration &
Supervision

Education Administration Quarterly

Educational Law and Administration

Educational Leadership and Educational Record

Higher Education

Higher Education & National Affairs
Bulletin

Journal of Educational Administration

Journal of Higher Education

NEA Bulletin, NEA Journal, NEA
News

North Central Association Quarterly
Phi Delta Kappan

Public Administration Review

Public Personnel Review

Research in Administration

Studies in Management

The Chronicle of Higher Education

The College Blue Book

The Research Reporter

University Affairs

University and College Quarterly

University News and University
Quarterly

Academy for Higher Education
  Administrators: proposal,
  246-48
accreditation: salvaging, 104-10
American Association of Uni-
  versity Professors (AAUP),
  131, 134
American Civil Liberties
  Union (ACLU), 220
American Council on Education
  (ACE), 153
American Medical Association
  (AMA), 204
Americans United for Sepa-
  ration of Church and State
  (AUSCS), 220
anxieties in academe: editor's
  comments, 117-18, 147-48
Association of American
  Colleges, 219

Bailey, Richard, 202
Baird, William, 226-27
Barbe, Richard, 43
Blackmun, Harry, 204
boards of control: external
  influences, 7; function, 7;
  representation, 5
Brooks, Glenn, 74
Browne, Michael, 160
Buford, Warren, 154

campus: center for offenders,
  178-94; classifications, 63;
  extension into community,
  211-18
Carl, Mary, 92
Carnegie Commission on Higher
  Education, 63

Case, Charles, 33
case studies: approach, 9-12;
  utility, 11, 15-16
chairperson: function, 169,
  174-75; leadership role,
  166-77; perspective, 14;
  position, 165; relations with
  administration and students,
  175-76
challenges of change: editor's
  comments, 151-52, 195-97
Chickering, Arthur, 153
Chucker, Harold, 202
collaborators: classification,
  12-15
colleges and universities: University of Bridgeport, 104;
  University of California,
  Berkeley, 53, 160; Colorado
  College, 73; University of
  Delaware, 92; University of
  Florida, 22-23; Georgia State
  University, 43; Goucher College, 166; Hamline University,
  202; University of Idaho, 160;
  University of Illinois, Chicago
  Circle, 54; Louisiana State
  University, New Orleans, 78;
  University of Maine, Orono,
  226; University of Michigan,
  Dearborn, 53; University of
  Minnesota, 140; University of
  Mississippi, 140; University
  of North Dakota, 211; Seton
  Hall University, 130; University
  of South Carolina, 153; Uni-
  versity of Vermont, 33; Uni-
  versity of Washington, 178;
  Western Maryland College, 219

GEORGE J. MAUER is currently serving the State of South Dakota as senior policy analyst in the Department of Executive Management, Office of the Governor. An academician as well as public administrator, he has taught at five private and public universities and has held positions in federal, state, and local government.

In addition, he has served the academic community as director of three government research agencies and head of public administration and public service internship programs. He has published dozens of articles in a variety of professional journals, and has authored numerous special studies under contract research.

He planned, compiled, and edited this book during his recent year of postdoctoral work at the University of California, Berkeley, under the sponsorship of the Institute of Governmental Studies.

Dr. Mauer received his B.A. in Political Science from Oklahoma State University, his M.A. in Public Administration from the University of Kansas, and his Ph.D. in Government from the University of Oklahoma.

COMPARATIVE HIGHER EDUCATION ABROAD: Bibliography and
Analysis
edited by Philip G. Altbach

DESEGREGATING AMERICA'S COLLEGES: A Nationwide Survey of
Black Studies, 1972-73
William M. Boyd, II

EDUCATIONAL POLICY-MAKING AND THE STATE LEGISLATURE:
The New York Experience
Mike M. Milstein and Robert E.
Jennings

WOMEN IN ACADEMIA: Evolving Policies Toward Equal Opportunities
edited by Arie Y. Lewin and Elga
Wasserman